Being and Becoming

Other books by Franklyn Sills

Craniosacral Biodynamics, Volume 1: The Breath of Life, Biodynamics, and Fundamental Skills

Craniosacral Biodynamics, Volume 2: The Primal Midline and the Organization of the Body

The Polarity Process: Energy as a Healing Art

Being and Becoming

Psychodynamics, Buddhism, and the Origins of Selfhood

Franklyn Sills

North Atlantic Books
Berkeley, California

Published by
North Atlantic Books
P.O. Box 12327
Berkeley, California 94712
Cover and book design by Jan Camp
Printed in the United States of America

Being and Becoming: Psychodynamics, Buddhism, and the Origins of Selfhood is sponsored by the Society for the Study of Native Arts and Sciences, a nonprofit educational corporation whose goals are to develop an educational and cross-cultural perspective linking various scientific, social, and artistic fields; to nurture a holistic view of arts, sciences, humanities, and healing; and to publish and distribute literature on the relationship of mind, body, and nature.

For more information about Franklyn Sills, contact
The Karuna Institute
Natsworthy Manor
Widecombe-in-the-Moor
Devon
United Kingdom TQ13 7TR
www.karuna-institute.co.uk

North Atlantic Books' publications are available through most bookstores. For further information, visit our Web site at www.northatlanticbooks.com or call 800-733-3000.

Library of Congress Cataloging-in-Publication Data

Sills, Franklyn, 1947–
Being and becoming : psychodynamics, Buddhism, and the origins of selfhood
/ Franklyn Sills.
    p. cm.
ISBN-13: 978-1-55643-762-5
ISBN-10: 1-55643-762-5
1. Psychotherapy—Religious aspects—Buddhism. 2. Buddhism—Psychology.
I. Title.
BQ4570.P76S56 2008
294.3'422—dc22

2008011673

2 3 4 5 6 7 8 9 10 UNITED 15 14 13 12 11 10 09

Table of Contents

ৡ Contents

Acknowledgments

My deep gratitude goes to Dr. William Emerson, who has been an inspiration, mentor, colleague, and friend over many years. It was William who introduced me to the work of Dr. Frank Lake, with its clear perspective on earliest human experiences. I am also deeply appreciative of the work and writings of W. Ronald D. Fairbairn, Donald Winnicott, and Daniel N. Stern, all of which can be viewed in an integrated and congruent way within a Buddhist self-psychology framework. I want to acknowledge the Bridge Pastoral Foundation, that carries on the work of its founder, Frank Lake, and keeps his writings available through its online website. I deeply appreciate my colleagues at the Karuna Institute who have read and responded to this work and taught the paradigm and its practical applications in classrooms, and whose feedback has been immensely important.

My spiritual journey has been incredibly enriched by my early teachers. I would like to acknowledge Master Lui Hsu Chi, who introduced Ch'an teachings to me and offered his students an inspiring interpretation of Lao Tse's *Tao Te Ching* from the original archaic Chinese. Most importantly, I would like to acknowledge, with deep humility, my root teacher, the Venerable Taungpulu Sayadaw of upper Burma (Myanmar), who taught direct knowing and the primacy of awareness in all spiritual process. Sitting in his presence, receiving the transmission of Dharma through a depth of resonance and stillness, was formative to my healing process. I would also like to thank Rina Sircar both for her insightful meditation teachings and for introducing me to Sayadaw.

Finally, and most importantly, I would like to acknowledge, with profoundest appreciation, my wife Maura Sills, the founder of Core Process Psychotherapy, whose deep knowledge and experience of the human condition has clarified and enriched my understanding of life. It is through her relentless inquiry into the nature of suffering that I owe my orientation to the inherent health that is always with us even in the midst of apparent disturbances. She has given much needed and helpful guidance in the drafting of this book and has been a pivotal influence on its content.

Foreword by Maura Sills

MEETING FRANKLYN IN LONDON IN 1973 AT A CH'AN CLASS, I NEVER imagined the journey of learning we would travel together. From this shared journey, the work of the Karuna Institute and Core Process Psychotherapy was birthed. This book is the expression of many years of teaching, psychotherapeutic practice, and exploration in the profound territory of Buddhism.

Core Process Psychotherapy is deeply informed by Buddhist principles and practices. It is founded on understandings central to the Buddhist view of the nature of suffering and how healing occurs. The training of psychotherapists at the Karuna Institute pivots on these principles and focuses on the ability of therapists to hold and transform their own arising processes while maintaining a spacious awareness of their own thoughts, feelings, body states, and subtle energetic experiences, as well as the client's.

This work is psycho-spiritual in nature, as it orients not just to developmental psychology and the formation of selfhood, but to our deepest spiritual roots. As psycho-spiritual psychotherapy, Core Process is mindfulness-based psychotherapy. It may be the only new form of therapy developed in Britain that incorporates the phenomenology of a major spiritual tradition with a secular form of psychotherapy.

In Core Process work, the practice of psychotherapy is undertaken as a joint practice between client and therapist in the context of the present moment's experience. It is based on a deep experiential understanding of emptiness in the Buddhist tradition. Emptiness, or *shunyata,* is the basic ground underlying all form and from which all form manifests. Thus it points both to the process nature of selfhood, and to the inherent spaciousness and openness of the human condition. Emptiness unifies. We are not totally discrete, distinct, and separate beings; we are all deeply interconnected. Thus there is no individual experience that does not affect, and is not affected by, the experience of others. In the words of Ven. Thich Nhat Hanh, we *interbe*.

The nature of interbeing must be understood by the psychotherapist. The malaise and sense of disconnection many of us experience in relationship to our partners, friends, and children, and to the planet must be acknowledged. Psychotherapy can no longer be seen as only the individual's journey. Our atrophied ability to experience ourselves as belonging to a whole, which has been displaced by extreme feelings of separation, must be addressed as a central concern. Our ability to abide in silence, confusion, fear, or uncertainty must be viewed not as a problem, but as a doorway to mutuality, wisdom, and health. Sensitizing ourselves to our human condition is no longer optional. To continue to see problems, suffering, and confusion as outside and separate from ourselves only perpetuates alienation and dis-ease. It is time for us all to own the suffering that afflicts us and collectively participate in its transformation.

In this book, a radical reinterpretation of developmental psychology, combined with an embodied knowledge of Buddhism, provides a basis for the analysis of consciousness. I deeply believe that the approach to psychotherapy described here meets the call for a means to an ethical awakening to, and reckoning with, the troubles of our times.

Introduction by Franklyn Sills

THIS BOOK HAS ITS ORIGINS IN A FORM OF PSYCHOTHERAPEUTIC practice called Core Process Psychotherapy. In Core Process practice, Eastern and Western understandings of being and selfhood are integrated with the intention to alleviate the suffering that emerges from our conditional self-forms.

My interest in the nature of suffering and the human condition has been fueled by my own healing journey, which began when I had a breakdown at age twenty-one. I found myself sitting in the university library, stuck, blank, brooding, and diligently depressed, as I stared for four days straight at the same picture of a cell. For me, it was both terrifying and stupefying to find myself sinking into an abyss that made no sense, yet felt eminently familiar. Many years later, I realized that I had been cast into the disconnection, meaninglessness, and non-being that Frank Lake, an analyst who explored ways to access and heal unresolved prenatal and birthing experience, calls the transmarginally stressed state, a dissociative state that arises due to very early trauma. I left school, went home, and entered psychoanalysis. I met with an analyst three times a week, and in the course of the analysis felt myself held in a truly non-judgmental listening space. This fostered a sense of safety and a renewal of trust, so that I could begin to explore myself and the causes of my suffering with more freedom. Over time, some sense of empowerment evolved, and that was the real start of my journey of self-inquiry.

Around the same time, I discovered Zen meditation and Buddhist mindfulness practices, which also became essential to my personal journey. Over time I explored various other personal growth, psychotherapeutic, and body-oriented healing modalities. With these various forms of support, I learned to explore my suffering with greater objectivity, curiosity, and interest. My guess is that many readers may relate to this experience: What seems to get us interested in the nature of suffering is our own suffering.

My wife Maura Sills, whose vision in seeing the connections between Buddhist and Western psychologies was groundbreaking for its time, initiated the development of Core Process work. Her unstinting belief in the primacy of awareness in healing processes has been inspiring to witness. The paradigm presented in these pages is based upon this work, as well as many hours of teaching, clinical practice, reading and integrating the thoughts and research of others, wonderful conversations with colleagues, and my own direct experience of the roots of being and selfhood.

As we undertake an inquiry into the nature of suffering, inevitably we must confront the nature of the conditioned self and the need to find the meaning of our lives. We find ourselves asking, "What does it mean to be?" I begin this book by inquiring into the nature of being through my interpretations of Martin Heidegger and Buddhist and Taoist concepts. Most of the book, however, is about the nature of self and selfhood as a process of becoming, rather than being. The nature of self, the principal concern of any psychotherapeutic form, must be understood and penetrated to some extent before the reality of being can be known.

Here we investigate the nature of being and the development of selfhood by weaving together concepts from object relations theories, pre- and perinatal psychology, and Buddhist self-psychology. Object relations help define the structure and nature of self-systems, while Buddhist psychology describes their moment-to-moment cycling. Thus I refer to the works of W. Ronald D. Fairbairn and Donald Winnicott, along with insights from Daniel N. Stern, and discuss them within the context of Lake's pre- and perinatal psychology and Buddhist concepts. I focus on Fairbairn's object relations as he maps out territories that are both straightforward and flexible to work with and, most importantly, congruent with Buddhist self-psychology. Likewise, Winnicott and Stern's insights into the nature of the early holding environment, the infant-mother relational field, and early perceptual dynamics inform both the psychotherapeutic process and the journey of self-discovery. As interpreted and integrated here, they each and all contribute to a more cohesive paradigm of being and selfhood.

Further, the healing journey is explored within the context of Buddhist self-psychology, which holds a process view of self that brings psychodynamics into the present moment of experience. From this evolves a paradigm for understanding personality development and for healing personal wounding. Although the paradigm offered here certainly is not the only one to describe this territory, its particular understanding of being and selfhood provides unique help to both client and therapist in understanding the nature of personal suffering and its alleviation.

The Wider Context

Growing up in the 1950s in the South Bronx, the local community was strong, even in the midst of a huge city. Its center was a shopping area whose shopkeepers knew all the local families' children by first name. Older brothers and sisters looked out for the younger ones in the streets; the local school was a focal point in the neighborhood; religion was a theme in everyday life; and a sense of cohesiveness prevailed. One had a clear sense of place and belonging, of one's particular part in it all.

Today, many of us are experiencing a breakdown in our families and communities, even in smaller towns, along with a loss of any sense of connection to each other, to the culture we are part of, and to the world at large. This alienation is amplified by our disconnection from the earth we live on that sustains all our lives, yet is at risk of being destroyed by our neglect and abuses. When any such critical structures break down, a shift occurs from being-to-being relatedness to self-defensiveness, with vast implications for life in all forms.

If the wider holding field for mother and other primary caregivers breaks down, this disharmony will be directly mirrored in the more local field they provide prenates, infants, and children. If the community, the family situation, or the holding field provided by primary caregivers to the infant in early life is fragmented, not cohesive, non-responsive, or inconsistent, or worse, rejecting, then self will form in fragmentation, in defended and defensive forms.

The breakdown of community and family, the growing isolation of individuals, the loss of cohesion seen in many cultures, and the loss of connection to the earth we live on have pervasive effects, which might include, for example, the increase we're seeing in autism and divorce rates, as well as the general sense of cultural malaise. Here we look at this malaise from a particular vantage point, one which considers the nature of being, the importance of the early holding environment, and the creation and dynamics of selfhood.

In order to heal the alienation in our culture, each of us must embark on our own healing journey, asking such questions as these: How do I generate suffering, both for myself and others? How do I contribute to the fragmentation and disconnection that I sense within me, in my immediate surroundings, and in the world at large?

And then the individual's healing journey must be considered in a wider context. The wider holding field and mutual interdependence of family, community, and culture plays a critical role in any inquiry into the nature of selfhood. Our personal journeys thus interrelate with and contribute to a larger healing process in the world around us. Within a Buddhist framework, we all *interbe*. We are all mutually interdependent, and all processes, even our self-self interactions, co-arise on a vast scale.

I hope that this book, in its own way, can help orient its readers to the possibility of the inherent freedom that is present in the midst of all of these seemingly intransigent conditions that surround us.

Intrinsic Health

As we delve into the nature of self and suffering, it is all too easy to pathologize the issues and particular personality forms under examination. The foundation of Core Process Psychotherapy is the experientially derived premise that, at the foundation of our human condition, there lies inherent health and a spiritual ground that, however obscured, are always present and available to us. In Tibetan Buddhism this ground is sometimes called Brilliant Sanity; and in Zen, True Mind. In Christianity, it is the ever-present Sacred Breath, or Holy Spirit. This intrinsic health infuses and supports life process and personality forms, no matter how distorted these may seem. One can learn to sense the presence of this spiritual underpinning no matter what the conditions are of one's life at any given moment, no matter how much one is suffering. As prenatal and early childhood woundings are resolved in session work, this inherent ground of health naturally comes to the forefront. I find that it naturally and spontaneously comes into play in all the deepest healing processes. It is a common experience that personal inquiries into the nature of suffering orient people not just to "what went wrong," or "what was not good enough," but to a deeper appreciation of spiritual connection and basic okay-ness.

The resolution of suffering entails more than just an expression of emotions, a clearing of trauma impacts and neural dysfunction, or a recognition and letting go of defensive or adaptive processes. On a deeper level, it involves realignment and reconnection to something often obscured by our subjective experience of life: our innate spiritual nature. In this vein, Maura Sills calls psychotherapy work the *reclamation of being*. Clients often remark that a greater sense of connection, joy, and equanimity emerges, as their suffering heals within the context of a wider truth. They find it easier to be compassionate both to themselves and to others.

In Core Process Psychotherapy we call this inherent state of health the Core State. As we shall see, this state naturally emerges as the therapist maintains a non-collusive ambiance of presence, acceptance, warmth, attunement, resonance, and responsiveness within the clinical setting. This ambiance orients the client to the unmet needs of the inner prenate, infant, and child, and helps direct session work not just to unresolved issues, but also to the inherent health that supports wellbeing even in the midst of these conditions.

1

Starting Points: Source, Being, and Self

There is something very important about being here in this present moment: At the root of our human condition, at the core of our very being, we are already free and fully realized. This inherent state of freedom and luminosity is called Big Mind or True Mind in Zen Buddhism. Its obscuration is the plight of our human condition. This book sets out to develop a cohesive paradigm of being and self that acknowledges the freedom at the root of our human condition and maps out the process of development of self and personality in relation to this deeper truth. This paradigm integrates concepts from Western and Eastern philosophy, object relations theories, pre- and perinatal psychology, and Buddhist self-psychology. Moving from the theoretical to the practical, we then conclude by addressing the questions: Given this understanding of our human condition, what heals the wounded self? And, how can a therapist be trained to facilitate this process? But we start where the Buddha began his inquiry, with the nature of suffering and its origins.

Suffering

The world is unstable. Natural catastrophes—hurricanes, earthquakes, storms—arise, accidents happen, and suffering is inevitably experienced. We are contingent and transient beings who are born, may become ill,

1

and certainly will die. Our loved ones will also get ill, grow old, suffer, and die. The likelihood is that things will hurt at times. However, life is not totally bleak. Pain is balanced by the joy and beauty also present in this world of ours, and the possibilities for love, compassion, and real companionship within the experience of being. It is imperative to form a relationship to the natural impermanence and instability inherent in our lives, and the pain that results from them.

Perhaps the hardest thing to understand and relate to is the suffering that we as human beings create for ourselves and others. Our tendencies to form fragmented and split selves, to become oppositional, territorial, and alienated, to lose contact with the inherent connectedness of all life, seem the cruelest of all causes of suffering. This inquiry points to possibilities, interrelationships, and processes that can address these causes and help alleviate them.

Four Noble Truths

I have always found solace and great inspiration in the Buddha's Four Noble Truths. They are a wonderful starting point into any journey that explores the nature of self and the human condition. One does not have to be a Buddhist to appreciate and benefit from the wisdom in them and the depths of inquiry that they open one to. In reading the original text of the Four Noble Truths, I have always been struck by their process-nature. Each of these four propositions is always coupled with an inquiry by which its truth can be realized.

In the First Noble Truth, the Buddha states that *there is suffering and it must be understood.* He did not state that all life is suffering, but that suffering is part and parcel of our human condition and, if we do not understand its origins, we will fall victim to it. The root of suffering in this framework is ignorance, a profound misperception and ignoring of what is many times clearly presenting itself to us within the pain of our relationships and the turmoil of our inner and outer worlds. The intention here is to become aware of our personal and interpersonal processes, to gain insight into the nature of suffering, and to find ways of letting it go.

The Second Noble Truth states that *there is an origin to suffering and it must be relinquished.* This origin is said to be clinging and attachment, which can also be understood as the basic drive that solidifies one's identity. The Buddha points out that it is attachment to the self and ignorance of its deepest underpinnings that are the foundations of suffering.

The psychotherapeutic journey also digs deeply into the roots of selfhood and suffering. The arising of the self-system is the basic ground of inquiry. Fairbairn, in presenting his object relations theory, stated that it is the closed and cyclical nature of self, with its inner loyalty and attachment to an internalized world of objects and conditions, that causes resistance to change and healing in psychotherapy and blocks the experience of greater freedom (Fairbairn, 1994a). In the course of this inquiry, we shall also see how attachment to self and its inner object world obscures natural luminosity and openness and conceals our deepest spiritual roots.

The Third Noble Truth affirms that *there is the possibility and presence of freedom, and it must be realized.* Here the Buddha points to a state called nirvana, a "blowing out" of the tendencies that lead to suffering. This blowing out can occur through an inquiry by which one comes to understand that the self, which seems so solid and stable, is really an ephemeral, contingent process in which any particular form or identity has only momentary existence. In this inquiry, one mindfully observes the process of the arising and passing away of the self and finds ways to simply be with this process that are liberating, allowing one to let go of the deepest wounds.

That is not to say, however, that this is a nihilistic journey. It is possible to discover a luminosity and freedom at the hub of the self-system that is often largely obscured. This sentience is an expression of life itself; an inherent openness of being not contingent upon the conditions of any particular moment.

In psychological terms, Winnicott stressed that an empathic holding environment provided by mother and other primary caregivers in early life allows the little one to settle into and explore, in an undefended way, the state of *simply being*. This allows for the development of a cohesive state of being at the hub of the developing self-system (Winnicott, 1965). Lake noted that in the presence of and reflection provided by the mother's being, the infant learns about its own being and spiritual nature. In later life, settling into the stillness of basic being opens the perceptual field to greater potential, the roots of the human condition, and the possibility of living without suffering.

The Fourth Noble Truth, *there is a path and it must be trod,* outlines an ethical approach to living and a process of inquiry that in our times, I feel, must take into account cultural and clinical needs, and the use of personal and interpersonal skillful means. The psychotherapeutic journey, coupled with the clarity of mindfulness practice, can do that. This orientation leads us into a very deep inquiry in which life's central questions—What does it mean to be? Who am I? Who have I become? Why do I suffer? Who suffers? Is there a way out of suffering?—naturally arise.

Source, Being, and Self

In initiating this inquiry into self and suffering, I will outline three territories I refer to as Source, being, and self. These terms are derived from the Buddhist concepts of *bodhicitta*, the already enlightened ground state; *citta*, the manifestation of that state as the core of our human existence; and *atta,* the self that is generated in response to life conditions. These are not mutually exclusive territories, but are holographically enfolded and spontaneously co-arise.

The nature of human-beingness cannot be reduced solely to genetic, neurological, or developmental processes; but must encompass the whole of human experience. In the context of this inquiry, life is seen to be an inherently spiritual journey, and being and self are clearly differentiated. I propose that *being* manifests as an innate core of sentience that is the true agent of awareness; while *self* represents the psycho-emotional-energetic constellations that are generated as being meets its relational world.

More specifically, *Source* represents a field of interconnection and openness at the heart of the human condition. The concept and experience of Source takes us into the realm of the archetypal energies described by Carl Jung, who oriented his psychology to the universal underpinnings of the human psyche. In some forms of Buddhism, Source is understood as an inherent emptiness, or the radiance of pristine awareness, a naturally enlightened, open ground that connects and informs all beings. In other spiritual traditions, Source is understood as a personal or an impersonal God, a Universal Principle or Creative Intelligence that permeates the human condition and all of creation. Given the premise of this book that life is essentially spiritual in nature, the greatest wounding any of us can experience is the obscuration of Source and the subsequent disconnection from, or dislocation of, being.

Being refers to the sentience or awareness underlying all self-constellations. It is the heart of I-am, a spontaneous center of presence that manifests from the moment of conception, is inherently connected to all other beings, and by its nature seeks to know the essence of its own being and the world it finds itself in. Coherency and continuity of being are fundamental aspects of a centered and responsive self-system. Its essential felt-nature is that of presence, or *sati,* as it is called in Buddhism. Being is not separate from the world it inhabits. Mutual interdependency is a central principle in Buddhist thought, in which things are understood to co-arise interdependently, and all beings are fundamentally interconnected. We interbe and are never truly out of relationship.

Fairbairn noted that we are never autonomous selves, but are always engaged in mutually interdependent self-other interchange. It is this basic state of interbeing that is at the root of relation-seeking. This archetypal being-to-being interconnection is critical to understanding early developmental experience, the infant-mother relational field, as well as therapeutic process. In essence, we seek other beings to know ourselves. If self is a wheel that spins in response to relational life, then being is the hub of that wheel. Being is both innate and developmental in nature and must not be confused with the self that constellates around it. As we shall see, being arises from Source, and it is Source that mediates being-to-being interconnection. Source manifests through being as natural compassion and loving connection. Source bestows meaning and allows being to imbue relationship with compassion.

Self is a constellation of psycho-emotional-physiological processes that we generally identify as me or mine. It is a dynamic and inner felt sense of I-am-this from which we tend to relate to others and the world around us. Self is not a discrete thing so much as a dynamic matrix of energy-exchange processes that organize internally in what I call self-constellations. Self-constellations are largely held together by the energies of conditioned tendencies, historical perceptions, and the charge of past experience called feeling tone in Buddhism. Feeling tone is a basic urge, a cellular imperative, towards or away from an object. Self is not just a mental construct, but a tonal, embodied feeling-experience: I am what I feel myself to be.

The self is relational in nature. It mediates being's relationship to the world and seeks to maintain that relationship under all conditions. As we experience self as I-am-this, we tend to shift identification from our natural being-state to the seemingly more solid feeling of selfhood. In this process, our being-nature becomes obscured to everyday perception. This will be discussed in greater detail later.

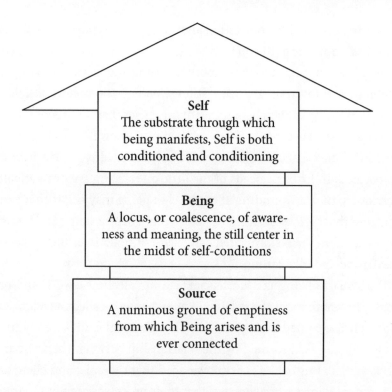

Fig. 1.1 Source—A numinous ground of emptiness
from which being arises and to which it is ever connected

Universal Axes

In following sections we will orient to two universal axes of relational process. The first is an inherently personal and spiritual one, that of Source-being-self. When being maintains its connection to its Source, and self is organized around that connection, then a sense of continuity and cohesiveness of being infuses the self. If being comes through the developing self-system as a stable presence, then all beings are seen to arise from the same Source and be interconnected and non-separate. This second important axis is an interpersonal one, the being-to-being axis. Here interbeing is directly experienced and interpersonal relationships are grounded in mutuality and compassion.

This being-to-being connection allows the archetypal maternal relational field to attune to the infant's being, its inner states and basic needs. It also allows the infant to sense mother's being and feel acknowledged, accepted, and loved at the deepest level. When the maternal field is attuned to the little one's being, the infant senses that it is unconditionally received and accepted and so can begin to know its own being and connection to Source. If the maternal holding field is poorly attuned or breached, if the basic needs of the little one's being are dramatically overridden, then a wounding at the level of being may occur that casts him* into the tragic experience of non-being. Then, as being and Source are obscured in the resulting defensive self-constellations, life is experienced as devoid of meaning.

The being-to-being axis is a crucial factor in all clinical work. In Core Process Psychotherapy, this relational interchange is called the *relational field,* a phrase coined by Maura Sills. The relational field is a conjoined being-to-being field formed by the relationship between therapist and client. Within this field it is acknowledged that therapist and client are on a mutually interactive journey, that their processes are not separate, and that what arises between them arises from the mutuality of their relationship. On the therapist's side, this being-to-being field has a dual archetypal nature. The maternal aspect is that of unconditional acceptance and nurturance and the paternal, that of protection, reassurance and safety. Therapists must be able to generate a true being-to-being holding field in order for a meaningful therapeutic process to unfold.

---

* I will refer to the prenate and infant in the male gender as "he" or "him" to more easily differentiate the infant in the written text from its mother.

Axes of Relating

The Source-being-self axis is universal and interactive. At any time we may orient to others from our self-position, feeling isolated and separate, or from innate being, through which we sense our connection and interbeing with others. When self is organized around a cohesive sense of being, then true being-to-being relatedness is possible. Self-self axes of relating are most common in everyday life, as we tend to relate to others from the viewpoint of the relatively fixed position of selfhood. Self mediates being's relationship with its outer world, and in that exchange relates the current relational encounter to past experiences. A particular form of selfhood then arises contingent on the situation, the nature of the current relational exchange, the past experience associated with it, and the particular internal organization of self that is activated. Self assumes the form that is most appropriate to the situation, or most comfortable, or most defended, given its inner organization and felt sense of the present moment.

However, being is never lost, and will shine through in safe, empathic relationships and situations. We may relate to others from our being-state in a being-self relational exchange, or we may find ourselves in true being-to-being relationship with intimate, attuned, safe others. Entering the being state with another allows the experience of true relatedness, where self-self interchange softens into interbeing.

Perhaps you have had the experience of meeting a stranger in a café. At first you are defended, protective of your space, unwilling to show them who you really are. Perhaps you're there to meet someone else, or fear that you may not be acceptable. All your self-forms are on-the-ready to protect you. Yet something happens. Perhaps it is a smile, or a kind word; and suddenly both you and the other person feel connection, maybe for a brief few moments before you part ways, or maybe as the start of an enduring friendship. Certainly I have met other beings in such a way and found it no small thing in the daily slog of life.

Likewise, we all know the company of those safe others—perhaps partners, family, or good friends—with whom we can settle into an undefended state and simply be. Within the context of psychotherapy, the therapist must learn to consciously settle into their being-state and hold the client in a being-to-being field of acceptance and non-judgment. As we shall see, the creation of this field influences session work in particular and both the client's and therapist's lives in general.

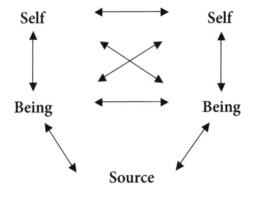

Fig. 1.2 Source-Being-Self Interactions.
Being arises from Source. At any time we may be in
Being-to-Being, Self-to-Self, or Being-to-Self relationship.

Territories of Therapeutic Work

The self-being-Source interplay is non-hierarchical, dynamic, and holistic in nature. Each state interpenetrates the other. They naturally co-arise in therapeutic work. Hartman and Zimberoff refers to these states as the ego, the existential level, and the transpersonal level, respectively (Hartman and Zimberoff, 2003). Work at the level of self orients to the experience of I-am-this and the dynamics associated with it. This is the territory of self-image, self-forms, self-defenses, and related relational processes. Here the basic wounds of selfhood are held by both the client's inner resources and the environment of the therapeutic relationship. As the self-forms generated by wounding emerge within the ambiance of trust and what is called *witness consciousness* in Core Process Psychotherapy, they can soften, and self-other boundaries can clarify as greater fluidity and ease emerges in self and self-other dynamics. The client moves from a defended and fragmented sense of selfhood to a more cohesive state centered in innate being.

Work at the level of being orients to the larger existential questions of life: Who am I? What does it mean to be? What is the nature of being? Issues of life and death emerge, insight into the angst or anxiety generated by the inherent impermanence of life arises, and a loosening of identification with selfhood and self-image has the potential to occur. As these issues are held within the resources of the client and the holding presence of the therapist, the potential for the reclamation of being truly unfolds.

Work at the level of Source is about reconnection to the deepest roots of life. Here our most painful wounds have the potential to heal. Lake called those tragic impairments *wounds at the level of being* (Lake, 1986a, 1986b). This level of wounding can only be healed by reconnection to spiritual essence or Source. When this reconnection occurs in the course of therapy, it's recognized as a state of grace by both therapist and client, as the experience surpasses any concepts or understandings held by either. With this opening in the therapeutic space, the potential for truly transcending the most painful and distorted conditions held within the self-system emerges.

Again, the levels of Source, being, and self are not clearly separate one from the other, and work at any level co-arises with that at each of the other levels. The following chapters suggest a paradigm for holding these Source-being-self interactions that I hope will provide a useful framework both for clinical and personal exploration.

2

Sentience and
Early Experience

What is sentience? I am proposing that sentience, as the determining factor in human existence, is an inherent ground state of consciousness independent of perceptual relationship to any object. It is a state of innate beingness or, as the Buddha described it, an innate luminosity. It is from this that the self emerges. It is essential not to reduce sentience to neurological and biological processes. We are more than the sum of our parts, and sentience is not just the result of having a central nervous system. Indeed, sentience is the very core of our being.

Prenatal and Perinatal Sentience

In the past, orthodox medicine and psychotherapy have held that infants and prenates could not remember their experience or perceive and respond to difficulty in the womb or during birth process. Over the last thirty years, however, much evidence has accumulated to show that prenates and infants are aware of their environment and register and respond to their sensory experiences. Infants in the womb have been shown to respond to loud noise, uncomfortable pressure, and strong maternal emotions. I have seen an amazing video of an eight-week-old fetus pushing away an amniocentesis needle! There has been research showing that infants remember

13

music played to them in the womb and also learn to orient to mother's voice in utero. It has also been shown that bonding and attachment processes begin in utero, not just after birth (Chamberlain, 1998; Maret, 1997; Verny, T. 1981).

I consider prenates and infants to be sentient, conscious beings capable of having experiences and processing those experiences. I believe this is true even at the embryonic stage of development, that there is sentience and response to relational experience right from the moment of conception. In this context, the prenate will protect himself from painful or stressful impingement and will respond and take shape relative to it. Lake was convinced that personality tendencies were already in place by the end of the first trimester in utero (Lake, 1979). In Buddhist psychology, personality tendencies called *sankhāras* are thought to be present from the earliest moments of incarnation (Payutto, 1994).

That most people do not acknowledge the sentience or intelligence of the yet-to-be born child is a great tragedy. This blindness to the reality of prenatal and infant intelligence leaves the little one in an extremely vulnerable position. In their sentience and openness, prenates and infants are especially attuned to their relational environment and are easily overwhelmed by lack of stimulation, denial of their basic needs, inattention, non-responsiveness, perceived danger, and powerful emotions in the field around them.

Historical Precedence

In the field of psychology, an acknowledgment of the sentience of newborns and the psychological importance of the prenatal and birth experience can be traced back to the early theories of Freud and Otto Rank. A strong belief in the preeminence of the birth experience was one of the causes of Rank's break with Freud. Later, psychiatrists Francis Mott and Nandor Fodor wrote extensively about pre- and perinatal experience as the foundation of personal suffering and personality formation (Fodor,

1949; Mott, 1964). Ronnie Laing, a well-known British psychotherapist who came to prominence in the 1960s and 1970s, also believed that the prenatal and birth experiences are fundamentally important in the formation of personality (Laing, 1976).

In the 1960s, Lake, originally a classical analyst, found, first in LSD sessions and later in breathwork and guided visualization, that his clients were accessing what seemed to be their earliest womb experiences. Lake developed a detailed paradigm of prenatal and birth experience and clearly linked it to personality development.

In the same period, another clinician and researcher, Stanislav Grof, was pivotal in bringing this area to the attention of a wider audience. Grof, initially via LSD research and later via breathing techniques, also discovered that clients could access what seemed to be very early prenatal and birth experience. He developed psychological theories and constructs around four basic stages of prenatal and birth experience he called basic perinatal matrices (Grof, 1979).

Other researchers and clinicians such as Swartley and Emerson followed this orientation and confirmed the importance of this earliest experience. Primal Integration Therapy has its roots in their work. Emerson has been very pivotal in my own understandings of this territory (Emerson, 1996). In a similar vein, Graham Farrant, a pioneering psychotherapist and associate of Emerson, believed that his clients were accessing memories of pre- and perinatal experiences held in the consciousness of the cells. The concept of cellular sentience is a useful starting point in our inquiry into early experience.

Sentience, Cellular Consciousness, and Memory

That personality tendencies may be generated from the earliest moments of life implies cellular sentience: that individual cells have the ability to perceive and respond to experience. From this implication many questions may arise: Who or what is having experience? What is consciousness? How are early experiences remembered? etc. Laing offers a poetic starting point from which to explore these questions when he writes:

> The environment is registered from the very beginning of my life, by the first one cell of me. What happens to the first one or two of me may reverberate throughout all subsequent generations of our first cellular parents. That the first one of us carries all my "genetic" memories … It seems credible, at least, that all our experience in our life cycle from cell one is absorbed and stored from the beginning, perhaps especially in the beginning. How that may happen I do not know. How can one cell generate the billions and billions of cells I now am? We are impossible, but for the fact that we are. When I look at the embryological stages in my life cycle I experience what feel to me like sympathetic vibrations in me now … how I now feel I felt then. (Laing, 1976)

Llinás, in his seminal work, *I of the Vortex: From Neurons to Self,* postulates that subjectivity, the ability to uniquely perceive and respond to the world, is a property of the single cell. According to Llinás, volitional movement or intention, and the need to predict the nature of the environment that the organism moves in, are what drive evolution. The organism needs to be able to predict the outcome of its intentions and actions for survival and to make subjective decisions about the world around it.

Perception and subjective experience are thus properties of the single cell, and feeling-shapes that Llinás calls "qualia," are generated within it as experience unfolds. These, in turn, allow the organism to know the current state of its environment in the context of past experience. It is thus critical to understand that cells perceive, feel, and respond to their environment, and that cellular perception is not dependent upon the presence of a fully formed central nervous system (Llinás, 2001).

This points to the real possibility that the single cell at conception is sentient, has subjective experience of its relational world, and responds to that experience. As the brain later develops, this early perceptual experience may be incorporated into the developing self-system as information about its environmental and relational milieu. As a closed self-referential system develops, this information may thus contribute to the form the organism assumes. This is really not such a strange concept as it may at first seem. Theorists in pre- and perinatal psychology have postulated that cellular memory begins with the single cell at conception, is held holistically as a field state, and is passed on to every subsequent cell (Emerson, 1996; Lake, 1979; Laing, 1976).

Research supports that cells are extremely sensitive to their environment, respond to the conditions present, and learn from that experience (Stone, 1989). This implies memory and true intelligence. We tend to assume that intelligence is a manifestation of the brain and intellect exclusively; yet this research shows that intelligence is much deeper than mental processes. The single cell "is" and has similar needs to multicellular forms. Safety, acceptance, and ongoing sustenance are needs present at all stages of embryonic development. Echoing this understanding, embryologists such as Erich Blechshmidt and Jaap van der Wal are convinced that the earliest processes of human formation are not determined by genes, but by forces present within the fluids of the embryo. They further believe that at each developmental stage, the embryo is complete in itself, a fully functioning being doing what it needs to do. Van der Wal also affirms that embryological development is a response to the play of consciousness. Thus there is being from the moment of conception (Blechshmidt, 1978, 2004; van der Wal, 2002).

Cells have the physiological ability to perceive the emotional environment they are in. Even the single cell at conception has receptors for stress hormones and other neuro-active chemicals that help it monitor and respond to the environment. The inner structure of the cell is supported by microscopic connective tissues called microtubules. When the neuro-hormonal receptors for catecholamines and other stress-related hormones are full, these microtubules may contract in response to the perception of a hostile environment. This information may then be passed on in subsequent cell divisions and impact and sensitize the developing nervous system. Even at this most earliest stage of life, the being may become sensitized to its womb environment, perhaps even manifesting autonomic hypersensitivity after birth. I propose that this may be an important factor in later hyperactivity and insecure attachment processes.

Field Consciousness and Fluid Memory

In considering early sentience, the interplay of consciousness with what takes place in the surrounding field is an interesting area to explore. I recently attended a conference in London in which Masaru Emoto presented research that showed that water is directly affected by thoughts and emotions and can hold memories of its experience. Water forms different kinds of crystalline structures depending on the environmental factors, including thought and emotion, impacting it. If water is in the presence of wholesome environmental factors, or wholesome thoughts and positive emotions, beautiful crystalline structures result. If unwholesome environmental factors or negative thoughts or emotions are present, the crystalline structures break down or fragment. In other words, thought and emotion directly impact the structure and form of water at a molecular level. This impact remains as a kind of fluid-crystalline memory (Emoto, 1999).

At the same conference, Mae Wan Ho, a biophysicist and geneticist, presented research that showed that memory may be held within the water molecules that surround and interpenetrate all cells. Ho postulated that water may even be a vehicle for consciousness itself. She also presented research that showed that microtubules, which help to maintain the shape and movement of living cells and the transportation of material within them, resonate and vibrate to the information received from the surrounding environment. All cellular microtubules vibrate together as the unstruck strings of a piano resonate together with the other strings that have been struck. Through this resonance the microtubules rapidly pass information from cell to cell throughout the body. They may also hold memories of the initial encounter as vibratory forms in the surrounding fluids.

Ho also researched quantum-level field phenomena in living organisms. Her research with single-cell and invertebrate animals shows that all these organisms are organized within stable quantum fields of light (Ho, 1998). In fact these fields seem to organize all life forms. They seem to order the anatomy of the organism and are intelligently responsive to the environment. For example, when toxins are placed in the fluid that an organism resides in, the quantum field responds first by distortion and reorganization, and then the anatomy and physiology of the animal follow suit. Then when the toxin is removed, the field again responds first. It reorients to its own midline, and then the anatomy and physiology of the animal respond in kind. The quantum field responds to the environment and does the 'intelligent thing,' and it seems to hold the memory both of the ideal form of the organism and of the events or conditions it encounters over time.

Ho believes that all organisms, including humans, are formed in such an intelligent, responsive quantum field. She has undertaken research to show that the fluid field within organisms is a medium for quantum-level information exchange at nearly the speed of light. She suggests that fluids and tissue in the human body function together as a unified liquid-crystalline structure that holds memory. Here we have evidence of field organization, field memory, and consciousness at work at both primitive and the most highly evolved levels of organization.

Rupert Sheldrake proposes a similar kind of field consciousness whereby memory is held holographically and is available simultaneously to every cell. Sheldrake postulates that personal and ancestral memory are passed on through a field of energetic interconnection that he calls the morphogenetic field. He rejects the idea that memory is stored solely in the brain and central nervous system and sees the brain less as a container for memory than a receiver for tuning into the morphogenetic field. The morphogenetic field holds the memory of all experienced conditions, and the brain accesses this memory via resonance. If we consider that the information held in this field is available to each and every cell of the organism, then the idea of earliest memories being accessible even to single cells is not so farfetched. In keeping with the Buddhist understanding, all phenomena are understood to co-arise within a unified and ubiquitous field of interconnection and interbeing. This field holds the memory of all past events and all potential futures. In this way past, present, and future are simultaneous and accessible at each and every moment, and memory is held in a much wider field than that of the individual human being. Each being's life and ancestral history is seen to be totally interconnected and interdependent with that of every other being.

In research at the Heartmath Center, human placental DNA was placed in a container within which changes in the DNA could be measured (www.heartmath.org). It was discovered that the DNA changed shape relative to the emotional field generated by the researchers involved! When researchers felt love and gratitude, DNA strands seemed to relax and unwind. When anger, fear, or stress was present, the DNA strands became shorter and tightened up. It was also observed that DNA coding seemed to become inactive in the presence of strongly negative emotions. These codes reactivated when the field changed to positive emotions of love, gratitude, joy, etc. It does not seem unreasonable to suppose that this responsiveness of DNA to changing conditions may be at the heart of the evolutionary process and provides further evidence of a cellular, field, and memory process that far surpasses the functioning of the central nervous system.

Applying this research to human psychology, here we are looking at the possibility that not only might the fluids within the cell hold the memory and emotional tone of early experience, but the conceptus might actually hold the tonal quality of both father and mother's state of consciousness at the time of conception! And perhaps the embryo and prenate are organized by the intelligence of quantum fields, and these fields and the fluids within them, hold memories of environmental processes, including the emotional environment of the placenta and surrounding womb. Thus prenatal and infant memories may be held as field phenomena transmitted to every cell of the body. This would be an extremely efficient form of memory retention and information processing, with the implication that cells are not separate entities, but are interconnected in all their experiences. These fields may even be expressions of the universal aspect of consciousness itself. The biophysicists involved seem to believe that this is the case. Such possibilities support the Buddhist concepts of non-separateness and of karmic memory, whereby the personal, familial, and cultural influences are all present right from the beginnings of life. And all of these ideas point to the possibility that consciousness is an ever-present ground of being, rather than solely a product of the central nervous system. It seems feelings and emotions are a universal language resonant at all levels of being. Thus cells may thus exist within a unified matrix of energetic interchange that connects all of creation.

Sentience in Frank Lake's Prenatal Paradigm

It is my belief, supported by my experience as a clinician, that cellular memory is a real possibility, and that memory is also maintained as a field state in the human body-mind system. I perceive this reality at work as I hold a receptive and gentle awareness of the field around and between a client and myself, and information is passed subliminally between us. In this circumstance I have learned to trust what I sense, as I see no reason to negate the possibility that memory imprints may be communicated within this interactive field. I believe that a human being is more than the composite of their anatomy and physiology; that his or her nature is defined at subtle levels of sentience, spirit, and life-force; and that it is crucial for those in the healing professions to keep an open mind about the nature of being and sentience.

As Lake was one of the fathers of modern pre- and perinatal psychology, his ideas on sentience have particular importance. In many ways, sentience is the first and most important aspect of Lake's prenatal paradigm. As his work unfolded over many years, he became convinced that there is sentience from the moment of conception. He refers to cellular consciousness in his writings and was clear that the prenate is a conscious being having and processing experience even during the embryonic period. Lake believed that memory is not dependent on having a fully formed central nervous system and that the memory of the single cell at conception is enfolded within the whole human being. To support his insight, Lake referred to the ideas of Karl Pribram, a scientist who researched memory as a holographic phenomena (Pribram, 1970, 1971), and David Bohm, a physicist who developed what is known as the holographic paradigm (Bohm, 1980).

Pribram postulated that memory is held holographically within the brain and central nervous system. Memory manifests in the organism as a field phenomena and is not necessarily linked to specific neurons, cells, or sites in the brain or body. Information is held and accessed via interactions that are state—not place—specific. Lake extended this concept to postulate that memory is present as a cellular field state from the moment of conception; that every cell shares in, or is a manifestation of, a unified field of holistic consciousness.

Bohm envisaged the universe as a conscious holographic entity with information of the whole enfolded in every part and held as an implicate order that underlies reality. Thus all of us are connected by and are part of this vast implicate order. Every cell holds the past and present experience of the entirety of being, from the level of the smallest living thing to that of the universe as a whole.

Lake, teeing off on these ideas, proposed that memory may be holographically encoded by the protein molecules present in every cell and transferred with every cell division from conception onwards. He extrapolated that memory is a holographic field state present from the first moments of life and is held as field phenomena accessible through that life's duration. In this framework, every cell has access to the memory of the whole and individual human consciousness is not separate from the universe we inhabit.

3

The Nature of Being

Sentience implies a quality of being, the presence of something. In this vein, the German philosopher Martin Heidegger marveled, "Why is there something as opposed to nothing?" He wrote,

> … the wonder (is) that a world is worlding around us at all, that there are beings rather than nothing, that things are and we ourselves are in their midst, that we ourselves are and yet barely know who we are, and barely know that we do not know all this. (Polt, 1999)

For most of us, a basic beingness and selfhood is at the heart of our experience of life. We feel ourselves being. There is the sense of I-am. In developmental psychology and objects relation theory, the nature of being and the self-sense are fundamental to understanding suffering and personality formation. Yet when one begins to inquire into the nature of being, it can be like trying to grasp flowing water. As you immerse yourself in water, you sense its supportive nature. You perceive its presence, you sense temperature, motion, and fluidity; yet its true nature is difficult to describe and even more difficult to define. Being is very much like this. As this inquiry into being and Source may take us into a basically unanswerable mystery, I approach this subject with great interest and some trepidation; for the one seeking to understand the nature of being is also the being itself.

The nature of being is one of the great philosophical conundrums. Aristotle and Plato inquired into it, classical Indian and Chinese philosophies dwelled upon it, and modern philosophers are still debating it. I will explore the nature of being from a number of perspectives. I would like to open this inquiry with the thoughts of two German philosophers.

Husserl and Heidegger

What is does it mean to be? The German philosopher Husserl explored the question of is-ness, or being, within the context of present-time awareness. He was a phenomenologist who inquired into the essential nature of things, their being-nature, or what really exists. He said that as you pay gentle attention to things, their essential nature clarifies. Things are naturally *self-showing;* they *unconceal* themselves to you. They give you evidence of their existence. This natural process of unconcealment is at the heart of all therapeutic and healing processes.

To Husserl's understanding, perception of the phenomena related to a thing or entity, its *being-nature,* can lead you to its essence, its timeless and perfect nature. That is to say that being is innate, present at the heart of things, and not bound by time or history. Being is an essence that is complete in and of itself and, in the right circumstances, will unconceal itself to you. My experience in clinical practice, as well as through meditative and contemplative practices, seems to confirm Husserl's understanding of the essential nature of being.

Husserl's eminent student Martin Heidegger, while deeply influenced by his teacher's ideas, did not engage in a metaphysical exploration of the innate nature of being, but undertook to understand the context in which being could be understood. For Husserl, being manifests as an is-ness that is deeper and wider than any particular attribute or content. Heidegger, however, believed that being could only be understood and experienced within the context of time and the nuances of personal, familial, and cultural meaning. Time and history lend context and meaning to being's existence. A car may be a certain shape, color, and model; but the is-ness of it for any particular person is something else. Its meaning is far more than its shape or performance. It exists in inter-being with our psyche in the wider context of the world we live in.

Heidegger uses the German term *Dasein*—literally, "being there"—to indicate the entity that can have an understanding or perceptual sense of Being and its world. Each being as *Dasein* has a way of being that is different from every other way-of-being, whether that of another human, or of a cat, dog, or tree. This way of being has a context, a world it finds itself in. *World* for Heidegger means not just places and things, but the inter-relational meanings and purposes that enable one being to relate to others. Thus in Heidegger's thought, being is relational in nature and can only be understood within the context of time and history (Heidegger, 1992; Polt, 1999).

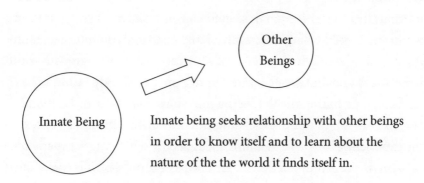

Fig. 3.1 Innate Being Is Naturally Relation-Seeking

In psychological terms we might liken *Dasein* to the self. As we've previously defined it, self is the conditioned form that develops as being meets its world of contingencies. Self mediates being's relationship to the world and is, in turn, shaped by that encounter. As this occurs, being develops a *way of being*. In this context, self can only be understood in terms of the being that manifests through it, and being can only be understood in terms of its way of being and the world it inhabits. In other words, being cannot be separated from its context of relationships, history, and time. Heidegger considers time not just as the sequential passing of moments, but as all of history, all of the past and its implications, and all potential futures, right here in this present moment. According to Heidegger, being cannot be known separate from this context.

Heidegger describes *Dasein* not as a thing, but as a process that manifests a particular way of being. This parallels our definition of self as process-oriented and not as a fixed entity and echoes Buddhist concepts of self-nature. Furthermore, self holds a sense of there-ness that refers not just to the world around it, but to an inner sense of there-in-here. Self internalizes its relational experiences so that being there includes the inner meanings we give to "world" and our relationship to it. Self can only function within the context of its internalized world of meaning and form. Thus, on a deep level, we are our own "there." In various object relations theories, the infant is seen to take in, or internalize, its relational world and to split what is internalized into good and bad internal objects. As a result, the developing sense of self is also split or fragments as different ways of being are generated in response to this dynamic.

Heidegger maintains that being must have *Dasein* in order to manifest, to be at all. In our terms, being can only arise within the context of the experiential world of meaning mediated by self. Being is experienced as I-am, while self filters that experience as I-am-this. Thus the context for being is self and the context for self is a world of meaning, and being and self are mutually interactive. Being needs self in order to manifest in the relational world of form, and self needs being as the fulcrum for a cohesive I-am experience.

Being in Buddhism and Taoism

Buddhism denies the solidity of self, but addresses the nature of being in various ways dependent on the particular tradition. In early Buddhism, being-nature was described as a center of awareness and knowing, the *knowing faculty,* a function of what the Buddha called *citta.* The term citta has many connotations and is usually translated as mind and/ or mental states and activity. Rune Johansson, a Swedish psychologist and Buddhist scholar, likens citta to a locus of awareness within the movement of ego or personality. He writes, "It [citta] is not the same as "personality"; rather a centre within personality, a conscious centre of activity, meaning, and emotionality" (Johansson, 1979). It is a stable center of knowing that has continuity in the midst of all conditions and manifests as *presence,* a deeper sense of I-am. Note that it is being that holds true meaning, not the conditioned self that organizes around it. This core of presence is at the heart of the understanding of sentience in Buddhism.

Buddhism states that all beings are sentient from the first moments of life. It is this sentient core that is said to migrate from life to life. This nucleus of beingness is a universal presence within each and every life, from that of your neighbor, your pet dog, and the bird you see flying in the sky, to that of the earthworm in your garden. Being is a locus of presence and sentience, a *knowing* that pervades consciousness. Being can be thought of as a coalescence of awareness that orients to the world through being-self interactions. Being needs self as the mediator of experience, and self needs being for coherency and continuity. Being lies at the hub of the self-system, and orients to the world through self's perceptual processes.

In an early discourse, Buddha states that citta is inherently luminous and free, but that this luminosity is obscured by conditions that come from the outside (Pali Canon: *Anguttara Nikaya,* I:10). Being, in this context, is seen to be inherently pure, radiant, and empty of self. At the heart of human experience is an essence of luminosity and openness. In Zen, the understanding that beings are inherently enlightened and liberated reflects this truth. In Mahayana Buddhism, citta is also understood as a coalescence of a wider presence called Bodhicitta, the already free and enlightened state, a pristine awareness ever present within all forms of sentience. It is being that manifests the peace and interconnection of this awareness, rather than the conditioned self we tend to identify with. When a person attained their freedom, or enlightenment, the Buddha would say, "Citta is free." It is not the self that is liberated, but the deeper beingness at the heart of a life. When citta is liberated, its Source is known.

When being comes to the forefront, felt qualities of openness, vibrancy, warmth, and radiance are directly experienced and the heart opens as a loving presence pervades the immediate moment. The inherent interconnection of all beings and things makes itself known, and compassion naturally flows as an expression of this interbeing and gives true meaning to life. The tragedy of human life is that we, more often than not, identify with our conditioned self or ego, and being becomes clouded over, concealed, obscured, as does our natural connection to other beings. Heidegger's term for this is *ontic obscuration* (Heidegger, 1992).

In Taoism, the source of being is Tao. Tao is a numinous unseen essence that underlies all of existence. We are empowered by Tao to be. A mysterious presence called Te mediates this empowerment. Te is sometimes translated as virtue, as in "by the virtue of the power invested in me." In Taoism, the relationship of Tao, as the essence, to Te, as an innate center or agency of beingness, is in some ways similar to the relationship in Buddhism of Bodhicitta, as boundless awareness and true reality, to citta, as the personal expression of that truth. Te is the inner power that is the fulcrum and agent of our being nature. When this fulcrum is aligned to Source, it manifests as a center of stillness, empowerment, and resource. Each and every one of us is truly empowered to be. If this core of beingness is not completely obscured as self coalesces, then a coherent center of being that has continuity throughout life's journey can be sensed at one's core. Even in the midst of painful and seemingly chaotic experience, coherency and continuity of being is present. Our being-nature is sensed when we dis-identify with conditioned self-constructs and self-view. This can only occur in a state of knowing or presence, which allows our self-constellations to soften and open. This, as we shall see, lies at the heart of Core Process Psychotherapy and of all healing processes in general. The essence of being can only be known in the stillness of presence and the manifestation of being can only be known in the context of the phenomenological world. As Heidegger stressed, being only has meaning in relationship and time, and relationship is the heart of the experience of life. Being arises from Source and the context for its development is its relational world.

Being in Christianity

The Christian tradition orients to the soul-nature at the core of human experience and its relationship to God-as-Source. Jesus spoke in Aramaic, and Douglas-Klotz has done beautiful work in translating and reinterpreting the New Testament from the original Aramaic texts (Douglas-Klotz, 1999). Aramaic is a language whose words have many connotations and nuances, and translation will always be interpretive. The Aramaic word *naphsha* has been variously translated into English as soul, self, and life. In the original Aramaic, naphsha has the connotation of a deeper subconscious self, a locus of consciousness beneath particular self-experience. In Jungian terms, this might be similar to the archetypal Self whose presence is obscured or distorted as the conditioned self takes form. Douglas-Klotz writes, "… the soul-self naphsha is really a continuum that connects the 'heavenly' or vibrational aspect of being with the 'earthy' or particular aspect." On the Source-being-self axis, naphsha is a continuum of being not separate from the Source of its creation. Thus naphsha, as our essential soul or being-nature, is neither an isolated form nor separate from all of existence. As Douglas-Klotz points out, in Jesus' Aramaic world a person was not thought to *have* or possess a soul, but *to be* the soul whose essential nature is a direct manifestation of *alaha*, Sacred Unity, One-ness, the All, the God-within. In the Aramaic world, heaven and earth, God and person, are not separate. All is one as Sacred Unity reigns supreme.

Douglas-Klotz suggests that the way to know Sacred Unity is to surrender the experience and attachment to separateness and to attend to, or be present for, the love at the core of one's being. This love is not separate from God's love that permeates all of existence, an understanding that resonates with the Buddhist teaching that compassion underlies and supports all of existence. From Douglas-Klotz's translations of Mark:

> Everyone who desires to give energy
> to his separate, subconscious self (naphsha)
> will eventually find that self surrendered,
> extinguished in the Only self. (Mark 8:35–36)
> Let compassion unfurl from your inner womb
> for Sacred Unity *(alaha)*
> in the form that impresses you most deeply,
>> inside or out.
> Send this love with and through your whole passionate self,
> your whole awakening, subconscious self,
> your whole instinctive mind,
> and with all of your life energy. (Mark 12:30–31)
> (Douglas-Klotz, 1999)

This is a radical reinterpretation of Mark, where *giving energy* is understood as being present both for the direct experience of one's deepest soul-nature and for the love that connects us to Source and to other beings. The teaching is to direct that love to every expression of being and to give oneself to the Sacred Unity, the ground from which love emerges. The spiritual journey is understood as the relinquishment of the conditioned temporal self and a turning inward to allow the love at the core of one's being to shine through. Father Keating, the developer of Centering Prayer, a modern form of contemplation based upon the medieval text, *The Cloud of Unknowing*, writes as follows:

> Christian life and growth are founded on faith in our basic good-ness, in the being that God has given us with its transcendent potential. This gift of being is our true self … God and our true self are not separate. Though we are not God, God and our true self are the same thing. (Keating, 1986)

Here again being-nature is described as innate, naturally manifesting transcendent potential, the potential to directly know its Source and the Sacred Unity that informs all things. God is not separate from creation and beings are not separate from the God-within.

The great Christian mystic Meister Eckhart wrote this about the nature of being and Source:

> God's being is my being and God's primordial being is my pri-mordial being. Wherever I am, there is God. The eye with which I see God is the same eye with which God sees me. God created all things in such a way that they are not outside himself … Rather, all creatures flow outward, but nonetheless remain within God … Being is God's circle and in this circle all creatures exist. Every-thing that is in God is God. (Fox, 1983)

Here we are again cast into the primordial mystery of life: In our dif-ferentiation, we are not separate. All beings arise from the same Source and abide in Sacred Unity. The Source-being-self axis is forever one. This resonates with the Taoist concept that all things arise from and return to Tao. Nothing exists outside of Tao, and all things are direct manifestations of its intentions. Once again, the great challenge of life is to relinquish our apparent separateness and all that obscures our most basic being-nature, to reclaim this essential core, and to know our direct connection to Source in the heart-felt experience of being.

Being in Object Relations and Self-Psychology

Object relations theorists have largely avoided discussion of innate being, transpersonal energies, and spirit, perhaps because such concepts seem unscientific. Nonetheless, the subject of being has, to some degree, been explored. Although concepts of ego, self and being are commonly conceptually intermixed in object relations theory, there are some strands of thought that have grappled with the concept of being. I relate briefly below the ideas of a number of psychological theorists, including Fairbairn, Winnicott, Kohut, Jung, Bowlby, and Lake.

Fairbairn

Fairbairn was the first theorist to propose a full object relations theory. He stated that there is an *original ego* at birth that is whole, has agency, and is inherently relation-seeking. He retained the term ego to acknowledge the roots of his analytic work, but his use of the word was very different from Freud's. For Freud, ego has no inherent energy, but is a mechanism that mediates the tensions between instinctual impulses and the constraints of family and society. Fairbairn, on the other hand, defines ego as having its own energies and agency and as inherently object-relation-seeking and directly responsive to the impact of external experience. His concept of original ego is very close to that of being as defined above; that is to say, it's a holistic locus of presence or awareness that has agency, is inherently connected to other beings, seeks relationship and is impacted by experience.

Fairbairn believed that original ego becomes fragmented or split due to the ambiguity of primary relationships, the perceived goodness or badness of the maternal field, and breaches in empathic relating by mother and other primary caregivers. In our terms, it is innate being that is a holistic center of sentience. It never becomes split, though it can become deeply obscured to everyday awareness. What does manifest in split and fragmented forms is not being, but the self that coalesces as being meets a world of contingency.

Winnicott

Winnicott, a contemporary of Fairbairn, believed that a continuous sense of being was essential for a cohesive self-system. He held that continuity of being is developmental in nature within the acceptance, warmth, and appropriate responsiveness of mother and other primary caregivers. As mother and others generate a holding field that is sufficiently attuned to the infant's needs, the little one can rest in what Winnicott calls the unintegrated state. This is an undefended and open state within which the infant can simply be. Winnicott believed that the infant shifts from an undifferentiated state merged with mother, to individuation, the process of developing a discrete and separate sense of being in the world. In this way a "self-experiencing being" develops (Winnicott, 1965, 1987).

Within the safe holding field, what he calls the *true self* can arise. This is a self that is organized around a continuous sense of being and is in mature relationship with others. It can negotiate its needs while responding to the needs of others in appropriate ways. This being-sense is independent of life circumstances, and is whole and self-referring even when facing negative conditions. On the other hand, if the maternal holding environment is not adequately attuned to the infant, then what Winnicott called the *false self* arises. The false self cannot differentiate its needs from the needs of others and organizes its relational field in defensive and distorted ways.

Kohut

Kohut, like Winnicott, believed that a cohesive sense of being could only arise within the safety of an empathic relational field. Contrary to Winnicott, however, he believed that the infant is not initially lost in some undifferentiated or merged state from which he then shifts into individuation, but is a unique individual from the start who is seeking and taking part in relational experience (Kohut, 1978, 1984). This mirrors concepts in found in Fairbairn and Lake's work and in Core Process Psychotherapy. Echoing Fairbairn and also Heidegger, Kohut asserted that there is no experience or sense of self that is not derived from relationship to another. The developing sense of being is dependent upon at least one essential other who functions as an empathic touchstone. Self is so dependent on the external other that Kohut called self's outer object the *selfobject*. Self only experiences a center of being in the presence of the selfobject, and being only knows itself by reflection. Similar to the dynamic described by Winnicott, through the mirroring of an empathic primary relationship, a sense of personal being develops in relation to the selfobject. This sense of being is internalized and then the external selfobject is no longer needed for continuity of being to be experienced throughout life's vicissitudes. A cohesive *nuclear self* emerges and a *nuclear program* that gives meaning to life clarifies. The nuclear self, somewhat similar to Winnicott's true self, is seen to be the self-principle around which the person's sense of being is organized and from which his or her life plan is generated.

Jung

Jung, on the other hand, differentiates between self as ego and Self (with a capital 'S') as the mediator and organizing principle of life (Jung, 1976). Self is seen to be a deeper transpersonal center with multiple relationships to ego process, to the divine, and to archetypal realms. It is from this Self-center that self, or ego, springs as the various conditions of life are encountered. Self is the seat of being and has direct connection to the archetypal forces that the ego draws upon. In Kohut's term's, Jung's Self might be a kind of internal selfobject that is present from the beginning of life—not just a developmental structure, but innate, transpersonal, and already connected to the ordering and organizing forces of life. It is Self that is reflected within the relational field of the empathetic caregiver, whose attuned field is the context that allows Self to emerge in the world of conditions. It is through empathetic mirroring that Self is supported, connection with divine and transpersonal forces is maintained and a coherent sense of being upheld. A healthy and fluidly functioning self is based upon alignment with Self and its deeper resources. In Jung's work we again see that being, as Self, is both innate and relational.

Bowlby

John Bowlby was an English psychoanalyst who worked primarily with children. He was unhappy with the existing psychoanalytic theories of child development: object relation theories based on Melanie Klein that saw the development of personality as a largely internal process fueled by the child's fantasies, defense mechanisms, and projections. He felt that the actual, living relationship between mother, other primary caregivers, and the child were not fully taken into account or given enough weight. From his observations he developed what has become known as attachment theory.

Bowlby discerned that there were distinct stages related to the child's development of feelings of security, continuity of being, and wellbeing. Like Winnicott, Bowlby believed that a safe and empathic holding environment is essential. When the primary caregiver maintains an attuned, resonant, and appropriately responsive relational field, the infant or young child can experience a *secure base,* a responsive relational environment within which needs are met in an adequate way. From this secure base, the infant can begin to explore his world.

Initially, this is a spatial process in which the child seeks to maintain a certain minimum distance from its secure base. This is called *proximity seeking.* If the distance is too great from the secure base of primary caregiver, the child experiences *separation anxiety,* a term originated by Fairbairn. The child becomes anxious and expresses his need for contact and reassurance by protesting in some way. This is called *separation protest,* which has four basic levels. The child may initially appeal for contact through voice and motion and through reaching out towards the caregiver. If an appropriate response is not offered, then this may change to crying and anger. If the contact and responsiveness of primary caregivers is still withheld, or not present, then this may shift to withdrawal or, in the extreme, detachment and dissociative processes. As we shall see, this mirrors the fight-or-flight response and Lake's concept of the transmarginal stress hierarchy.

If the relational environment is safe and largely responsive to the child's needs, then the child will internalize this sense of safety as an *internal secure base.* He then brings this inner security to bear on all of his relationships and develops an ability to clearly discern if particular relationships meet his needs. The child further internalizes its relational experiences as an *internal working model* of his world and develops an inner continuity of being organized around the internalized secure base. An attuned and responsive holding field generates an inner sense of security called *secure attachment;* inconsistent, unresponsive, or abusive holding fields will generate *insecure attachment.* In insecure attachment, the child develops a self-system based upon relational wounding and will play out his internalized insecure base in all primary relationships (Bowlby, 1969; Holmes, J, 1993, 2002).

Lake

As already discussed, Lake believed that there is sentience present from the earliest moments of life and that our earliest experiences create the ground for the later development of selfhood. Lake defined the nature of being in terms consistent with his Christian background. Being, he suggested, develops in relationship to a divine Source, and Christ is the divine transpersonal selfobject at the heart of being. Life is sustained by Christ-love. This is similar to the idea in Mahayana Buddhism that compassion is the archetypal force that sustains life and moves us, if we are resonant with its presence, to respond to suffering. In Lake's paradigm, the *womb of spirit* is the early relational field that reflects this nature. It is within the empathetic, safe, and reflective field of mother-as-source, that the connection to divine Source is maintained and being is nurtured. Lake believed that the womb of spirit is one in which the maternal presence reflects mother's own spiritual essence and in that reflection the child discovers his own being and connection to Source. Here again, being only knows itself via relationship to other beings.

In Lake's work, the sentience of the prenate is a given. In pre- and perinatal psychology, the prenate can only exist in the context of the maternal womb-field surrounded by all of mother's psycho-spiritual-emotional-physiological processes and the wider world that mother inhabits. The prenate exists in interbeing with all of this and, indeed, cannot be separated from it. Lake affirms, as did Winnicott, that the infant's coherency and continuity of being is dependent upon the presence of a safe, trustworthy, and responsive early holding environment. The good enough empathic holding field provided by mother and primary caregivers allows his sense of being to develop and mature. Initially, the little one recognizes his own beingness only in relation to mother's presence and being. Within the good enough womb of spirit, a coherency and continuity of being begins to develop. After birth, the infant's beingness is further reflected in mother's tender gaze and by other primary caregivers within the larger familial and societal field. In mother's loving presence, the infant knows *it is* and deserves *to be*. As the infant later explores his world, the safe holding environment of being-in-relationship allows it to develop a sense of *being-in-itself,* a coherent and continuous sense of being with self-reflective ability. The little one now senses his own being as a stable inner presence. According to Lake, as well as to Kohut and Winnicott, at this point being no longer needs reflection from another, but is fully empowered *to be* in the world.

4

Source

Being has a source. In all traditional healing and spiritual traditions, an understanding and relationship to Source is the key to wisdom and happiness. The exploration we are undertaking in this volume is grounded in the understanding that the human journey is essentially spiritual and some acknowledgment of Source must be included in any inquiry into the nature of that journey.

The following is an introduction to some traditional concepts of Source. In the end, the experience of Source is a unique one for each of us whose truth cannot be realized by intellectual inquiry alone. In the words of Lao Tzu, "Those who know don't speak, those who speak don't know" (Lui, 1974). So, as one who is speaking, I enter this territory with great humility.

Source in Buddhism and Taoism

In some Mahayana traditions, Source is understood as emptiness, a state of primordial potential beyond all concepts of being or non-being. It manifests as Bodhicitta, a numinous ground of pristine awareness from which all activity emerges. Bodhicitta is a field of coherency and presence from which the experience of interconnection and non-separateness arises. If being is like a coalescence of awareness within the mind-body process, then Bodhicitta is the field from which it coalesces. This innate ground of pristine awareness is called *Rigpa* in the Nyingma tradition of Tibetan

Buddhism. Its felt-experience manifests as the *Brahma Viharas,* the illimitable states of consciousness. These are inherent qualities of consciousness that naturally emerge as self-view is even momentarily dropped. They manifest in equanimity and presence, in the flow of compassion and loving kindness, and in a direct experience of joy-in-relatedness. These are a direct experience of the alignment of the Source-being axis, which manifests as true interbeing in open-hearted compassion, loving kindness and joy.

Likewise, the Ch'an and Zen traditions of China and Japan elegantly orient us to Source. Taoist thought strongly influenced Ch'an Buddhism and a wonderful synergy of spiritual gnosis resulted. In Ch'an, the ground state or Source is called Buddha-nature, or True Mind. In the Ch'an text, the *Straightforward Explanation of the True Mind,* Chinul (1158–1210) writes:

> … the basic substance (essence) of the true mind transcends causality and pervades time. It is neither profane nor sacred; it has no oppositions. Like space itself, it is omnipresent; its subtle substance is stable and utterly peaceful; beyond all conceptual elaboration. It is unoriginated, imperishable, neither existent nor non-existent. It is unmoving, unstirring, profoundly still and eternal … Neither coming nor going, it pervades all time, neither inside nor outside, it permeates all space … all activities at all times are manifestations of the subtle function of true mind. (Cleary, 1997)

This is one of the clearest descriptions of Source that I have ever encountered! In the Ch'an teaching, true mind is the heart of awareness itself. It is an omnipresent and vibrantly still ground-field from which our very being arises. It is profoundly still, yet dynamically present. Permeating all space and all activities, it is an implicate realm of potential from which all form arises.

These are the words of Hongzi, a twelfth-century Ch'an Master:

The field of boundless emptiness is what exists from the very beginning ... Vast and far reaching without boundary, secluded and pure, manifesting light, this spirit (essence) is without obstruction. Its brightness does not shine out but can be called empty and inherently radiant. Its brightness, inherently purifying, transcends casual conditions beyond subject and object. Subtly but preserved, illuminated and vast, also it cannot be spoken of as being or non-being ... (Leighton, D. and Yi Wu, 2000)

The important thing to understand is that these Ch'an masters are not intellectualizing or theorizing; they are attempting to describe their direct experience of the essence of life.

Taoists use the term Tao to indicate Source. Tao is a spiritual essence, empty, yet pregnant with all potential. It is the *Dharmakaya* in Buddhism, the True Mind of Zen. Tao is the ground of emptiness from which all arises and all returns. Its presence may be sensed, but never grasped. In language similar to Hongzi's, Lao Tzu states in the *Tao Te Ching*, "All things originate from being. Being originates from non-being" (*Tao Te Ching*, chapter 40). Tao is an immanent ground from which being emerges. Lao Tzu writes:

The Tao that can be Tao'ed is not the eternal Tao
The name that can be named is not the eternal name
Nameless: the origin of heaven and earth
Named: The mother of all things
Empty of desire, perceive the mysteries,
Filled with desire, perceive the manifestations.
These have the same source, but different names,
Call them both profound—
Profounder and yet profounder:
The gateway to all mystery.
(Lui Hsu Chi, 1974)

Tao cannot be separated, multiplied, or dissected. As the origin of all being, life arises from it moment-to-moment in the ever-lasting present. Interestingly, Tao can only be known in a state free from desire, a principle later echoed by the Buddha. Empty of desire, in a state of interior stillness, a profound gateway opens.

Source in Christianity

The Christian contemplative tradition has much to offer in its orientation to the direct knowing of Source as Sacred Unity. The wonderful mediaeval Christian writer of *The Cloud of Unknowing* encourages us to put aside all created things, literally everything that is known, and enter a cloud of unknowing in order to know God; for it is only in this kind of interior stillness and freedom from concept that the truth of God-as-Source may be comprehended.

In Douglas-Klotz's radical translation of the Aramaic Gospels, Jesus points us to our Oneness with God, the non-separation of creation from Creator, and to Sacred Unity as the truth of life. Created finds its connection to Creator through *Holy Spirit.* The word for Holy Spirit is *ruha* in Aramaic and *ruach* in Hebrew. Ruha has the connotation of a number of English words: spirit, breath, wind, air. In the Jewish/Aramaic tradition of Jesus, it is the *Sacred Breath,* or *Breath of Life,* that quickens all of creation. It was when John saw the Sacred Breath descending and alighting upon Jesus that he proclaimed Jesus the Son of God. From John:

> God is Breath.
> All that breathes resides in the Only Being.
> From my breath
> To the air we share
> To the wind that blows around the planet:
> Sacred Unity inspires all. (John, 4:24)
> (Douglas-Klotz, 1999)

The numinous presence of the Sacred Breath mediates our relationship to Sacred Unity, the presence of God in all things. Similar to the Taoist concept of the empowerment to be arising from Tao and returning to Tao, it is from the ground of Sacred Unity that our deepest being-nature arises, and it is to this ground that all beings return. Douglas-Klotz translates a section from Matthew:

> Ripe are those who reside in breath;
> to them belongs the reign of unity.
> blessed are those who realize that breath is their first
>   and last possession;
> theirs is the "I Can" of the cosmos. (Matthew 5:3)

It is the Sacred Breath that empowers us to be, and it is via its mediation that Sacred Unity is known. Source, Breath, and being are not separate. God is Breath, and all things exist in the Oneness mediated by the Breath of God as "Sacred Unity inspires all." When one resides in this knowledge, "theirs is the 'I Can' of the Cosmos." In the presence of the Sacred Breath, one's heart is cast open and a flow of love and compassion floods the present moment. In our terms, the Sacred Breath arises from Source and mediates the unity of the Source-being axis.

The Core State

In Core Process Psychotherapy, one orients to Source and being via what is called the *core state,* a pristine state of presence and potential that underlies each moment and all experience. The core state is a manifestation of the luminosity of Bodhicitta and is the direct experience of the coherency of being and non-separateness that emerges from Source. It is inherent health. In the core state, the emptiness of all forms, their transience and interdependency, becomes clear; it is understood that therapist and client are not separate, that their processes mutually arise, and that they are both of the same nature. The same truth that informs and supports one, supports the other.

Resonances with this idea are found in the analytical theories of the analyst Wilfred Bion in his concept of "O." O is associated with Absolute Truth and Ultimate Reality. In the development of a human being, universal, impersonal O becomes personal, emotional O. The goal of therapy is then, in essence, to gain knowledge of O and to transcend the limiting conditions of self (Bion, 1965, 1970, Grotstein, 2000). In Core Process Psychotherapy this is called *the reclamation of being*. From this perspective, even the most distorted personality forms are grounded in this state and are thus truly open and empty at their core.

The Core Process psychotherapist is taught to relate from this ground of spaciousness and stillness, to abide in presence and awareness, from which compassion, loving kindness, and sympathetic joy naturally arise. In this way, the therapist learns to balance the client's natural tendency to focus on her pain and suffering and identify with transient conditions. Orienting to the Core State aligns both therapist and client to the inherent health and okay-ness underlying all contingent phenomena, rather than pathologies. As self's changing and contingent nature is witnessed in relation to this ground of being and innate health, the self-system can open and self-identity can soften. What was initially taken to be me or mine is now seen to be a moment-to-moment open-ended process.

A similar idea is again found in Bion's writings. The therapist must put aside all needs, desires and understandings, must let go of all ego forms, and enter the state of O (the absolute, the universal). It is within the state-of-knowledge of O that the therapist orients to the client and can perceive the emergence of O in his or her process. It is the emergence of O as a field of coherency that allows the client to transcend the conditions of selfhood and to heal the deepest wounds (Bion, 1965, 1970, Grotstein, 2000).

The ability to be with self as arising process, rather than as a fixed form, represents a critical shift in the client's therapeutic work. It opens the door to their experiencing the being that underlies selfhood and so to healing their deepest wounding. It has been my experience that this kind of healing can only take place in the present moment, in the stillness that lies at the heart of their suffering. I have observed over and over again that the deepest changes in a client's process occur in this dynamic stillness. As both universal and conditional forces come into balance in this way, being emerges from the shadows, and the conditions causing the suffering can be transcended. Jung called this the *transcendent function,* the dynamic balance of personal and transpersonal forces from which suffering are transcended (Jung, 1970). In this context, therapy becomes a joint practice for both therapist and client where the self-system is held in a mutual and reflective field of awareness, coherency, and inquiry.

5

The Relationally Dynamic Self

Here we will look at the territory of selfhood, the process of self-formation, and the dynamic structure that is generated as being meets the world of contingency and form. We will inquire into the nature of the relational milieu present in early life, and the generation of self-forms that help manage the experience of it.

For the purposes of this discussion, self is defined as the conditioned form generated as being encounters its world, makes decisions about its nature, and organizes a way of being in response to the experience of it. Self mediates being's relationship to its world and attempts to predict the consequences of its needs and actions in that world. The first world we inhabit is the world of the womb, and the first other we encounter is mother, who, in turn, reflects the nature of her world to us. It is within this relational milieu that self is born.

In the inquiry below, we will use aspects of western object relations theory which, although structural in form, appreciates the nature of a relationally generated self. This will give us an initial sense of how, in response to the relational world, self becomes organized into various internal constellations that become being's way of being. We will discover that self or ego is a dynamically generated form that emerges out of the relational conditions and contingencies met in life. We especially focus on the work of Fairbairn and Winnicott, while aspects of both Stern and Gendlin's work will supplement the inquiry.

Contextualizing the Inquiry: Freud and Klein

In analytical psychotherapy and the development of object relations, there has been an ongoing debate as to the nature of the self or ego, and, by extension, the nature of the human being. The focus of debate is: does the ego form as a result of instinctual drives and the need to satisfy libido, or pleasure-seeking needs; or, because humans are innately relation-seeking, does the ego take shape in accordance with the nature of the relationships encountered? Object relations theories either take a pure object relations perspective, or a mixed view that includes both perspectives.

Freud postulated that the basic needs of infants are generated by pleasure-seeking impulses; while those in the object relations school see the infant as principally motivated by the need for relationship itself. Freud intended psychoanalysis to be a science and so took biology and the physical sciences as his starting points. In what is called *drive theory*, he contended that the human self-system and self-experience are based upon instinctual drives and energies. These drives are polarized in nature: Eros, the force of life, organization, cohesion, and creativity; versus Thanatos, the force of death, deconstruction, fragmentation, and chaos. Eros generates the drives of the libido, instinctual impulses that seek contact, cohesion, and, most importantly, pleasure. Freud believed that the developing human self-system is inherently conflicted and fragmented by the power of these innate forces.

From this premise, Freud conceptualized a three-part structure as the basis of self-dynamics. This structure is comprised of id, ego, and super-ego. The forces of Eros and Thanatos are contained in the id, or "it," a seething caldron of impulse and instinctual need driving human experience. These polarized forces of life and death generate an inherent tension. Libidinal drives motivate the infant to seek contact with outer objects in order to reduce this tension and gratify pleasure needs; for humans, Freud contends, are tension-reducing, pleasure-seeking beings. The sexual drive lies at the heart of libido, and its unfoldment is the basis for Freud's theory of ego development.

The ego develops to mediate between the impulses of the id and the current reality via what Freud called the reality principle. The ego, or the "I" in German, maintains homeostasis between the id, with its need for immediate gratification, and the concerns represented by the super-ego, or "above-I." The super-ego represents the forces of external reality and the related constraints imposed by primary caregivers, family, society, and culture. The ego is seen to be structurally separate from the energies of the id and superego with no energy or agency of its own, but functions to mediate and reconcile the id's instinctual drives with the super-ego's constraints.

As a structural theory of self that reduces a human being to biological drives, Freud's theory does not hold a holistic view of self that might include relationship, environment and, most importantly, the transpersonal and spiritual.

The Freudian viewpoint largely gave way, in the object relations schools, to a view of the self as formed by and meditating the world of relationship. Here the ego, rather than being simply a mechanism that mediates the relationship between the Id and Super-ego, is understood to have its own energies and to be inherently object-seeking. There is, however, no unified concept of ego and self in the object relations school.

Influential theorist Melanie Klein kept the Freudian framework of Eros and Thanatos and their instinctual drives. She believed that the self is inherently split due to the presence of these innate forces and is constantly engaged in an inner battle to maintain life in the presence of the death instinct. In Klein's world, the forces of life and death, and the inner battle to maintain integrity, are overwhelmingly intolerable to the infant. This battle is projected out onto relational others (initially mother), so that the experience of the inner split is sensed to be "out there," rather than "in here." These projections, experienced as part-objects, are then taken back in, or introjected, and the infant fantasizes about their nature. Klein used the word *phantasy* as it means not only thought or imaginings per se, but also the process whereby internal object relations are generated through which the external relational world is perceived and experienced. The inner world of the infant is seen to be tumultuous and inherently split, composed of conflicting internal objects based upon projection, introjection and phantasy. In essence, the infant is always relating to others in terms of its own projected reality, and legitimate relationship seems almost impossible.

For Klein, human beings seem fated to maintain a depressive position within which the forces of death, and the inner aggressiveness they engender are, at best, held at bay. The depressive position is one, however, in which the infant begins to experience the other as separate, and from that, the possibility of gratitude for having its needs met in a loving field may also arise. Klein thus saw love as a genuine motivational force arising from the life instinct, and, unlike Freud, the drive for contact with others is not just for tension reduction, but is also based on genuine loving feelings. Klein posited that these allow the infant to curtail its inner aggression in order to maintain contact with significant others and feel gratitude for their empathic presence. Those around Klein had deep respect for her clinical work, especially with children.

Sentience and Early Self-Other Relationships

Freud believed that there was no possibility of self-referential experience until after birth, and even then only after the negotiation of certain developmental stages. The infant was seen to initially exist in a diffused and merged state, the state of *primary narcissism,* with no differentiation between self and other possible.

Along similar lines, the American theorist Mahler believed that in the first two months after birth, the infant resides in an autistic stage where there is no differentiation possible between self and environment, and the satisfaction of needs feeds the infant's perception of its own omnipotence. At two to four months, in the symbiotic stage, awareness of others as outer objects emerges. Here the infant senses the relationship of baby-mother as a dual unity, a fused reality. Mahler held that differentiation between self and other is still not possible at this stage, but mother's presence is sensed via her holding behavior, and from this awareness, differentiation between self and other begins to evolve.

Lake's pre- and perinatal paradigm clearly differed from these viewpoints. The ability for self-referential experience was seen to be possible from the very beginnings of life. Kohut likewise makes the case for self-other experience from birth onwards, as does Stern, a keen observer of mother-infant interchange. Stern and his researchers stressed the ongoing moment-to-moment nature of infant-mother relational experience. He showed that there is self-other awareness and relational interchange from the very beginning. Infants will innately orient to mother and other primary caregivers from a self-referential core and are making decisions about that exchange on a moment-to-moment basis (Kohut, 1978; Stern, 1985).

It is clear that the newborn infant has all the neurological apparatus needed to experience itself as perceptually separate from mother and others. The infant organizes its feeling-experience relative to the feeling states of others, and there is a clear interactive learning process between the infant and others right from the beginning. The sense of selfhood, and the internal object representations of relational experience, thus grow and mature in the milieu of feelings experienced from the earliest moments after birth. The sharing of experience and affective states creates attunements and resonances between the infant and primary others, and helps both to moderate the infant's affective states and to shape the developing internal representations of his outer world. It is also clear that this perceptual apparatus is already in place in utero, which opens up the clear possibility of the impact of prenatal and birth experience as factors in both the developing self and in attachment processes (Stern, 1985, 1996; Schore, 2001a, b).

As we shall see below, Fairbairn likewise held that infants experience moment-to-moment self-other relational interchange from birth onwards, and possibly before, and that ego is an inherently holistic, sentient, and self-referential core. Self-other relationship is the basic motivational imperative that underlies self-development and personality formation. Fairbairn developed his object relational theories based upon these premises.

These ideas that the prenate and infant are sentient beings having and responding to experience, together with concepts previously introduced of cellular sentience and the possibility of early subjective experience, indicate that the prenate and infant clearly have the ability to discern their relational environment and to respond to and protect themselves from stressful experience. We are relational beings, relationship lies at the heart of all self-process, and this ability is present from the earliest moments of life (Verny, 1981; Maret, 1997; Chamberlain, 1998).

Fairbairn and the Dynamic Self

Fairbairn was the first analyst to develop a pure objects relations theory. His work is consistent with Buddhist self-psychology and is a useful starting point in our exploration into the nature of self and its relationship to being. He also clearly influenced the thinking of Lake, whose work we will later explore in some detail. Fairbairn's work elegantly describes the structural territories of ego and selfhood, which he describes as *dynamic endopsychic structure*. I find that endopsychic structure outlines the basic territories of conditioned self in ways that are both useful and flexible. We have clearly seen that an awareness of dynamic endopsychic structure can help both therapist and client hold their inner worlds with awareness and differentiation, and offers a clear and adaptable base to explore the conditioned nature of relational exchanges.

Over the course of his career, Fairbairn developed many ideas that were radically different from Freudian theory. He incorporated into his view the findings of the new physics that energy and matter are interchangeable and that the universe is a unified whole to assert that mind and body can't be separated. Unlike Freud who asserted the ego has no energy of its own, Fairbairn saw the ego as a dynamic and holistic energy form that cannot be separated from the basic drives of life. In essence, the ego or self *is* energy, and the drives of libido are a part of that energy. Ego is a self-referential sentient core from which intentionality *and* motivation arise.

In this context, Fairbairn claimed the drives of libido are not solely pleasure-seeking and tension-relieving, but are inherently relation-seeking, and that relation-seeking is the primary drive that underlies all others. Ego naturally seeks objects, or interpersonal relationships, to fulfill its basic needs. It literally takes in its outer world, makes it its own, and takes shape according to the nature of the relational exchange encountered. Mother is the first relational other sought as the object of relation-seeking, and it is through mother's field that the little one begins to get a sense of its world and take shape relative to that experience. Thus ego develops through relationships with significant others, and the nature of these relationships, and how they are perceived, is of paramount importance in personality formation.

Fairbairn's concept of self as a dynamic energy form is supported by recent research into brain function. Llinás, a neurologist and researcher, describes how the brain generates a self-referential core that, over time, produces a sense of coherency and continuity, the basic experience of "I-am-me." In essence, the self manifests as a stable internal energy form via the coherency of neuronal oscillation, entrainment, and resonance. The main function of this self is to reach out to its world, to internally organize in an appropriate form given the nature of its ongoing experience, and to predict the outcomes of future relational exchanges. This has obvious value in terms of survival and also creates a sense of selfhood that can be sustained through changing conditions. A unified self-referential nucleus that allows a stable experience of me-in-relationship, a self-sense that is both responsive and predictive of relational interchange, is one of the critical functions of neural processing (Llinás, 2001).

Another significant aspect of Fairbairn's understanding is that the ego is originally whole. *Original ego* is a unified center of sentience and agency—not split or fragmented, but obscured to everyday awareness by defensive responses to relational experience. This fundamentally positive and hopeful view of the human condition was a major departure from both Freud and Klein, who saw the human condition as inherently split and fragmented. In our context, however, the wholeness of original ego is a manifestation of a deeper wholeness, that of innate being.

The Generation of Selfhood

Basic Ambiguity

In Fairbairn's terms, the generation of selfhood is totally relational in nature. Original ego is inherently relation-seeking and it is the infant's felt-experience of its relational milieu that is the primary factor in self-formation and self-organization. He observed that the relational field encountered by the newborn is inherently ambiguous: Sometimes needs will be met; other times, not. The one who is needed to lovingly provide all basic needs may also be experienced as inadequate, indifferent, invasive, hostile, or abusive.

In Buddhism, this ambiguity is at the root of what is called *dukkha,* usually translated as un-satisfactoriness or suffering. The Buddha described dukkha as one of the three constants of relational life, along with *anicca,* impermanence: that everything is in constant flux, including self-other relationships; and *anatta,* no-self: that self is not a thing, but a process organized around the conditions met in life. These assertions presaged modern research in neurology and developmental psychology by 2500 years (Varela, 1991; Stern, 1998; Llinás, 2001; Schore, 2001).

Dukkha points to the unstable, changing nature of life. Everything is changeable: Sometimes we are comfortable, other times too cold; sometimes we are happy, sometimes sad; sometimes we get what we need, sometimes not; sometimes we are responded to, other times not; sometimes mother is kind, sometimes angry. In Lake's terms, it's an inherently mixed and unpredictable bag of experience (Lake, 1979). Fairbairn saw this to be a basic truth permeating the developing relational field between baby and mother.

Vedanā, Feeling Tone, and Affect

In Buddhist psychology, basic ambiguity, or dukkha, leads to the experience of polarized feeling tone called *vedanā,* a basic positive, negative, or neutral charge that arises in response to an object. Simply put, a positive charge generates good feelings and a drawing towards the object; a negative charge generates unpleasant feelings and withdrawal from the object; and a neutral charge elicits no strong feelings nor movement towards or away from an object. The more intense the negative feeling tone, the more polarized the relationship to the object becomes.

Basic ambiguity and the polarities generated by positive and negative feeling tone produce inner experiences of goodness and badness, which, in turn, generate inner tensions that underlie all defended personality systems. These tensions manifest as the polarity of wanting and not wanting, or loving and not loving, the fundamental push-pull of attachment and aversion. Vedanā underlies the experience of the goodness or badness of relational exchanges; the generation of affect, the feeling response to those exchanges; and the organization of the inner world of object relations that is the foundation of the developing self-system.

The Role of Affect

Modern research into the development of the brain is clarifying the role of affect in the generation of attachment systems and personality in general. For the first three years after birth, the right hemisphere of the brain is in prominence. This hemisphere mediates non-linear holistic states of consciousness and the experience and encoding of self-object/ self-other interchange. It is in prominence in unconscious processing of affect-evoking emotional stimuli. During infancy and early childhood, an internal felt representation of self-other exchange is built up via right brain processing that is the foundation for the formation of the self-system and attachment behavior (Schore, 2001, 2003).

Most importantly, affect is primary in the development of selfhood. The young child *feels* its way into its world. In the field of self-other interchange, feeling tone is generated towards objects in the field resulting in movement towards or away from those objects. If the relational field experienced is empathic, reflective, and appropriately responsive in a good enough fashion, it feels good, and internal self-other representations are generated that reflect this experience. Simply put, relational exchanges generate feelings. These are experienced as relational goodness or badness, and internal self-forms are generated that reflect this interchange. Through these dynamics the young child also learns to regulate his affects as he comes into resonance with primary caregiver states. This is the stuff of self-formation. Fairbairn saw affect to be the glue of all self-forms.

Goodness and Badness

The terms goodness and badness in object relations have experiential and relational connotations and do not imply value judgments. The experience of relational attunement and responsiveness to basic needs generates positive feeling tones and the felt experience of goodness.

Alternately, the experience of unmet or overridden needs generate negative feeling tones and the felt experience of badness.

Lake saw that it is the relative experience of the intensity, duration, and repetitiveness of the affects of goodness or badness that sets the stage for the development of either a fluid and responsive self, organized around and oriented to innate being; or a defended self-system organized around the need to protect, distorting the natural process of relation seeking. These are the roots of insecure attachment and oppositional and dissociative personality forms.

Primary Trauma

Fairbairn believed that the infant is an inherently loving being and its most basic need is for his love to be unconditionally received. The infant also needs to know that he is unreservedly loved purely for himself, without provisos or stipulations. This echoes Lake's concept of the basic needs of being: recognition, acknowledgment, and unconditional acceptance. As we have seen, however, the relational field that the infant finds itself in is ambiguous and inconstant. Inevitably the infant will, at times, feel unseen or unaccepted. The experience of relational ambiguity, and the polarized feeling tones that arise with it, are the source of what Fairbairn called *primary trauma*.

Primary trauma involves perceived empathic failures in a primary relationship. These are breaches in the good enough holding field that impel the infant, in order to protect his integrity, to withdraw from an open, relaxed, and whole-hearted connection to others. In Winnicott's terms, the little one is forced to shift from an open state of simply being to internal defensive processes. In Fairbairn's concept, primary trauma is unavoidable as the relational field is an inherently mixed experience and, as in the Buddhist concept of anicca, constantly in flux.

Although both Fairbairn and Lake stress the importance of needs deprivation and separation anxiety in the generation of primary trauma, it may be generated by anything that disrupts easy and open contact with primary others. It may be physiological deprivation, low oxygen or poor nutrition through the umbilicus, physical trauma such as an accident, or the experience of overwhelming emotion from mother or another primary caregiver. Lake believed that overwhelming maternal anxiety and other negative emotional states perceived in utero or early infancy can be the origin of primary trauma and strongly defended personality systems (Lake, 1979, 1981, 1986).

The Generation of Internal Object Relations

As feelings of relational goodness and badness are generated in response to an ambiguous relational field, self-territories begin to coalesce in order to manage the experience. This occurs via the generation of what Fairbairn called *internal object relations.* An internal object relation is not a *thing*, but a subjective matrix of feeling tone and affect representing the felt-experience of self-other exchange. The more ambiguous and polarized that felt perception is, the more intense the experience of primary trauma will be, and the more polarized and defensive internal object relations will become.

The Internalization and Splitting of the Object

Fairbairn believed that the experience of the badness or inadequacy of mother and primary others is intolerable to the infant, who needs them to be unambiguously good and unreservedly loving, accepting, and responsive to his needs. In order to keep the other all-good, he must manage the experience of badness in some way. According to Fairbairn, "the first defense adopted by the original ego to deal with an unsatisfying personal relationship is mental internalization, or introjection, of the unsatisfying object." (Fairbairn, 1954) Fairbairn suggests that the felt-experience of the self-other experience is managed by generating an internal representation, the internal object. The internal object is not a thing, but a subjective image-feeling-form, the "all-about-ness" of the relationship. This internal representation of the outer other is then split into three aspects: the aspect of the object that is experienced as rejecting, another aspect that is sensed as exciting or potentially fulfilling, and a third aspect that is relatively satisfying. This is called *the splitting of the object*. This split inner landscape mirrors the infant's experience of mother and other primary caregivers as mixed objects that are sometimes experienced as fulfilling, and sometimes as rejecting.

Now original ego must organize itself relative to these three internal object representations. Fairbairn's says it does this by splitting into three ego territories. This is called the *splitting of the ego*. Splitting was considered by Fairbairn as unavoidable, the most primal adaptation to relational dissonance, and the root of all subsequent defensive personality processes.

Thus, all self-systems are inherently split and defensive in nature. The more intense the ambiguity experienced, the more intensely split and defended the self-system becomes. This concurrent splitting of the object and ego is both the basis for the internal object relations of selfhood and of the repression of conscious knowledge of the now internalized badness. As the internal object world is established, a perceptual shift occurs. The badness that was originally experienced to be out-there is now felt to be in-here. The good-bad conflict now resides inside and can be held in some kind of dynamic balance separate from relations to others. It is now *my* badness, not theirs. Making the badness his own allows the infant to maintain an unambiguous relationship to mother and other primary caregivers. Fairbairn called this the *moral defensive*. This could be viewed as not just a primary defensive process, but as a compassionate act: "I take on the badness in order to keep the other all-good." The price to pay for this is, of course, an inner experience of badness that can lead to low self-esteem in later life and, in the extreme, narcissistic depletion, a rupture in self-worth, and feelings of humiliation, guilt, and shame (Matos, 2002).

The Holding Field and Direct Energy Attunement

The dynamic described above occurs in the field of interaction between prenate or infant and primary caregivers. If we extend Fairbairn's understanding of self as energy, we see that this relational field is not an inside-outside dichotomy. Quantum physics tells us that all things and processes are energy-based, interconnected, and mutually interactive. In Buddhist psychology this dynamic is recognized as the principle of mutuality and non-separateness. As the ancient sage Chung Tzu maintained, as a butterfly flaps its wings in China, a storm gathers on the other side of the world. The intertwined fields of infant and mother are thus not energetically separate, especially on the level of feeling tone and affect. This state of mutual resonance is a manifestation of the natural being-to-being interconnection inherently present at all times.

If mother is supported to settle into her relationship with her child, there is a natural shift to a state of being that is attuned to and resonant with the infant's inner states and able to respond appropriately to them. Stern calls this a shift to the *motherhood constellation*. Likewise, in such a holding field, the infant can also attune to mother's inner states, and a reciprocal, interactive field of attunement results (Stern, 1985, 1998).

This observation is supported by recent brain research, which indicates that one person's thoughts and feelings may be directly sensed by another person, brain-to-brain. As one participant thinks certain thoughts or has particular feelings, the brain of another participant lights up in the same areas, or comes into EEG resonance and convergence (Laszlo, 1996, 2003, 2004; Radin, 1997, 2003, 2004; Grinberg-Zylberbaum, et al, 1987, 1988, 1992). In recent studies it has also been shown that the right brain activity of mother and infant comes into resonance, particularly on the level of affect, as they engage in relational exchange (Schore, 2003). The right brain is the holistic, non-linear aspect of the brain and may be the area that also mediates what Freud called the unconscious. Sheldrake has shown that consciousness itself is a field phenomenon yielding mind-to-mind resonance (Sheldrake, 2004).

Thus, the internalization of an outer object may not be a defense per se, but a natural process whereby the infant's subjective inner world begins to coalesce and mirror the energetic connection with its outer one. Fairbairn originally maintained that it is only the bad object that needs to be internalized. Here I am suggesting that it is not a matter of internalization of an outer object at all, but that all relational experiences, whether good or bad, resonate within the developing psyche of the infant through energy attunement. The infant senses his outer mother as a subjective felt experience that, in turn, manifests as an internal mother. This same dynamic applies with all primary others. In Kohut's paradigm of the selfobject, the developing sense of being and selfhood is dependent on and always held by an essential other who functions as an empathic touchstone. As with Fairbairn's primary identification and Lake's being-in-relationship, a sense of personal being only develops in the empathic presence of the other, and the little one only knows its own being by the reflection of the selfobject. The important point here is that self and selfobject are energetically continuous, and the selfobject is directly sensed as in-me.

If the essential other as selfobject is attuned and empathic in a good enough fashion, the infant senses this as an inner experience. Likewise, if mother as selfobject is oriented to her own being, then this quality of beingness is sensed inwardly by the young child, and the possibility of developing a cohesive sense of being is enhanced. However, if the wounded nature of the other as selfobject is more present in the relational field, then that wounding is also sensed as an inner state. Then a cohesive sense of beingness does not have the opportunity to form, as self must organize defensively all too early.

Splitting and Dynamic Endopsychic Structure

As an ambiguous relational milieu is encountered and internalized, self-territories begin to evolve to manage this now split inner landscape. Ego-territories are set up to manage the object's split aspects, its rejecting aspect, its exciting aspect, and its satisfying or fulfilling aspect. In Fairbairn's concept, as the object is split into its acceptable and unacceptable aspects, the unacceptable aspects are split off altogether from conscious awareness and repressed. This repression is a natural consequence of having to manage relational ambiguity by maintaining outer others as all-good. As the internalized object is split into three aspects, original ego, naturally whole, must also split in order to manage this divided inner landscape. Fairbairn called these ego territories *central ego, libidinal ego,* and *anti-libidinal ego.* Although he employed classic Freudian terms, his meanings were very different. The libidinal ego manages that aspect of the object that was experienced as exciting and is driven by unresolved need. The anti-libidinal ego manages the aspect that was experienced as denying, rejecting, or abandoning. It is driven by the need to protect, denies all need, and opposes the natural relation-seeking imperative. Central ego emerges oriented to the satisfying aspects of the object and the goodness experienced. It becomes the conscious persona, or self-sense of the person, holding the general feeling of I-am-this. Central ego, as the conscious aspect of ego, still seeks relationship in some form and maintains an idealized and fixed sense of self and other. The bad internal object relations, those oriented to the unsatisfying aspects of relational exchange, are repressed into the unconscious, only to emerge and influence the everyday experience of relating to others in distorted ways.

These three self-territories are infused with their related affects and are driven by a deep neediness, a distortion of the innate drive for relation-seeking that manifests in a spectrum ranging from satisfaction, joy, and hope, to fear, anxiety, and anger, or, at the extreme, terror, rage, and the overwhelming experience of emptiness and non-being. Each self-constellation's way of being holds volitional intention and the felt meaning of relational experience, and is organized around a triad of confusion, attachment, and aversion, the classic Buddhist roots of suffering. Each self-constellation is composed of the following:

1. a self-view with particular volitional intentions that are basically a coalescence of the energies of repeated relational exchange;

2. the energies of the mother or primary other as an internalized felt-object; and

3. the affects generated by the relational experience.

These three form an internal object relation and define inner territories that are dynamic and are continually being generated moment to moment.

All aspects of a self-constellation co-arise and are not separate territories. It is important to reemphasize that the process of splitting and generating internal self-other constellations is not pathological. It's a natural response to the goodness and badness experienced and allows the infant to maintain a relationship to the outer other as an ideal, unambiguously good object.

As Fairbairn's concept of ego is so different from Freud's, conferring ego with wholeness, agency, and its own energies, it is better called *self*, and this is the term I will use in the sections below. I will call the three self-territories that emerge as a consequence of early relational exchanges, *central-self*, *needy-self* and *rejecting-self*. As introduced above, all self-constellations are reflections of the movement of vedanā, the basic push-pull response to experience that, in Buddhist psychology, can be considered to be the glue that holds self-constellations together.

Innate being as a locus of sentience and object seeking

Meets an inherently ambiguous relational environment

The outer other is experienced as the inner felt-other in the wholeness of ambiguous relational exchange

Vedanā or feeling tone is generated.
(Positive neutral, or negative feeling tone)

Affect is likewise generated and relational goodness and badness experienced

The external object is sensed as a subjective inner felt-object and is split into three object-territories; self is likewise split into three self-territories in order to manage these splits and the intensity of relational ambiguity

These manifest in the object relations matrix of dynamic endopsychic structure:
- Central-self matrix with the idealized aspects of the other and satisfying, positive affects
- Rejecting-self matrix with the rejecting and abandoning aspects of the other and the affects of frustration and anger
- Needy-self matrix with the potentially fulfilling aspects of the other and the affects of longing and neediness

Fig. 5.1 The Generation of an Internal Object Relations Matrix

Central-Self Constellation

Central-self organizes around the good object, those aspects of the relational field that are experienced as fulfilling and good. These manifest within central-self as an idealized, unambiguously good internal object, *the ideal object.* This allows the little one to maintain a sense of the goodness of the maternal holding field, even when its needs are not being met or are overridden. Central-self holds the experience of goodness in a dual fashion: as the ideal object or an idealized sense of others who might completely and totally meet self's most basic needs; and as the idealized sense of me as a self that is attractive to others and whom others would wish to give to. Thus central-self maintains a self-image and self-sense, an idealized sense of me-as-self, that is both an expression of how we wish to be and how we wish others to see and relate to us. This is similar to Jung's concept of persona.

Central-self mediates relation-seeking needs, and it is through central-self that relational contact with essential others is initiated and maintained. Central-self is thus motivated by the need to maintain relationship, is oriented to the outer world, and seeks others in order to fulfill basic needs. It manifests ways of being that allow it to remain in relationship without having to feel undue aggression, anger, or neediness. Defended forms of personality manifest through central-self, as does self-image and self-view. Processes of projection, ego inflation, low self-esteem, dissociative states, depressive forms, etc., all may present as central-self's way of being. Indeed, central-self manifests our overall personality shape at any given time. It is the core of the I-am-this experience.

Central-self perceives others with the immature expectation that external others will meet its needs, only to be continually disappointed. In Buddhist terms, central self is veiled by confusion. How many of us can resonate with this idea? I have certainly noticed myself idealizing others, projecting expectations on them, assuming that they can and will meet my needs, treating them as objects whose role is to satisfy me. Many people wait for the ideal other who will make their lives better, only to be continually disappointed. This behavior of central-self is a distortion of the deeper, most basic need for contact and relationship.

Central-self also functions to maintain the repression of bad object relations. Lake called central-self's modes of repression *reaction pat-*

terns. These are personality forms that protect the person from bad object relations and their powerful affects, particularly emptiness, terror, and rage. Repression protects the person from the worst of the internalized badness, but it may resurface when the defenses of central-self are challenged, or it may even become incorporated into central-self's way of being.

Central-self, however, also mediates life-affirming processes. Initially, central-self constellates around the relational goodness experienced as primary needs are met, or even anticipated as being met. Relational goodness experienced in later life is further incorporated into the positive object relations at the heart of central-self, and this strengthens the sense of cohesion and continuity of being in the self-system as a whole (Scharff & Scharff, 2000). As a cohesive being-state is experienced at the core of selfhood, being-to-being interconnection mediated by central-self is also supported.

As central-self incorporates further experiences of relational goodness, self-esteem and positive self-view are strengthened and the self's own goodness is reinforced. This allows central-self to seek relationship for needs fulfillment in a more mature and constructive way. Central-self mediates the shift from immature dependency, in which one cannot differentiate one's own needs from those of others, to mature interdependency, in which separateness is experienced within a matrix of interconnection and the needs of others are of equal value to one's own. Central-self mediates relation-seeking, relational learning, affect management, and the repression of other self-constellations.

The central-self constellation is comprised of the following:

1. an idealized self-view that represents the self others will want to give to, how we wish others to see and relate to us. It is a self-view veiled by confusion;

2. the energies of an idealized internal object, or idealized other, the other who is all-good and will meet all of our needs as though they

are their own. This idealization veils outer relationships in confusion, as no outer other can ever meet the projected expectations;

3. the affects and feelings generated by the experience of relational goodness, satisfaction, hope, wellbeing, positive feeling tones, etc.

Central-self holds the potential for reorientation to being, renewal, and the possibility of moving to real present-time relating.

The next two self-constellations, needy-self and rejecting-self, are generated in order to manage the experience of badness. They mediate the polarities that relational ambiguity sets up and the push-pull of feeling tone that arises as relational badness is encountered. Needy- and rejecting-selves manifest the dynamic generated by the experience of relational badness, the need to protect and the need to maintain contact.

Needy-Self Constellation

Needy-self is organized around the *exciting object,* those aspects of relational experience that still holds the possibility of basic needs being met. It orients to the energies of relational others who tantalizingly hold out the possibility of fulfillment, and to the energies of the original unmet need. It is energized and excited by the experience of mother and other primary caregivers who might provide fulfillment within the felt-experience of deprivation and lack of abundance. It is terrified by the breach in the holding environment and the resulting internalized sense of badness, yet still desperate for contact. Needy-self is infused with the affect of longing, energized by unmet needs. In everyday life, as a tantalizing, potentially fulfilling other is met, exciting fantasies about the person may arise, longing may become sexualized and clinging and attachment becomes the predominant mode of relating.

In Buddhist terms, needy-self is driven by attachment, a desire for fulfillment that pulls it towards the object. In the extreme, this manifests as hysterical clinging. The needy-self longs for connection and intimacy, yet never truly attains it. When it pervades central-self, excessive neediness and fear of loss drive relational experience. This need is either projected out as longing and clinging, or held inwardly as an overwhelming sense of shame.

Needy-self clings to outer others whether or not its basic needs are really being met, in terror that they never will be. It is the energy of this neediness that inevitably pushes others away and so is self-defeating at its core. I am sure that many readers can empathize with these energies. I can remember myself in teenage years trying to make contact with girls while coming from an incredibly needy place in myself defined by a deep terror of abandonment and betrayal. Inevitably, my neediness would drive the objects of my desire away. I also remember clinging to unfulfilling and even negative relationships, driven by that same fear and neediness. So powerful is the longing of needy-self that leaving relationships can feel like a life-or-death decision.

The needy-self constellation is comprised of the following:

1. a self-view that is identified with the possibly-fulfilling and tantalizing aspects of the other, and that longs for contact even if that contact is painful or unfulfilling;

2. the internalized energies of relational experience that tantalizingly hold out the possibility of fulfillment, the exciting or potentially fulfilling object;

3. the affects of longing, clinging, and distorted attachment. Needy-self is terrified by the possibility of the loss of the other.

When it pervades central-self, excessive neediness and fear of loss drive relational experience. This need is either projected out as longing and clinging, or held inwardly as an overwhelming sense of shame.

Rejecting-Self Constellation

The rejecting-self organizes around the rejecting object, that other in relational exchange that is experienced as rejecting and denying. It is oriented to the frustration and distress generated by the betrayal of unmet or overridden needs. Rejecting-self is a deprived and angry self-territory that denies interbeing, rejects the need for contact, pushes significant others away, and also rejects needy-self and its tendency to cling to others. It becomes an internal saboteur that experiences intimacy as dangerous and painful, and pushes those who hold out the potential for fulfillment away, as frustration and anger pervades relationship. When it pervades central-self, rage and hatred may be projected onto others, or a depth of self-persecutory guilt may be experienced.

In Buddhist terms rejecting-self is driven by aversion, negative feeling tone that pushes the object away in the denial of need. In its most intense forms, it manifests as paranoid withdrawal or aggressive behavior. Rejecting-self withdraws or disconnects from relationship, seeks artificial independence, and claims it can do without others. It holds both the pain of the original insult and the energies that protect it against further wounding. Perhaps the reader may again be able to resonate with that part of themselves that may have pushed intimate others away when the sense of the goodness of the relationship was somehow challenged or impinged upon; or have had difficulty in committing to intimate others. When a truly fulfilling relationship presents itself, earlier relational woundings are unconsciously activated, danger is sensed, and rejecting-self emerges to sabotage any possibility of real intimacy. In the extreme, intimacy is experienced as a source of anxiety and danger, and the other is rejected or hated as the cause of that pain. The real truth is that which is feared as out-there is really in oneself.

The rejecting-self constellation is comprised of the following:

1. a self-view that is wounded and protective against further wounding. It is organized around the pain of the wound and withdraws from further relational contact, denying any relational needs;

2. the internalized rejecting object or other, the energies of the experience of rejection, denial, and abandonment;

3. the affects of frustration, anger, and rage.

Repression, the Shadow, and the Interplay of the Constellations

Central-self manifests our persona and functions to mediate being's relationship to the outer world of relationship and meaning. It is similar to the Buddhist concept of self-view. It is a self-territory that manifests our overall way-of-being and our overall experience of selfhood. In Heidegger's terms, it is being's way-of-being, the way being is "worlding" and "being-there." On the other hand, needy- and rejecting-selves, the self-territories that coalesce around the badness experienced, are repressed into the shadows. In Fairbairn's terms, repression is the means by which the intolerable feeling affects of badness are pushed into the deeper reaches of the mind, out of everyday consciousness. This echoes Freud's concept of the unconscious, a territory of mind underlying but usually unavailable to everyday consciousness. It is the shadowland of everyday life and is the territory from which dreams and implicit memory and feeling emerge.

Fairbairn's understanding of repression also echoes Jung's concept of the shadow, those aspects of self that are hidden in the unconscious, yet underlie and color much of relational experience. Although Fairbairn's shadow realm orients specifically to repressed badness, we can also include the essential nature and experience of being that commonly becomes obscured from everyday consciousness. As being-nature falls into shadow, Source and the archetypal forces it generates, including those of loving connection, are also obscured or distorted to emerge from the shadows in our dream world.

Although repression pushes bad object relations and related affects out of everyday consciousness, it cannot get rid of them completely. Rejecting- and needy-selves may be pushed beneath present awareness, but they can resurface to pervade central-self when circumstances impinge upon them. Either central-self's idealized sense of self and other, or the needy- or rejecting-selves who hold the pain of unmet or overridden needs, may become dominant ways of being; or a person may shift from one to the other. These inner splits are commonly projected out so that the inner tensions are displaced out-there and form a distorted ground for relational interplay. It is not uncommon, for example, for a person to idealize another as the "one who will make my life better" and cling to the other with needy-self's longing for fulfillment, only to reject them later, when needs are unmet or the relationship becomes otherwise challenging.

Central-self, with its idealized sense of selfhood, will commonly manifest self-forms—what Lake called reaction patterns—that are the antithesis of what has been repressed. For instance, a person may have an underlying and repressed sense of worthlessness and low self-esteem, yet show herself as confident and happy self to the world; or counter a sense of inner emptiness by taking up causes in a self-righteous, holier-than-thou face to the world. This mask, as Perls calls it, may dissolve under stress and challenge, and the repressed energies and affects of the split-off badness will then flood into present awareness.

Fairbairn observed that the rejecting-self also represses the needy-self and its attachment to others. He called this *secondary repression*. It is clear to me that the repression can go either way. Depending on the relational context, either the rejecting-self may repress the needy-self, or the needy-self may repress the rejecting-self, or one or the other may pervade central-self. This process of splitting and repression is the ground of all other defenses.

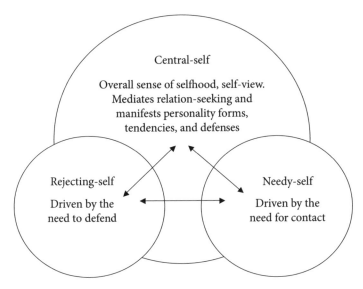

Fig. 5.2 Territories of Selfhood
Central-self manifests the overall self-form, reaction patterns, and defensive tendencies, and mediates Being's natural relation seeking, while the energies of rejecting- and needy-selves, although repressed, may drive self-defenses and emerge within the self-sense at any time.

Guilt, Shame, and Blame

While reaction patterns may protect the individual from the intense experience of repressed affects, guilt, shame, and blame may never be far away. Fairbairn's work gives a clear context for understanding and relating to the powerful affects that infuse many personality systems and behaviors. As badness is incorporated into the self-system, the guilt of the other is also taken on. As rejecting-self mobilizes its need to defend and push away, infusive feelings of guilt may arise, while needy-self may feel shame in its wounded need for another. Both guilt and shame are among the negative affects that are repressed by central-self and projected out at others as blame: "If I project this out on others, I won't feel it in me."

The guilt-shame-blame interplay generated by introjected and repressed badness is the basis for what Karpman calls the *drama triangle,* which is defined by three interrelated positions: *persecutor, victim,* and *rescuer* (Karpman, 1968). Each self-position is a manifestation of Fairbairn's internal saboteur, and each is an expression of the repressed badness mediated by needy and rejecting-selves. As these positions arise in interpersonal exchanges, the persecutor projects blame, while the victim and rescuer are driven by shame and guilt. True intimacy becomes impossible. Each position feeds into the other, and the cycle of guilt-shame-blame is maintained as a manifestation of the low self-esteem engendered by internalized badness.

While a particular drama triangle position may dominate certain personality adaptations and become central-self's main relational way of being, it is not uncommon for a person to shift from one position to another depending on circumstances, personality tendencies, and the nature of interpersonal exchanges. The shame and anger of the victim may become the damning energies of the persecutor. The rage of the persecutor may, in turn, become the guilt of the rescuer, etc. Although assuming these positions may help keep rejecting and needy-selves repressed, they will also greatly contribute to continued relational pain and wounding.

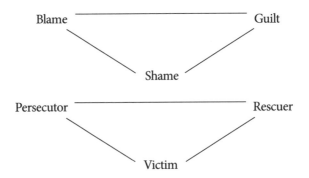

Fig. 5.3 The Blame-Guilt-Shame Triangle Generates
Central-self Positions of Persecutor, Rescuer, and Victim.

Endopsychic Structure:
The Schizoid and Depressive Positions

As we have seen, relational ambiguity and primary trauma are managed
by the infant's taking in and incorporating the goodness and badness
experienced, splitting off and repressing the traumatic impingements,
and internally organizing himself in some way so that the he can carry
on relating to outer others as unambiguously good. This splitting and
repression produce an inherently fragmented inner state that Fairbairn
called the *schizoid position.*

There is, however, a further price to pay for defending the self in this
way. The splitting off and repression of relational experience generate an
inner tension. This dynamic tension between the longing for relational
intimacy on the one hand, and the need to protect oneself and push away
relationship on the other, sets up what Fairbairn called the *depressive
position,* an inherently conflicted position relative to contact with others:
the one who is loved is also dangerous, the one who is longed for is also
rejected, as the good-bad dichotomy is actualized within.

This concept is markedly different than Klein's, who saw the depressive position as a consequence of the inherent conflict between Eros

and Thanatos. In Klein's world we are intrinsically split and conflicted beings, while in Fairbairn's, we are originally whole beings who use the splitting process to manage the ambiguity of real relationship. It's interesting also to note that Fairbairn, unlike Freud and Klein, did not believe that aggression is innate, but saw it as part of a protective response to unsatisfying or overwhelming circumstances; so the potential response is innate, but aggression is not.

A fragmented and conflicted inner landscape is present in all human beings and is the root of all personality dynamics. As we shall see in later chapters, the schizoid and depressive personality strategies are the fixed expressions of the schizoid and depressive positions, and all other defended personality forms are built upon their foundations. The diagram below depicts the basic interrelationships of Fairbairn's triad of self-constellations.

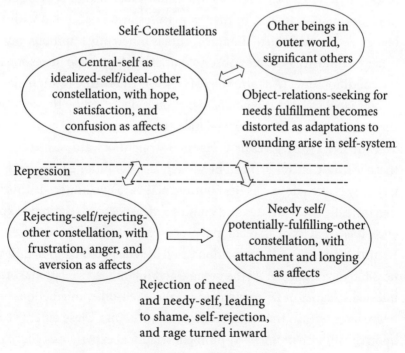

Fig. 5.4 Fairbairn's Schema of Relational Ego Splitting

Reframing Splitting: Central-self as a Field State

Our understanding of innate being supersedes Fairbairn's concept of original ego as a more holistic paradigm. As we have seen, being is inherently whole, innately connected to Source and to other beings, and seeks contact with others in order to know its own nature and the nature of its world. It manifests as a unifying field of sentience that is the root of the I-am experience. Self constellates as being encounters its relational and environmental world, and is the mediator of that experience. Being can be thought of as both the fulcrum of that life experience and as the field within which it occurs.

In Buddhist thought, being, as citta, is a center of presence, a knowing faculty at the hub of the self-system. In some schools of Buddhism it is seen to be a manifestation of a wider universal field of pristine awareness, Bodhicitta, that is, in turn, a manifestation of Source within all beings. As the Buddha maintained, citta is inherently luminous, but this inner luminosity becomes obscured as self takes shape in response to the conditions met (*Anguttara Nikaya*, I:10). Thus being is originally and always whole; but this wholeness becomes obscured by the self-forms that are generated to manage relational experience.

Fairbairn's work gives us a clear and straightforward way to orient to these forms. Central-self can be viewed as a conditioned self-field, or a territory that coalesces as life contingencies are encountered. This field dynamically incorporates and contains *all* aspects of relational experience. It is a matrix of all relational processes that yield an overall sense of I-am-this and, given the conditions met, has the potential to manifest all possible ways of being. As the prenate and infant meets relational others, internal schemas or representations of these self-other interactions begin to coalesce within the wider field of innate being. These emerge based upon the infant's moment-to-moment relational experiences. Stern calls these *schemas-of-being-with* (Stern, 1994). Similarly, in Buddhist self-psychology, these schemas are considered to be embodied relational experiences generated by contact with outer and inner objects. They are composed of perceptions, feeling tones, sensations, mental formations and predispositions that manifest as dynamically structured internal self-forms.

Stern's schemas-of-being-with manifest as internal constellations of "what it is like to be in relationship." There may be *schemas-of being-with-mother*, or of *being-with-father*—schemas from which different attachment modes may be generated. They may also be organized around affects, like schemas of *being-with-sadness*, or *being-with-over-whelming-mother-emotions*; or around needs fulfillment, like *being-with-waiting-for-something*, or *being-with-inconsistent-others*, etc. All of these are internal representations of outer relational experiences that constellate into a general sense of I-am-this and this-is-how-it-is-to-be-with-others.

The idea of original splitting then widens to the formation of a central-self that is comprised of many schemas-of-being-with held in a kind of dynamic tension that is either organized around a cohesive and integrated sense of being, or around past impingements and primary wounding. Central-self can thus be thought of as a dynamic matrix that is a holding field for *all* schemas-of-being-with and all self-constellations. In any given moment of experience, central-self will manifest a particular way of being relative to the relational context encountered. I am sure that all readers have had the direct experience of seeming to be one kind of self at work, and a different kind when with friends or family, or in difficult circumstances, etc.

In this way of thinking, the rejecting- and needy selves manifest schemas-of-being-with-badness and are not split off per se from central-self, but are part of its overall matrix. Although they are repressed, each can infuse central-self and become an overarching way of being at any time. Repression in this sense is not a linear process, but is more like stew in a stewpot. If central self is the whole of the stew containing all of the ingredients of selfhood, then repression is like chunks of stew that settle to the bottom of the pot, only to rise up when the stew is stirred. Central-self will take an overall self-form, or modus operandi, that is dictated by personality tendencies generated in early life in response to the relational environment encountered.

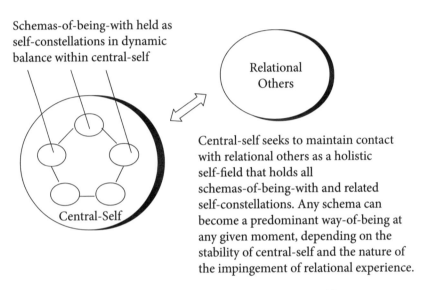

Schemas-of-being-with held as self-constellations in dynamic balance within central-self

Relational Others

Central-Self

Central-self seeks to maintain contact with relational others as a holistic self-field that holds all schemas-of-being-with and related self-constellations. Any schema can become a predominant way-of-being at any given moment, depending on the stability of central-self and the nature of the impingement of relational experience.

Fig. 5.5 Central-self as a Holistic Self-matrix Holding
the Sense of "I-Am-This" and "Who-I-Am-in-Relationship"

If relational experience has been of a largely empathic, attuned, and responsive relational field, then a central-self will develop that both expects that kind of relational milieu to be present and can discern when it is not. Within the conditions met and the ambiance of empathetic and attuned others, central-self can rest in innate being. If, however, relational experience has been one of a fragmented, cold, unresponsive, or inconsistent field, then a self-system will evolve that will expect a similar kind of field, and will be on constant guard to protect against further pain. In this kind of relational ambiance, central-self cannot rest in being, is constantly oriented to danger, and organizes around relational wounding. The self is, in essence, set up to become what it has already learned to be, and will constantly perceive the world through this same veil. This concept lies at the heart of clients' resistance to change that Freud noted in his early work and of insecure attachment processes.

Qualities of Central-self

Central-self can be thought of as having momentary existence with the overall sense of selfhood arising moment-to-moment, as internal and external objects are perceived. This concept of the moment-to-moment-self has clear ground in neurophysiology and is also congruent with Buddhist psychology, which sees the self as a fleeting existence within a process of constant flux. As we all know from our everyday experience, our sense of selfhood does, however, have continuity. I generally feel myself to be the same self as I was yesterday. The brain is set up to generate this kind of continuity. As noted above, all organisms, from the single cell to the human being, have a survival imperative to be able to predict the nature of their relational and physical environment. In this sense, the central-self has predictive functions. It is set up to foresee the likely outcomes of relational and environmental processes and respond to relational encounters in appropriate ways. A stable sense of selfhood is thus essential for survival (Llinás, 2001).

As we have seen, it is central-self, holding the overall sense of being-with-others, that mediates being's natural connection to other beings. As Fairbairn highlighted, if the person is still relating in an immature way, through what he called immature dependency, central-self relates to the other in an unrealistic and idealized fashion whereby others are experienced not as separate individuals with their own needs, but as objects existing solely to fulfill central-self's needs. This is then the main schema-of-being-with that central-self manifests, as idealized self-other interactions become its main mode of relating.

In Fairbairn's concept, as a person shifts into a mode of relationship called mature interdependency, central-self shifts to real, present-time relationship with others. Central-self then manifests a way of being that is more oriented to innate being, can perceive others as separate yet interconnected, and can negotiate needs-fulfillment with the other in a mutually fulfilling way. In other words, innate being-nature becomes the hub of one's experience. Central-self, the overall sense of I-am-this, will either be relatively stable and organized around a cohesive and integrated sense of being, or a more fragmented and potentially unstable self-field organized around primary trauma, basic wounding, and personality defenses.

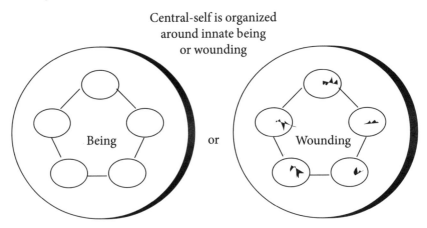

Fig. 5.6 Central-self Orientation
Central-self will either be oriented around and connected to innate being, or organized relative to relational wounding and manifest adaptive self-constellations that are defended and largely disconnected from being.

Fairbairn has been accused of being overly involved in theory making (Greenberg and Mitchell, 1983). When one first meets his concepts, they may seem overly intellectual or artificial. However, it is clear to me that he was a keen observer of our human condition and that his theoretical developments directly mirror his understanding of client process and human nature in general. And they clearly resonate with Buddhist self-psychology. If one really lets the guts of these ideas inside, a resonance with one's own process may be sensed. The problem, as always, is how to make these ideas a living, useful reality in clinical and interpersonal process. I find his concepts incredibly helpful in ongoing therapy work and in my own personal processes of introspective and contemplative practice.

For instance, it has been very helpful to tease out the nature of my central self-organization, its modes of defending and ways of being, as well as to sense and name the push-pull generated by rejecting and needy selves, as they either come out of repression, or subtly infuse central-self with their affects and needs. Once the feeling tone of these inner movements can be held in some awareness, their driving imperative lessens and space opens for something else to arise.

In clinical work, it is imperative to develop sensitivity to the organization of central-self, its particular tendencies and modes of relating and protecting, and how the energies of rejecting- and needy-selves manifest through central-self in the client's life. This becomes the focus of the practitioner's mindfulness practice. and the felt-sense of the personal nature of I-am-this.

Expressions of Suffering

All defended personality forms are built on the play of endopsychic structure and its various modes of relating, such as disconnection, projection, and introjection, which may infuse a relationship at any time. The inherently fragmented and split nature of endopsychic forms leads to splitting in everyday life. This may be expressed as taking sides, forming cliques, getting others to support your position in opposition to others, seeing things in terms of black or white, not being able to discern the wholeness or subtleties of a relational process, and even as conflicts in families, cultures, and societies. It can be painful to see this splitting played out both in everyday life and in therapy sessions.

If I can be aware of the nature of my own wounding, what basic needs have not been met, the basic forms and tendencies of my endopsychic dynamics, and my capacity to become any of it at any time, the possibility of not becoming it may actualize. This awareness, coupled with the settling into a deeper state of being, can bring real healing. I am sure that some readers have known the wonderment one feels when one settles more deeply into being, when everyday worries, anxieties, and fears release their grip on one's reality and real transformation takes place. Perhaps you have also had the experience of the deeper relatedness that emerges as this occurs. From this point of view, an ongoing, expanding awareness of one's own self-forms and tendencies becomes very liberating.

In essence, the journey is about acknowledging and healing one's wounds, allowing unresolved inner processes to complete, and returning to a more direct experience of innate being as the hub of existence. Once being begins to manifest in a client's process, its presence generates an inner witness, and the tightness of self lessens as its contingent forms can be held in present-time.

6

Self as Process:
Buddhist Concepts

In our previous discussions on the nature of self, we discussed Fairbairn's ideas about the splitting of self into a dynamic triad of self-constellations and introduced Stern's ideas about self-process as schemas-of-being-with. We saw that Fairbairn's basic self-constellation is composed of a self-form (e.g., rejecting-self), an internalized relational object (e.g., the possibly-fulfilling-object), and a related feeling tone or affect (e.g., frustration, anger, etc.). We also defined central-self as a holistic matrix of schemas-of-being-with, the overall sense of I-am-this, or self-view in Buddhist terms. We did not, however, discuss what holds all of this together, and what self-constellations, as schemas-of-being-with, are really composed of. In Buddhist psychology, *atta,* or self, is considered to be a dynamic process driven by volitional energies, whose form is held together by conditioned perceptions and affects. This mirrors Fairbairn's triad of self-constellations generated by the need for contact and the perceptual experience of an ambiguous relational field, held together by the affects spawned by this encounter.

Buddhist Drive Theory and the Self

This next section orients us to the formative forces that underlie relation seeking and the formation of selfhood. In most schools of analytical thought, the root of the self is found in instinctual drives and impulses or dynamic object relations-seeking, or a combination of both. In Buddhism, what drives being and self is understood in a much wider context as not separate from the forces that create stars and solar systems. Innate being *(citta)* and the personal self *(atta)* are seen to be in an ongoing moment-to-moment process of creation as expressions of a profound archetypal force that drives all becoming. This force, called *tanhā,* or *trishnā,* generates the basic *urge-to-become.* The urge-to-become permeates life. It is seen as the plant emerges from the seed and pushes itself up to the sun, as life evolves into newer and better adapted forms and, indeed, as the earth itself circles the sun. It is this urge-to-become that is behind all our self-processes and is at the root of all volitional actions. In Buddhism, the intrinsic motivation underlying selfhood is not rooted in instinctual drives, or relational object-seeking per-se, but is an expression of this motivational drive, or urge to become. Each expression of self-process is both conditioned and conditioning and, if awareness is not fully present, will spin in endless cycles of conditioned self-becoming. Attachment to conditioned self is considered, in Buddhism, to be the root of suffering. It is this attachment that obscures innate being and Source from everyday perception.

On a more personal level, the drive underlying self-process is considered to be volitional impulses and conditioned predispositions *(sankhārās).* In essence, these are personal expressions of *tanhā,* the urge-to-become, and are motivational energies that underpin self-formation. As relational experience is encountered, these drive us to enact personal expressions of selfhood. In other words, it is *intentionality* that drives the self-system. This concept is mirrored in modern brain research. Llinás notes that the intention to move and explore the environment, and the need to predict the nature of what is encountered, drives the evolution of all organisms. The brain has evolved around the being's need to reach out and relate to the environment it finds itself in and to predict the outcomes of that movement, especially in terms of relational experiences (Llinás, 2001).

A further and important extension of these ideas are the Buddhist concepts of mutuality and interbeing. As stated earlier, all beings arise from the same Source and are not separate from other beings. In Buddhist terms, all beings mutually co-arise and interbe. Thus in their shared drive-to-become, there is a natural interconnection from one being to another. Being seeks contact with other beings and is thus deeply relational in nature. Life is, in essence, about relationship, and self takes shape around and through relational encounters.

The Skandhas in a Psychodynamic and Psychological Context

It could be said that the Buddha was the first pure object relations theorist. He saw that self coalesces in relation to external and internal objects. The heart of the organization of selfhood is called the *khandhas* in Pali, or *skandhas* in Sanskrit. The khandhas, or personality aggregates, are five co-arising matrix-like aspects of the self-system that manifest via our physical, emotional, and mental faculties. All arising self-constellations, like Fairbairn's triad of central-self, rejecting-self, and needy-self, are considered to be composed of these five aspects shaped into particular manifestations of I-am-this. Buddhist psychology stresses that what we take as a continuous personal self or ego is nothing more than the dynamic arising and passing away of these five co-arising processes.

The five skandhas are 1) *consciousness,* the moment-to-moment awareness of internal and external objects; 2) *perception,* the conditioned arising of present and past perception as the all-about-ness of an object; 3) *feeling tone,* the impulse towards or away from an object; 4) *volitional impulses,* tendencies and predispositions that become driving forces and convey an underlying meaning and narrative storyline; and 5) *body processes,* physical form, energetic factors, physiological and sensorimotor processes, and sensations. In more detail they are as follows:

Consciousness (viññana) can be considered to be the field within which the other four skandhas arise. It is both field and the awareness of the particulars in the field. It allows coherent moments of experience to emerge, as objects and people are perceived in the present along with an onrush of schemas or matrices of experience from the past. Consciousness in its most basic form is an emergent micro-moment of pure perception that quickly becomes veiled by past perceptions and predispositions to generate particular self-forms and responses. An example of the process of consciousness would be a physical object that is seen through the eyes and known via the faculty of awareness before the influx of past experience and perceptions intrudes. It is important to note that self is seen to arise as sense objects are perceived. This is the essential premise of a pure object relations theory.

Consciousness is said to arise when three factors—*sense door, sense object,* and *knowing,* or the *knowing faculty*—come into contact *(phassa).* The sense doors are those of the five physical senses and that of the mind, or *mind door.* The mind in this understanding not only receives input, but spews out internal objects like thoughts, images, and symbols—just as the seeing sense has light and form as its objects, and the hearing sense has vibration as its object—these internal objects, in turn, become objects of consciousness. Knowing is the locus of awareness at the core of conscious experience.

As we have discussed earlier, citta, or innate being, is a center of presence and sentience at the hub of perceptual processes. Knowing is thus a function of citta, *and* citta is the heart of the I-am experience that manifests through consciousness as a center of pure awareness. Being then knows and responds to its world and relational conditions through the skandhas, and, as this occurs, the skandhas organize into particular self-constellations. Perceptual processes arise, decisions about the nature of the world are made, and the skandhas organize into particular self-forms. The felt-sense of self as I-am-this then emerges. In a similar fashion to the process described in object relations theory, consciousness is shaped by the impact of relational experience as the knowing faculty perceives the objects of being's world. Self-formation is based on inner and outer object relations and the internalization of interpersonal experience in an inherently ambiguous relational field.

It is important to understand that the brain processes the totality of a particular experience all at once. The objects of interpersonal relationship will yield a complex interweaving of *all* of the senses and sense doors that, in turn, give rise to the generation of complex self-forms, tendencies, and strategies. Stern calls the totality of a perceptual experience an *emergent moment*. He notes that the brain simultaneously processes a huge amount of sensory information in any relational experience, describing the arising and parallel processing of volitional shifts, visual images, auditory input, touch, sensation, affect/feeling tone shifts, autonomic states of arousal, internal images, memories, language, sense of place, time and space, etc., taking place all at once. Thus in the simple act of perceiving another, a huge amount of information is holistically processed by different parts of the brain to be received as an emergent moment representing a coherent relational experience (Stern, 1994). The five skandhas manifest this emergent moment as a co-arising matrix of self-form.

Perception (saññā) is the perceptual all-about-ness of an object. Consciousness (viññana) is colored by the nature of past perceptual experience. New perceptual experience is mediated through the veil of past perception as the self-system manifests in repetitive forms, recycling past impingements. The object is experienced in the totality of history and past conditions. As in Heidegger, being has no meaning outside of time and history. Stern discusses these integrated emergent moments of perceptual experience as *emergent properties of mind*. The present-time perception of an object is taken in by all of the senses at once, the brain processes all the input in parallel, organizes it all into a cohesive perceptual experience combined with any past constructs, memories, ideas, images, feeling tones, sensations, etc. that relate to the perceived object. This cohesive perceptual experience arises as an emergent property of mind and underlies the experience of a unified and continuous sense of selfhood, the sense of being a particular person (Stern, 1994). As the world and its objects are taken in, perceptual processes are engaged that are both conditioned and conditioning, and the nature of the object, composed of many interrelated bits of past and present perceptual, cognitive, sensory, and feeling processes, co-emerges with the subject that perceives it in any given experience. The resultant self-form is infused and largely maintained by the next factor, *feeling tone* (vedanā).

Feeling tone (vedanā) is, as already defined in the discussion of dynamic endopsychic structure, the basic charge or valence given to a perceptual experience. It manifests as a positive, neutral, or negative push-pull relative to contact (phassa) with the inner or outer world, and is at the heart of the movement towards or away from any object. From this basic tone or coloration given to an object, more complex feelings, psycho-emotional processes, and self-forms develop. In this sense, it is the charge that determines experiences of goodness and badness and the resultant generation of internal object relations. Along similar lines, Fairbairn saw that every self-constellation has an affect component that is its defining force. For instance, the rejecting self-constellation is infused with anger and resentment and the strong urge to push both the internalized other and the perceived external object away; while the needy-self longs for contact and is drawn towards the exciting or potentially fulfilling other. This is a manifestation of the internal push-pull of feeling tone (vedanā) that arises with each moment of consciousness.

Stern describes a process by which a matrix of feeling, the *temporal feeling shape,* as an internal organizing form experienced over a period of time, lends subjective tone and quality to any particular perceptual experience. It functions like glue that gives a feeling-contour to any emergent property of mind. Similar to Stern's concept, vedanā, or feeling tone, is the root of the basic affect-matrix that permeates all self-constellations and schemas-of-being-with, and colors the emergent self-form with feeling quality. As feeling tone is considered to be the glue that holds personality together, there are many Buddhist meditative practices that orient people to an awareness of feeling tone and related sensations as the first step toward dis-identifying with the conditioned self and reclaiming basic luminosity and freedom of being.

Volitional impulses/predispositions (sankhārās) are all of the global motivational forms, mental constructs, conditioned tendencies, and predispositions found within the psyche or mind-body system. They are infused by perceptions and feeling tones that impel us to see and respond to the world in repetitive ways. Volitional impulses are the most basic organizational energies of self and become active as internal or external objects are perceived. As stated above, volition, or intentionality, is considered to be the driving force of the self-system and of evolution itself. Motivational forces are behind all object seeking, object relations, and self-organizations. These include all of the habits, tendencies, or predispositions to think, feel, say, do, react, or respond to almost anything and everything, such as the tendencies to perceive or see things in fixed ways, to be attracted to or repulsed by someone, to take a specific personal stance relative to a specific experience, to believe certain things, to express particular emotions, to structure and defend our selves in particular ways relative to different experiences, etc.

Volitional impulses are the organizing centers of all self-constellations. Like the still point on which a child's teeter-totter balances, the personality process is poised on volitional impulses. Sankhārās represent the volitional intention to fulfill a need and the meaning this carries for us.

Stern describes a similar concept, the *protonarrative envelope*. By protonarrative he means that the narrative theme involved is non-linear and may have been formed prenatally or in infancy, before linear thought or language skills arose. When the infant reaches out to its world to explore and to get his needs met, he builds up, based on his encounters, an inner model of relationship that holds narrative and meaning. The protonarrative envelope is thus the overarching goal-based motivation and narrative meaning at the heart of any emergent moment of experience. It lends motivational drive and meaning to any temporal feeling shape, and is, in turn, infused by that shape. This is sankhārā, or volitional impulse. It is from this that schemas-of-being-and self-constellations emerge.

Volitional predispositions arise as experience impinges upon the psyche. Here psyche denotes the totality of both innate being and the human mind/self as the center of will, intention, feeling, thought, and behavior. Current perception is filtered through the shroud of past experience, tendencies or predispositions are triggered, conditioned feeling tone or valence is given to the impingement, and a conditioned response is set off. For instance, we meet a particular person and this impingement vibrates at a certain level of perception. This is colored by past experiences and the feeling tones and meaning they hold. These, in turn, predispose us to certain feelings, emotions, and mental processes, and inflexible or reactive behaviors are activated. For example, I meet a man, and right away I don't like him. I even feel scared and want to run away. As I reflect on it, I realize he reminds me of my uncle who, in a fit of rage, screamed and slapped me on the head. All of these behaviors are already present as volitional predispositions, the tendency to become or do in the present what we have become or done in the past. The fear and protective needs generated by the incident became an underlying tendency linked to the feeling tone and image of my uncle. Thus the whole of our personality system, with its adaptive and defended responses and processes, is based upon sankhārā.

Body/form (rūpa) relates to the physical body, its energies and sensations. The ground of manifestation of self *is* the body, and all of the above processes are mediated through the body. Self is seen to be an embodied experience, and no discussion of self can exclude the body. This assertion is echoed in many humanistic therapies such as Gestalt and neo-Reichian psychotherapies, that see the body as the container and reflector of personality process. Llinás affirms self as an embodied process and elegantly describes the generation of self and the *mindness* state, a self-referential feeling-state of "I-am." As the organism reaches out to its world, takes in perceptual experience on multiple levels, and processes it relative to past experience, a unified self-referential feeling state emerges and the organism orients to what is perceived and experienced with a unified sense of selfhood. Self is thus an embodied process that rests upon neurological development and physiological processes (Llinás, 2001). Basically, the body provides the substrate that being needs for incarnation, and this physical substrate is the basis for self-formation. In this context, body includes the physical form as well as its sensations, energies, shapes, tensions, and defensive processes.

Self coalesces as the interplay of these five co-arising factors. The ground of this coalescence is the moment of object-awareness. This sets up a cascade of conditioned perceptions (the all-about-ness of the object), tendencies, feeling tones, and body processes. In essence, self forms relative to the impact of external and internal objects, and the skandhas manifest those as particular self-constellations. While Fairbairn's endopsychic structure gives us the form and dynamics of selfhood, the skandhas orient us to its actual shaping process and the stuff of what selfhood is made of. Buddhist practice revolves around the opening up of this intrinsically closed system.

Meditative Inquiry

As we discussed the shaping of the skandhas into discrete self-constellations, we saw that this is based on a moment of knowing, which arises from citta, or innate being. As knowing meets a sense object through one of the sense doors, self-forms are generated and being becomes obscured from everyday awareness. One then becomes ignorant of one's true nature, one's inner luminosity and freedom. Yet, at the core of every moment of selfhood, there is that moment of knowing, which is never lost. Innate being lies at the hub of the skandhas, as the moment of knowing lies at the heart of Buddhist meditative inquiry into the nature of self and reality.

The particular usefulness of the Buddhist five-skandha schema is that it supports a meditative exploration of self. The Buddha encouraged meditators to develop sati, or presence, and to cultivate awareness of body processes, sensations, feeling tones, perceptions, mental states, and mental content. This is commonly called mindfulness practice. It allows a witness consciousness to develop that has its roots in being rather than in the self-forms that are witnessed. As one rests in presence, one begins to resonate with knowing, the heart of innate being.

In meditation on the skandhas, one simply maintains moment-to-moment presence while observing these five factors as they arise and pass away. Awareness of the skandhas via the development of an inner witness or observer gradually allows the meditator to sense the process-nature of self. In this process, identification with I-am-this is softened or dissolved and the space accessed encourages a dis-identification from the conditioned nature of the self-system Self's process-nature is intuited and innate knowing as a state of being is reclaimed.

We apply this understanding of the skandhas as the organizing factors of personality and related contemplative practices in Core Process Psychotherapy. Both therapist and client hold the client's process in present-time awareness and the potentials of being are awakened. It can be truly liberating and heartening when a person realizes that self is a process, not an entity or thing. A major change occurs in a client's clinical work when enough resource and space is accessed to allow a shift from, "I am so angry," to, "There is anger arising just now." The latter allows for a deeper inquiry into the nature of self and a possible dis-identification from its form. What has obscured the deeper truths of life then recedes, gradually allowing being-nature to shine through.

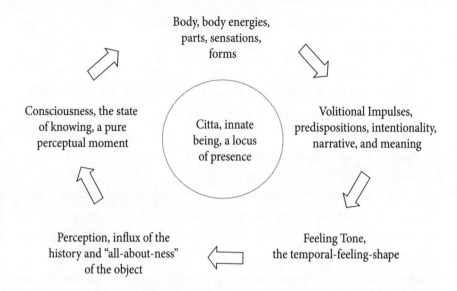

Fig. 6.1 The Five Personality Aggregates
These are the basic constituents of all self-systems. Innate being is the
locus of pristine awareness or presence at the hub of self.

The concept of the skandhas as the dynamic stuff of selfhood has strong resonances with the recent work of Stern. He describes self-constellations as composed of a network of six schemas that represent *emergent moments-of-being-with* others. These interweave to generate an overall self-sense of *schema-of-being-with-another-in-a-certain-way*. Stern's six schemas are:

1. *Sensorimotor*: motor acts and their coordination with sensory experience, sensations;

2. *Perceptual processes*: parallel moments of perception via all of the senses all at once in present time;

3. *Conceptual schemas*: symbols, imagery, and words;

4. *Temporal feeling shapes*: the subjective temporal feeling quality of experience; the felt affect that has feeling tone, or vedanā, at its root;

5. *Scripts:* repetitive event-sequences that generate conditioned responses and processes, and;

6. *The protonarrative envelope:* the overall form of the emergent property of mind that includes volition, motive, and meaning. This holds a narrative-like quality—the all-about-ness of something—and, as noted above, is similar to sankhārā, or volitional predisposition and impulse. (Stern, 1995, p.93)

As Stern describes the nature of the infant's moment-to-moment experience from this point of view, schemas-of-being-with are built up from many emergent moments of relational experience. Each relational moment is an emergent property of mind comprised of specific and various sensory experiences (e.g., perceptions, arousal, sensations, touch, affects, seeing, hearing, images, etc.) that are processed simultaneously. Each emergent moment conditions the next, until an overall schema-of-being-with, composed of the six schemas described above, is generated to form the overall *network* of a schema-of-being-with something or somebody. This overall network is the foundation of any self-constellation.

As with the skandhas, Stern's basic six schemas are held in multiple networks that arise in the immediacy of present-time relational experience and proliferate into particular ways of being. Central-self, the overall sense of who-I-am and how-I-am-in-relationship, is thus a dynamic process affected by our predispositions, rather than a structure, entity, or thing. As basic ambiguity is experienced, the skandhas become organized around that perceptual experience and its related affects. Thus all self-constellations and all schemas-of-being-with can be thought of as conditioned forms of the skandhas organized around the ambiguity of relational experience. These forms will either be fluid expressions of being, or become shaped relative to the distress and wounding experienced.

Self-Experience and the Felt Sense

You might ask, "What is the reality of all of this for me?" or "How is all of this actually experienced in the present moment?" or "How can I gain access to self-constellations and schemas-of-being-with in the healing process?"

I find the work of Eugene Gendlin to be of particular help here. Gendlin was a professor at the University of Chicago. He was working in the student counseling center with other psychotherapists whose orientations ran the gamut from classical analytic, psychodynamic, and humanistic therapies like Gestalt, to transpersonal therapies. In consultation with his colleagues, Gendlin observed that it did not seem to matter what kind of therapy was offered or what theories were involved; the students who got better got better because of something that they themselves were doing internally. It seemed that some students were better able to internally process their experiences than others.

Gendlin then headed a research project that set out to discover if this was true and, if it was, if the skill could be taught to others. It turned out that these students who showed the most improvement had the ability to access a realm of embodied experience that is less formed and more holistic than more obvious sensations, feelings, and emotions. Accessing this realm was based upon the ability to hold the whole of an arising process in a holistic kind of awareness. Gendlin called this inclusive experience the *felt sense*. The felt sense is the global perception encompassing everything, including meaning and felt energies, of any self-organization or schema-of-being within a given moment of experience. It is a direct expression of how one organizes and maintains the meanings of one's life as a holistic, coherent, and embodied all-about-ness.

Similar to Stern's schema-of-being-with, Gendlin stressed that the felt sense is a holistic realm of organization that underpins personal experience and personality shaping. It is a realm of subtle organization that precedes more formed sensations, feelings, emotions, and even thoughts and imagery. To perceive it is to directly encounter the most basic principle of personality: that self is an embodied experience. In the realm of the felt sense, the whole sense-of-me and the meanings given to the events and experiences of life is more available. This is a realm where the self-sense is not as formed and intransigent as usually experienced, more amenable to shifts in organization and beliefs, and more open to the possibility of reorientation to being-nature.

At the heart of felt sense lies what Gendlin called *felt meaning,* the embodied meaning of experience. This may be the meaning I give to relational exchanges, events, or needs, or the meaning I give to life in general. This is similar to Stern's protonarrative envelope and temporal feeling shape. It is the whole sense of selfhood at any moment. Felt meaning is akin to the Buddhist concept of sankhārā, the motivational force that holds meaning for and drives any self-formation.

The felt sense as an underlying reality is initially experienced as nebulous, unclear, tonal, and without clear form. Waking after a dream with a vague sense of something-about-it is a common experience of this realm. At first you struggle to name it, and then when you finally do, it's an "ah-ha!" experience. This is a realm that holds all the information necessary to resolve an inner conflict or concern. As you access this realm the concern or issue unfolds into its own resolution. The sense of the issue as a self-form shifts and opens into *knowing.* Gendlin called this the *felt shift.* It is not just a mental process; things *feel* different. As in Core Process Psychotherapy, health is at work in even the most distorted personality processes, and every personality issue holds the answer to its own question (Gendlin, 1996).

The felt sense is:

- the global, whole-body sense of something;
- organized around and holds felt meaning;
- not just physical, but underlies more formed sensations, emotional tones, feelings, senses, and even images;
- accessed within the body space;
- an expression of how one embodies and gives meaning to our experience;
- is initially nebulous, undefined, hard to grasp or name.

Gendlin discovered that unresolved issues, concerns, and qualities of selfhood are held tonally within the body in the felt sense realm. The felt sense is not, however, necessarily about something difficult or traumatic. It is a feeling realm that holds meaning and can be accessed via a natural movement of awareness. Orientation to the felt sense realm is an extremely useful adjunct to any kind of therapy, as it brings the client closer to the organizing center and felt-meaning of any self-form, issue, or arising process.

The five skandhas, as coherent self-constellations or schema-of-being-with, arise as a coherent moment of experience. Gendlin's felt-sense is the overall experience of this moment at the most formative level. It is perceived, by those who have the facility, as an overall body-sense that has at its core a felt meaning mediated by volitional impulses and temporal narrative content.

The focusing process that Gendlin subsequently developed is geared to help people make this implicit realm explicit. He developed a six-step protocol to teach people how to access this normally elusive layer of organization, orient to its overall felt-sense, and access the felt-meaning at its core. This brings the focuser to the organizing principle, protonarrative envelope, or volitional impulse (sankhārā) at the core of the arising experience. In Stern's terms, they are learning to sense the feeling shape of the protonarrative envelope and the motivational drive at the heart of the schema-of-being-with. Although some people already have access to this implicit level of experience, for others it may take some training in a therapeutic or group setting to learn how to access and work with the felt-sense (Gendlin, 1978,1981, 2003).

7

The Intransigent Self
and Dependent Co-arising

In each moment of consciousness, most of us have the experience of a discrete self that, for better or worse, generally feels as it did yesterday, last year, or even many years ago. The self-system that organizes relative to relational experience is very stable, even in its seemingly most distorted or unstable forms. Resistance to change is a known issue in all forms of psychotherapy and was even observed by the Buddha as a key stumbling block to personal freedom. In his early work, Freud noted that some clients manifest great internal resistance to therapeutic change, and even considered some conditions beyond the help of analysis because of this. He stated that the patient's resistance was one of the major things to overcome if therapeutic process was to succeed (Freud, 1914, 1925).

Fairbairn, again moving away from a Freudian perspective, noted that the intransigent and resistant nature of self is due to its being a "closed system of internal reality, a static internal situation ... which persist[s] unchanged indefinitely, and which [is] precluded from change by [its] very nature as long as [it] remain[s] self-contained" (Fairbairn, 1958, Guntrip, 1961). Self was seen to be an internal psychic reality that is a closed, relatively static, self-contained system, strongly resistant to change or regeneration. Self tends to become in the present what it had previously become in the past.

Fairbairn noted that self is resistant to change due to an intrinsic loyalty to its inner world of internal objects and object relations, the dynamic internal organization at the root of the sense of selfhood. In Buddhist psychology this is described as attachment to self-construct. We become identified with and attached to the sense of who we are, the history of our experience, and the way of being we have developed. "I feel myself to be myself," is our inner reality. Fairbairn's ideas echo Buddhist descriptions of the nature of self as a dynamic and closed process-loop that is both conditioned and conditioning, continually recycling itself through everyday perceptual experience. Each and every arising moment of self conditions the next and is in turn a consequence of past conditions and relational contingencies. In Stern's terms, our earliest relational experience is taken into an already self-referential internal system, which then becomes generalized and organized into schemas-of-being-with as stable forms through which our experience of relational others are mediated.

Llinás found that the concept of self as an internalized closed system has strong roots in brain physiology. He observed how the brain functions to generate a closed internal representation of the outer world that is self-referential, has survival value, and is a direct expression of the intention of the organism to reach out, orient, and move within and around its perceived world. The experience of our relational world is internalized and codified by the brain as a closed subjective experience of I-am-this and my-world-is-such. The brain generates a unified sense of self so that the organism can relate to the nature of its environment and predict outcomes of intentional actions in a moment-to-moment fashion. The generation of the self as a coherent self-referential experience is of paramount importance for survival and allows both infant and adult to predict the responses of others to their needs and actions. In Llinás' concept, the self is generated by the developing brain to be a stable system that 1) allows the intentions and needs of the organism to be actualized; 2) allows the organism to predict the nature of its environment and outcomes of relational interactions; 3) allows appropriate responses to those relational interactions; and 4) retains all of this as a stable self-sense that is prepared for the next relational interchange (Llinás, 2001).

This stability is both a godsend and a curse. It supports survival; but it also locks one into perceiving and reacting to the world and relational experiences in similar ways over time. Central-self's stable representation of one's relational world is inherently resistant to change and may generate confusion in everyday relational experience. It is important to stress again that self is not an enduring entity or thing. Self is process, and the stable self-referential experience is a factor of the properties of mind that arise from moment to moment. This seeming paradox between self as continuous experience and self as momentary process is the crux of our exploration.

The key to freedom, both in Buddhist terms and in the practice of psychotherapy, is to open this closed system in such a way that self is known as a process and not as an entity or thing, and identify shifts from I-am-this, to the simple fact of being. Self's intransigence must be held in an appropriately empathic manner in therapy sessions so that its closed nature may be reevaluated in the light of new relational experience. As being's way of being is held in the light of awareness within a trustworthy relational environment, the identification with self eases and the cloud of ontic obscuration clarifies.

Dependent Co-Arising

We are still left the question, What keeps all of this running? Buddhist psychology describes the self as a dynamic and cyclical cascade-like process, whose individual aspects co-arise and are mutually conditioning. The ongoing process that maintains the experience of an intransigent self is called *dependent co-arising* or *dependent origination*. Dependent co-arising describes the process of karma as psychological causality. In

Buddhism the term karma does not imply fate or predestined happenings, but points to the causal nature of all things. In our context, this means the co-arising and mutually interdependent nature of the factors that give rise to the experience of a continuous self. This understanding of causality is focused on the present-time, moment-to-moment generation of the self-sense, which makes it an excellent complement to Western developmental paradigms.

Dependent co-arising points to the total interdependence of all things, the vast web in which all beings interbe. I once heard a Ch'an Master say during a discourse, "If a single insect in this world was truly annihilated, the whole universe would disappear!" (Hsui Chi Liu, 1974, London.) Buddhism orients us to a vast non-linear web of causality in which no event can be separated out from any other. This concept is totally congruent with modern physics with its concepts of non-locality and quantum entanglement. The human personality system and sense of selfhood is one expression of this moment-to-moment interdependent causality. We are all beings who co-arise and whose essence is non-separate from the rest of the universe!

In the Pali Suttas, the Buddha took many approaches to explaining dependent co-arising. The most common version is a twelve-linked chain of causation that begins with ignorance, an absence of awareness of the true nature of self and its relational world. The concept of ignorance in Buddhism has the connotation of confusion, of not seeing things as they are. With ignorance, particular volitional impulses arise which, in turn, set off the whole self-cycle of dependent co-arising.

For our purposes, however, the most useful version of dependent co-arising is one that begins with a pure moment of perception or consciousness. This pure object-oriented moment initiates the generation of the self-system and is of the basis for all internal object relations. As consciousness of an internal or external object arises, a conditioned cascade of process is activated that gives birth to the experience of self as a stable entity. I call this the *perceptual cascade*. Current perceptual processes activate past perceptual knowing, as we become in the present what we have learned to be in the past. Here we are looking at the moment-to-moment generation of the self-sense of me, myself, and I-am-this. Dependent origination is a wheel of co-arising processes that keeps the self spinning in endless self-perpetuating cycles. The following description is based on a discourse of the Buddha's from the *Samyutta Nikaya* (II:73) of the Pali Canon.

The Perceptual Cascade

Contact with objects through mind-body processes is the means by which citta, or innate being, gains access to its inner and outer worlds and orients to other beings. This is an expression of viññana and is the starting point in our exploration.

The perceptual cascade starts with a moment of pure perception, pure awareness of an object. With this, an internal cascade of process is set off that maintains the "closed system of internal reality" that is self, as Fairbairn maintained. In the following description of the links in the conditioned chain of the closed self-system, you may recognize the five personality factors (skandhas) described previously. In the following nine-phase description of dependent co-arising, a basic ignorance of the true nature of the self is assumed, as are volitional impulses, the body, and its senses. The phases are as follows:

1. Moment of pure perception, or pure object-oriented consciousness

The first link in the perceptual cascade is a moment of pure object-awareness, not conditioned by past experience (viññana). This perceptual moment is based upon the *knowing faculty*, which is a function of citta, as a core of innate sentience and presence. Thus citta lies at the core of dependent co-arising, as well as the skandhas. This moment of pure object orientation occurs as a sense door, sense object, and knowing, come into direct resonance. This dynamic is the basis of all object relations. This is a moment of *contact*, or phassa, in Pali, at which a simple knowing of the object occurs, before the brain interprets the incoming data in terms of past experience and before a coherent emergent property of mind arises. The whole cascade that maintains a closed, intransient, and self-contained self begins with this pure object-oriented moment.

2. Influxes, secondary perceptions, perceptual tendencies

The next link in the perceptual cascade is an influx of recognition based upon conditioning, memory, and past perceptual experience (saññā). After the initial moment of pure perception, the all-about-ness of the object, situation, or circumstance floods in and all conditioned perceptions, judgments, and past knowing based upon predispositions and tendencies (sankhārās) infuse the emergent moment. As the brain processes all sensory input all at once, connections are made to past experience, relationships, existing self-constellations, schemas-of-being-with, and the historical sense of I-am-this. The object is recognized in the context of past history and conditions, and tendencies to relate to the object in certain ways are activated. The present relational moment is now experienced through the veil of past perceptions, needs, conditioning, internalized objects (relational others), and defensive tendencies. In this context, being's way of being as self begins to emerge. The new relational object is now seen through the veil of past conditioning and cannot be experienced purely in the light of the present moment.

3. Feeling tone

Feeling tone (vedanā) arises relative to the particular internal or external object or situation perceived as a charge, or valence; positive, neutral (indifferent), or negative. The quality of feeling tone is based upon the predispositions, tendencies, and volitional impulses (sankhārās) generated by past experience. Vedanā determines the experience of goodness and badness of the object, and the subsequent splitting both of the internal object and of the ego states that co-arise with it.

Feeling tone, as an expression of subjective experience, is a primordial response to conditions that is present even in single-cell and invertebrate organisms. Llinás describes the subjective experience of an object or situation as *qualia,* the inner tonal felt-experience of self and other that reflects the totality of neural processing relative to that object or situation. He stresses that subjective experience is a universal property of cells (Llinás, 2001). Even at the first moments of life in the single cell at conception, feeling tone may be experienced. If this is true, it supports Lake's belief that even our earliest experiences are accessible as embodied feeling tone and emotional affect, and that these may underlie the development of personality systems.

Feeling tone also correlates to Stern's *temporal feeling shape* and the emotional affects that Fairbairn observed with each self-constellation.

4. Urge/Desire Intensifies

The urge-to-become (tanhā, trishnā), the primary drive from a Buddhist perspective, intensifies as feeling tone arises. Movement is generated; urges, needs, and desires relative to the object are activated. The urge to become what one has already become intensifies. The push-pull likewise intensifies, and volitional predispositions further engage. In Fairbairn's terms, the energies of endopsychic structure resonate with the perception of the new object and the affects and internalized objects of central-self, and rejecting-self and needy-self are augmented, each self-constellation manifesting its own tendencies and urges. Urge and desire thus intensify the splitting already present.

5. Clinging: positional processes

As feeling tone and urge intensify, an inner clinging is generated that further reinforces the existing internal world of object relations and the closed and intransigent self-system. As the inner world of object relations resonates with the perceived object, it is clung to as a representation of selfhood and who-I-am in the world. Each new object then becomes a representation of who-I-am, and cannot be perceived for what it purely is. The feeling-sense of being a particular self is thus supported and reinforced. Clinging is at the heart of resistance to change, the intransigent nature of the self-system. One clings to and identifies with what one has become, to who one feels oneself to be, and the object is perceived within that context.

6. Incorporation and collecting

We then incorporate the object along with its history and all else that has arisen in relationship to it. In essence, we collect the things we cling to. This is similar to the object relations concept of introjection, or internalization. The new relational object is sensed through our internal felt-objects, or felt-others, and is integrated with these and incorporated into our conditioned sense of selfhood. Thus the process of incorporation supports and strengthens our existing self-sense as we begin to feel that the new object is just another expression of our internal object world. Psycho-emotionally, the incorporation of the object or situation helps generate a sense of the self's ongoing continuity. Again, this is, in essence, a reinforcement and re-assertion of our personality system. We continually cling to and collect our self-positions as we reinforce and re-collect our needs, tendencies, perceptions, ideas, views, opinions, beliefs, feelings, reactions, etc.

7. Becoming

This is a very subtle and deceptive process by which we believe that the experiences and things we collect, and the inner world that organizes in response to them, is who we are (Payutto, 1994). We identify with and become the very things that we have incorporated and collected. In essence, we become what we collect and identify with what we generate. There is no space or possibility here for introspection or knowing this as process. The present experience, seen through the lens of past conditions and tendencies, reinforces the collected sense of selfhood. We see the object through this lens and continue to become what we have already become.

8. Birth

Next is the birth of conditioned self in the present moment. Having collected, and become what we have collected, the whole process is solidified into self as I-am-this. The intransigent self is reborn as a fixed and contingent form that continually becomes being's way of being, its interface with the world of relationship. All schemas-of-being-with, self-constellations, and personality strategies are an expression of this moment-to-moment rebirth of self. In this rebirth, the skandhas, manifesting as internal object relations and schemas-of-being-with, emerge and all tendencies present within them are relationally reenacted. Characterological and defensive strategies come into play, projective processes arise, and conditional behaviors are acted out, all reinforcing further cyclic becoming.

9. Suffering

As the whole process proliferates, the experience of the current object or situation is mediated by intransigent self-constellations and perceived through past conditions. The truth of the present moment is obscured as the new experience reinforces ingrained modes of perception and ways of being. The protection and maintenance of the intransigent self literally becomes a way of life. If a deeper awareness is not present, we will totally identify with these self-constructs and perceive the world through them, defending our self-system as though our very lives depended upon it. As an object is experienced, conditioned self-constellations arise, personal imprints of wounding are triggered, and defended positions are taken, even when there is no need to defend. Attachment to I-am-this, self-view, and self-image, and the tendency to identify with self as I or me, rather than as a process of being here, then leads to pain and suffering, as the world shifts and changes in relationship to who we think we are. Citta, or innate being, becomes obscured by attachment to the self-forms generated in each encounter. It becomes harder and harder to see the truth of the present relationship as the self that mediates being's experience of the world gives a false reading of current relational process. All perceptual process becomes clouded by the influx of past perceptions, conditioning, and self-forms. Confusion reigns and suffering results in a seemingly endless cycle of being and becoming.

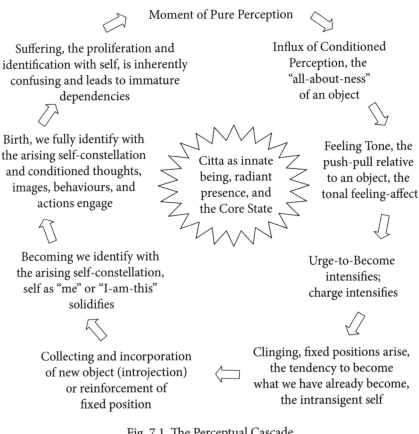

Moment of Pure Perception

Suffering, the proliferation and identification with self, is inherently confusing and leads to immature dependencies

Influx of Conditioned Perception, the "all-about-ness" of an object

Birth, we fully identify with the arising self-constellation and conditioned thoughts, images, behaviours, and actions engage

Citta as innate being, radiant presence, and the Core State

Feeling Tone, the push-pull relative to an object, the tonal feeling-affect

Becoming we identify with the arising self-constellation, self as "me" or "I-am-this" solidifies

Urge-to-Become intensifies; charge intensifies

Collecting and incorporation of new object (introjection) or reinforcement of fixed position

Clinging, fixed positions arise, the tendency to become what we have already become, the intransigent self

Fig. 7.1 The Perceptual Cascade
Dependent Co-arising is driven by volitional impulses that underpin the arising of conditioned perceptions and feeling tone. Citta, a radiant core of pristine sentience and presence, lies at the core of all self-experience.

It is important to understand that although dependent co-arising is presented as a chain of events, it is actually a non-linear process. All factors co-arise and are mutually interdependent and co-conditioning. In keeping with the principle of mutuality, each factor interpenetrates and infuses all others. If any factor ceases, the whole cycle ceases. It is this obscuration of being and interbeing that is the challenge of humankind and the heart of the meditative and psychotherapeutic journey.

Proliferation

This cyclical process fosters the proliferation *(papanca)* of the self. As dependent co-arising cycles, the self-system is both supported and further increases. Sensory processes occur, perception arises colored by volitional impulses, feeling tones surge, the self-sense develops, along with its affects, images, thoughts, and fantasies, and all are projected out as reality. This observation is a precursor to the Kleinian idea that we project out what we have introjected and then see the world via those projections, in projective identification. In Buddhism, this is an expression of *avidya,* ignorance of the real nature of things, which leads to confusion and suffering in relational interchanges. In this entangled process, we see the world that we have created, rather than the world as it is. As this whole cascade gets introjected into the next moment of experience, the self-sense spreads into the relational world like the roots of a tree. As this whole cascade gets refluxed or introjected into the next moment of experience, relational others are seen through the veils of conditioned perceptions, feeling tones, affects, beliefs and tendencies. This projected reality, coupled with the regressed needs of immature dependency, are the root of much relational pain, disharmony, and separation.

Dependent co-arising is a cyclical and holistic process that resembles spirals within spirals. The simplest description of the intention of dependent co-arising is this:

When there is this, that is.
With the arising of this, that arises.
When this is not, neither is that.
With the cessation of this, that ceases.
(*Samyutta Nikaya,* II:28, 65, as translated
    by P. A. Payutto, 1994)

You may already have glimpsed what can alleviate the suffering inherent in attachment to self, or as Fairbairn might call it, our loyalty to our inner world of objects and object relations. Healing occurs as we shift from identification with the proliferation of our conditioned self to a more attuned being-state. This shift holds the potential for realignment to Source and being and for the present-time experience of interbeing, and for transforming immature ways of relating to mature interdependency and compassion. This is, perhaps the sole hope we have as human beings to heal our personal, societal, and cultural splits—and the earth we inhabit and upon which we depend for life.

8

A Relational Paradigm

Now that we have a general view of the formation of selfhood, we can explore a more comprehensive paradigm that describes the generation and nature of particular personality systems and defended self-forms. For this, Core Process Psychotherapy builds on Lake's work, particularly his understanding of early life.

From his clinical work, Lake saw that the womb experience in general, and the first trimester in particular, is a period in which the prenate literally marinates in, and is permeated by, mother's spiritual, psychological, emotional, and behavioral life. By the end of his career, Lake was convinced that there is awareness from the moment of conception and that the prenate directly perceives and is affected by its womb experience. Lake also discovered that the prenate experiences the womb as a unique relational field, makes decisions about what it encounters in this field, and takes psycho-emotional and somatic shape accordingly. In this process, the prenate and infant are very vulnerable to environmental and relational input and to our mistaken assumptions about their awareness and intelligence.

Furthermore, the womb experience is a two-way street in which the prenate and mother are in a mutual exchange of feelings and emotions via the umbilical cord and placenta. In this reciprocal process, mother, too, is touched and affected, as are those around her. This profound interchange is responded to by the little one in various ways that are the ground of self and personality development.

Lake referred to the period from conception through the first nine months after birth as the womb of spirit. In this period the little one lives in womb-time, experiences his needs as though they are also mother's needs, and begins the shift from what Lake called being-in-relationship, the experience of being as mediated by mother's presence, to being-in-itself, a coherent and continuous experience of being not dependent upon mother's reflection.

I am convinced that this earliest experience of relational life directly impacts and conditions the little one's perceptions of the world he lives in. In clinical practice and in everyday life, it has become clear to me that many people live in womb-time—"womb as world, world as womb"—rather than real time. What follows is an interpretation of Lake's work that is directly based on my clinical practice in both individual and group therapy settings.

Five Basic Components of Lake's Paradigm

Although Lake was convinced that the first trimester in utero was most critical, his paradigm encompasses the wider developmental period of the womb of spirit. The paradigm is oriented to the needs and feelings of the prenate and infant and their responses to the experience within the womb of spirit. It includes: 1) the maternal environment the prenate or infant finds himself in and the relational interchanges within that field; 2) the fundamental, basic, or primal needs of the little one; 3) the responsive primal feelings that arise in the prenate or infant as basic needs are met or not met within the ambiguity of relationship; and 4) the repercussions to the developing self-system if these needs are not met, or if the related experience and the feelings generated from it are overwhelming. In the discussions below, I have divided Lake's paradigm into five basic components:

1. *The Empathic Relational Field and Basic Needs:* An understanding of the nature of the maternal field and infant needs, termed *basic* or

primal needs. Most importantly, basic needs are universal and trans-cultural, and are present throughout life. The womb of spirit is the first relational field that the new being encounters. This field ideally provides a good enough holding environment within which basic needs are largely met (Winnicott, 1965; Lake, 1979). These include relational needs such as safety, emotional warmth, acknowledgment, acceptance, recognition, nurturance, sustenance, attunement, resonance, and responsiveness. Whether the prenate develops a fluid and healthy personality system, or one organized around basic wounding, is dependent upon how these needs have been met, overridden, or denied.

2. *Umbilical Affect:* The influence of the inflow to the prenate of maternal sustenance and feelings via the placenta and umbilical cord, coupled with his feeling response or affect. This affect has three expressions: positive, negative, and strongly negative. This dynamic also extends to the womb of spirit as a wider energetic holding field of being, feeling, and emotion. The infant's umbilical connection to mother as a focus for affect runs very deep. For the first nine months after birth, he experiences mother's emotional states as though the umbilical connection is still present. During this time it is hard for the infant to separate mother's feeling states from his own. Fairbairn notes that this is a period both of primary identification, where the infant is emotionally continuous with mother's states, and of immature relating, where the infant cannot differentiate its needs from those of mother's. Ideally, a state of separate beingness is achieved by the ninth month after birth, as this is when, according to Lake, a transition occurs from being-in-relationship to being-in-itself.

3. *The Dynamic Cycle:* An ontological understanding of development that describes how the inflow of maternal being, emotions, and nurturance, and the relational environment in general, effect the being and wellbeing of the prenate. This understanding is expressed in terms of cycles of being, wellbeing, status, and achievement. As being and wellbeing needs are with us throughout life, this cycle continually renews

itself until the moment of death. Thus the potential for healing or wounding is always present, and the dynamic cycle can be renewed and be reclaimed at any time.

4. *Transmarginal Hierarchy:* An understanding of the repercussions of early experience and of the levels of response and defensive adaptations of the prenate and infant. Due to the inherently ambiguous nature of the relational environment, the infant experiences a "mixed bag" of relational interchange. The hierarchy describes the self-organizational and defensive processes that emerge as positive or negative affects are experienced. Under increasing relational stress, especially that of perceived breaches in the empathic holding field, more and more intense defensive responses are generated. The hierarchy is divided into four levels of response: ideal, coping, oppositional, and transmarginal. The generation of various personality systems relates to the level of the stress hierarchy that has been impinged upon and the defenses that have been engaged to protect against empathic failures and primary trauma. The stress encountered and mode of defending is directly related to the dynamic cycle and wounding at the level of being or wellbeing. The transmarginal level is one in which the shock level is so intense that a loss of being itself is experienced.

5. *Personality Systems and the Defended Self:* Lake's outline of the various psychodynamic strategies and related psychological response patterns generated as defenses against distress and perceived badness and based upon where in the dynamic cycle the prenate is affected (whether at the being or wellbeing levels). These are not pathological processes per se, but are attempts to remain in relationship, given the circumstances experienced.

The basic schema of personality development is then based upon the following:

1. Within the context of the safe holding environment, basic needs are more or less met;

2. As these needs are experienced as being met or not, a spectrum of umbilical affects is generated;

3. The intensity of these affects is experienced in a hierarchy of stress responses called the transmarginal stress hierarchy;

4. The developmental cycle of the infant is impacted in various ways dependent upon the increasing intensity of this stress hierarchy;

5. The infant is taken out of the state of simply being into the need to defend, which underpins the generation of various defended personality systems.

Our next few chapters will explore these developments in greater detail.

9

The Womb of Spirit and the Empathic Holding Field

The womb of spirit is a spiritual, psycho-emotional, and physical holding environment that is more or less nurturing and sustaining. As a *bidirectional interactive field* between child and mother, it includes both what is transmitted back and forth via the umbilical cord and the more energetic, instinctual, intuitive, and spiritual transmissions between mother and prenate or infant as a field experience. I have heard many mothers share that their experience of pregnancy, their child's birth, and the womb of spirit period, was a pivotal one for personal and spiritual recognition and growth.

It is important to understand that although mother provides an aspect of the womb of spirit and its interpersonal context, its holding environment is much wider than this. It also includes the holding field mother finds herself in and her support—father and his dynamics or mother's partner if it is not the father, her friends, the family around her, her society, its culture and history, and the time and circumstances of the pregnancy and in the world she inhabits. Thus mother's world of meaning and circumstance, the nature of the support and conditions around her, are as much a part of the womb of spirit as the immediacy of the mother-prenate/infant relationship. A breakdown in any of these interdependent and co-arising structures may adversely impact and impinge upon the young being, who is sensing all of this as a unified and interactive field of exchange.

The metaphor of the womb of spirit as an archetypal maternal holding field is found in many cultures. We see this archetype in the Virgin Mary, Kuan Yin, and Tara, to name but a few. These are images of the universal force of love that holds all creation in primal sympathy and manifests as compassion-in-action. The womb of spirit mirrors and reflects this archetype. The safety, empathy, communion, and nurturing experienced in a loving and responsive womb-field, generates feelings of spiritual connection and a sense of personal wellbeing. The safe holding environment of the womb of spirit sets the stage for the internalization of both a unified sense of being and an underlying sense of wellbeing. Being is sustained by the continued accepting and responsive spiritual presence of mother, and wellbeing is experienced as physical and emotional sustenance provided in a good enough fashion.

The Empathic Holding Field and the Development of Being

As we have seen, innate being is a locus of presence at the hub of selfhood and the I-am experience. But being is also relational and developmental in nature. The coherency of the Source-being-self axis is actualized in the relational field of accepting, trustworthy, and nurturing empathic others. In Lake's concept, it is only within the empathic mirroring of other beings that *innate being* becomes *personal being*. The first relational field met is the womb and the first relational other is mother. In Lake's terms, it is in mother's reflection and resonance that being and Source are known. In mother's loving gaze, the little one knows that "he is" and "deserves to be," and discovers the nature of his own being (Lake, 1979).

Lake maintained that an empathic relational field between mother and prenate/infant is essential for healthy personality development, a coherent sense of being, psycho-emotional maturation, and a fluid and stable self-system. The little one needs time and space to learn about this relational field and how to make, organize, and maintain contact with it. It is the nature of this field that is decisive in determining the way the infant organizes its self-processes relative to the interactions it perceives. If the relational holding field present is largely attuned and appropriately responsive, then a self-system begins to emerge that is organized around a way of being that knows and seeks this kind of empathic field throughout life. The little one begins to be able to discern the nature of the relational field he is in and the differences between empathic relational fields and those that are not holding or attuned. According to Bowlby's attachment theory, if mother and other primary caregivers offer a trustworthy and consistently responsive relational field, the young child can develop their own internal secure base and experience secure attachment processes.

The Nature of Empathy

The ability to empathize with another's state is an innate potential in humans critical to develop in the therapy setting. Empathy is not a conditioned feeling or intention. It is not a self-generated form, nor is it initiated through the self-system. It is not about changing inner states or conditional feelings. Nor is it a technique. True empathy arises from inherent being-to-being interconnection. It is a manifestation of the internal alignment of the caregiver, or source-person, to his or her own being and Source. When one is aligned to Source and centered in being, interbeing is known and a natural movement of compassion arises through direct resonance. Empathy allows the caregiver to respond to the being state of the prenate or infant, to accept unconditionally his presence and attune to his needs. Empathy is the heart of the maternal holding field. Mother, if supported by those around her, will naturally enter an attuned and resonant being-state.

Stern suggests that as she does this, a new self-constellation coalesces. This is a unique self-system, the *motherhood constellation,* which emerges during pregnancy and may last for many months or even years. He makes a strong case that mothers' self-process undergoes a marked change during pregnancy as this new psychic organization emerges. Mother's self-sense becomes largely organized around the presence of her baby, its wellbeing, and their mutual connection. In this state of primary receptivity, mother is naturally attuned to the inner states and needs of her infant, senses these via direct resonance, and can appropriately respond to them. Any issues she has concerning mothering and her own experience of being mothered will come to the forefront. Other relationships and self-constellations are still present and important, but tend to settle into the background (Stern, 1985, 1998).

In a similar vein, Winnicott stresses that mother's self-system shifts to *primary maternal preoccupation,* a state of heightened sensitivity, empathy, and clear attunement to the needs of the young infant within which the new mother naturally does the right thing as she directly knows the infant's inner state as her own (Winnicott, 1965). Lake suggests that mother undergoes a major change in self-state as she orients to her pregnancy and new child. If supported by family and culture, she will enter a being-state more closely aligned to Source and, in this state, be able to generate a good enough holding field within which the little one learns about the nature of his own being and the world in which he's incarnating.

There is a lovely myth from India that directly speaks to the archetypal nature of this empathic maternal holding field:

Garuda flew and remembered. It was only a few days since he had hatched from his egg and already so much had happened. … Who was the first person he'd seen? His mother, Vinata. Beautiful in her tinyness, she sat on a stone watching his egg hatch, determinedly passive. Hers was the first eye Garuda held in his

own. And at once he knew that that eye was his own. Deep inside
was an ember that glowed in the breeze. The same he could feel
burning beneath his own feathers. (Calasso, 1996)

In the loving reflection of mother's being, innate being knows itself and,
as relational experience unfolds, becomes personal being. However, if
there is a disruption in empathic holding, if the prenate or infant experiences denial, abandonment, threat, or overwhelming negative emotions,
then this mirroring will be interrupted or non-existent. The coherent
experience of Source, being, and self is disturbed, and a wounding at
the level of being may arise. This can plunge the little one into a depth of
terror, despair, and emptiness and, in the extreme, into the experience
of annihilation and non-being (Lake, 1979; Winnicott, 1964).

Winnicott's Holding Environment

Winnicott's concept of the *good enough holding environment* was directly
incorporated by Lake into the paradigm of the womb of spirit. Winnicott
believed that the infant experiences mother as a ubiquitous presence, a
hopefully safe and empathic holding field within which he can have the
experience of simply being. The infant can then rest in what Winnicott
called the *unintegrated state,* an open and undefended state of being.
From here, a cohesive and continuous sense of being may be experienced
that becomes the center of a healthy and fluid self-system. The holding
field provided by mother has the role of protecting and buffering the
infant from the impingements of relational and environmental experiences, especially in at the stage that Winnicott called *absolute dependence* and that Fairbairn termed *immature dependency*, as discussed
below. It is a period during which the infant is emotionally continuous
with mother and totally dependent upon her and other primary caregivers for all basic needs. Any impingement—it might be a loud noise,
bright lights, or most importantly, empathic failure—will take the infant

out of the state of simply being into a state of anxiety and fear. If the infant is not protected from impingement, then the experience of being is interrupted and he has to shift from the open and undefended state, to reaction and defensive processes. Due to the varied and uncertain nature of the relational and environmental field and the potential for intrusions or impingements, this risk is ever-present.

Confronted with this reality, Winnicott believed that the infant is constantly on the brink of anxiety. If he becomes overwhelmed by relational or environmental experience, he may be cast into a state of annihilation and the emptiness of non-being. Winnicott asserted that the experience of annihilation was at the root of psychosis and the most extreme personality distortions. It is the role of mother to protect the infant from relational impingements and the abyss of anxiety and anni-hilation. She and other primary caregivers do this by maintaining the good enough holding environment. Within this field of presence and containment, the infant is protected from jarring or shocking impinge-ments until he can manage the extremes of daily experience without shutting down his being, or being-nature. Winnicott recognized that holding begins in the prenatal period. Although he acknowledged the importance of the prenatal physiological environment, there is ample research that indicates that the prenatal emotional environment is just as important, if not more so (O'Keane and Scott, 2005; Perry and Pol-lard, 1998; among many others).

Winnicott acknowledged that all relational life has its ups and downs, but if mother maintains a holding field in a good enough fashion, then the little one will be able to rest in his being state and learn to trust rela-tionship. Lake called this the development of *basic trust* and considered it an essential aspect in the development of a fluid self-system.

Winnicott understood the holding environment as having three main aspects: holding, handling, and object presenting.

Holding

Holding relates to the quality of the relational field generated by mother and primary caregivers. Ideally the infant is held in a good enough fashion as mother contains and manages the baby's inner states through attunement to his feelings, needs and impulses. Mother generates a safe holding field by the way she holds, carries, feeds, moves, speaks to, gazes at, and responds to her infant. Within this field, baby is protected from the impingements and extremes of daily life. Although Winnicott did not discuss father's or primary support person's similar role to any great extent, their task is also critical. Father has the role of protecting the mother-baby relationship from outer relational or environmental impingement. In his protective field, mother can rest in her own being-state and sense her natural interconnection with infant's being.

If this attuned field is maintained in a good enough fashion, the infant gradually begins to trust mother and the holding field in general. Mother's empathic holding allows the *true self* to emerge, a self-system that can clearly differentiate its needs from others, with coherency and continuity of being at its core.

Within the empathic holding environment the baby can rest in unintegration, where all of the unintegrated bits and pieces of experience can be allowed to simply be. In this state the infant does not have to react to any particular outside stimuli, experiences a continuous sense of existing over time, and senses its separateness yet interconnection with mother. In Winnicott's paradigm, the infant can then move from the undifferentiated and unintegrated state to individualization, as it experiences an existentially integrated, unified, and holistic sense of being and selfhood.

If the holding environment is not attuned and resonant, if impingements and empathic failures are commonly experienced and the infant must frequently enter defensive and reactive states, then a *false self* begins to form. This is a self-system that is not in tune with its own inner needs, but exists via coping and compliance with the needs of others. A defended self results that is organized around reaction and defensive processes, without a sense of coherency and continuity of being. If there are continual empathic breaches, and the infant is not protected from jarring or sudden shifts in the relational or environmental field, he will be jolted into reaction and shock, and the terrifying experience of unintegration without holding occurs. In this relational ambiance, the little one is cast into the depths of annihilation and non-being.

Handling

Handling refers to the quality and nature of physical contact offered to the infant and the infant's resultant sensory/feeling experience. Within an empathic holding field, the attuned, sensitive, and appropriately responsive touch of mother and other primary caregivers allows the infant to feel acknowledged, recognized, and accepted, and yields feelings of wellbeing and satisfaction. Winnicott affirmed that with sensitive handling, the infant does not have to react or defend himself, and can continue to rest in being. With sensitive and loving contact, good feelings and emotions are experienced in a relational context, and an integration of mental, emotional, and sensory processes occurs. As a continuity of being is experienced, stability of mind and body results, along with the experience of being whole and connected to self and other in the midst of changing life conditions. The body and self are then experienced in an integrated fashion. The psyche truly inhabits the body and the boundary of the body is experienced as the dividing line between me and not-me.

If handling is managed in an insensitive, impersonal, or abusive fashion, then safety will be lost, as will basic trust in the holding field. In a field of impersonal and insensitive handling, the baby may feel disempowered, abandoned, and even betrayed by its holding environment. If insensitive handling is a common experience, it may become unbearable and, in the extreme, the infant may detach from body feelings and sensations and live in its mind cut off from physical reality. A sense of unreality and emptiness then will pervade the person's experience of life. They may feel disconnected, disembodied, and depersonalized. This dissociation is root of the schizoid strategy that will be discussed below.

Object Presenting

Object presenting is related to the way mother and other primary caregivers offer the things of the world to the infant. It directly influences the infant's growing sense of empowerment and agency. The sensitive other allows the infant space and independence to explore the objects of his world. If the infant senses a holding and handling environment that is attuned and responsive in a good enough way, then he can receive and explore what is presented in the context of his own pacing and needs. With sensitive object presenting, the infant is allowed the experience of getting his needs met via his own volition, exploration, and decision-making processes. The classic and critical example is allowing baby to find and attach to the breast or bottle in his own time, at his own pace.

Likewise, in a sensitive holding environment the infant is allowed to choose and reach for the toys or objects he's interested in. This encourages freedom to explore the world and a developing sense of agency in getting needs met, and so confers empowerment in relationship. The infant gradually learns that the interactive field is bidirectional, that he is separate yet connected to mother and others. Over time a sense of personal empowerment evolves by which there is, along with a cohesiveness and continuity of being, attunement to his own basic needs *and* the ability to sense and respond to the needs of others. If object presenting is insensitive, then personal empowerment and agency may not emerge or may become distorted. If objects are thrust at the infant, if he is not allowed choice, or if the environment is stark and impersonal, without mutual exploration between infant and primary caregivers, then insecurity and disempowerment may develop and the false self then generated will be constantly oriented to the objects and needs of others. A sense of agency will not emerge, as the person's own needs are subsumed in meeting the needs of others.

Winnicott notes a number of circumstances in which object presenting can adversely affect the infant's state of being. An anxious mother may override the infant's openness in reaching out and exploring the objects of its world. An unattuned mother or caregiver may lift the baby before he is ready or before he is awake, or may feed him before he's ready or hungry. An over-controlling caregiver may offer toys or objects to the infant that he is not interested in or does not choose to play with, or may force play upon him when he is not interested or ready for contact. A detached, depressed, or self-absorbed caregiver may not respond to the baby's needs, may be mechanical or cold in response to the infant, or override baby's need to reach out, make contact, and explore with indifference to non-engagement. In all of these cases, the infant will feel disempowered and will not develop self-confidence or agency. He may feel smothered or engulfed by his relational world, or isolated, unseen, and worthless, and, if the wounding is deep enough, may be thrown into annihilation and the emptiness of non-being. This kind of relational milieu is the firmament for the generation of insecure attachment processes (Winnicott, 1965a, 1965b, 1987). If impingements take the little one out of the state of simply being, then defensive processes will arise all too early, and an overly defended self, with no continuity of being at its core, will result.

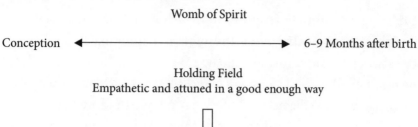

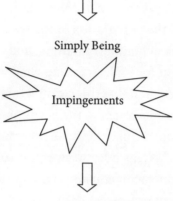

Fig. 9.1 The Generation of Defensive Responses

General Repercussions of Empathic Failures

Winnicott believed that empathic failures in holding, handling, and object presenting do not feel to the little one like the external failures of caregivers but, as the infant is not aware of its separateness from mother, as internal self-failures. In Fairbairn's terms, the infant is in a state of primary identification and immature dependency and so emotionally continuous with mother and other caregivers that external failures cannot be separated from the infant's inner world. Remember that any relational badness sensed out-there is felt by the little one as the play of endopsychic energies and their related affects. The bad object is not out-there, but in-here.

Winnicott believed that unmanageable stimuli and empathic failures easily overwhelm infants and impinge upon the state of unintegration and being, resulting in fractures in the wholeness of being itself. This has the further potential to cast the infant into unthinkable anxiety and the experience of annihilation and non-being. Winnicott suggested that the result of all of this is *false-self living*, a life in which one's own needs are forsaken, while the needs of others are adopted and attended to. This manifests as emotional isolation, a disintegration and fragmentation of the state of being, and the obscuration of the true self.

Winnicott's schema of holding, handling, and object presenting is a straightforward context for understanding what is relationally needed in early life experience. I find that this clear picture of the holding environment helps new parents orient to the needs of their prenate or newborn child. It gives them a context in to observe and explore their own processes and really helps engender an awareness of the need to provide the little one with attunement, empathy, and an environment that will foster secure attachment processes.

10

Basic Needs

In many ways, Lake's paradigm begins and ends with the concept of need. The prenate and infant have fundamental needs that must be met in a good enough way for continuity of being and a centered self-system to evolve. As we have seen above, an empathic holding environment is the prerequisite for the development of a fluid self-system organized around coherency of being. Within this holding field specific needs arise that must be held and negotiated, not just through the period of the womb of spirit, but throughout life. Primary, primal, or basic needs are with us our whole life. Due to the inevitable ambiguity and ambivalence of relational exchanges, different kinds of feeling-affects will be experienced. It is the interplay between need and affect that shapes the self-system.

The concept of need can be problematic in a Buddhist context. The self's needs are driven by volitional impulses, which are, in turn, a consequence of the ignorance of the true nature of selfhood. I contend that, once incarnated, there are certain needs that must be met for being to know its true nature, its connection to other beings, and its relationship to Source. This is the ground both of the spiritual journey and of a fluid and cohesive self-system that has being as its hub.

The Nature of Basic Needs

Basic needs are universal. If we strip away our particular patterns of conditioning, along with our related personality processes and positions, we may discover that we are more similar to others than we like to admit, and that the same basic needs are present in everyone no matter what the cultural or familial milieu.

In Lake's paradigm, basic needs are supported and provided for within the context of the good enough maternal holding field. They relate to the reflection and support of innate being, and to wellbeing, achieved by the sustenance and nurturance of being. If the needs of both being and wellbeing are supported within the womb of spirit, then a resourced, secure, and responsive self-system has a real opportunity to develop. One of the tasks of the therapist is to generate a holding field that acknowledges and is attuned to the client's basic needs. It is only in the trust that develops in this kind of relational environment that wounding generated by unfulfilled or overridden needs may be safely held and resolved.

The support of being and wellbeing has both universal and conditional aspects.

Universal Support of Being and Wellbeing

At a fundamental level, the little one is spiritually supported by life itself. Many traditions speak to this truth. Christ-nature, God, Bodhicitta, True Mind, Tao, soul-nature, all point to the tide of universality that we ride into life. In the Buddhist context, Bodhicitta is always present as the ground-matrix of life. The Taoists speak of creation as the *Primal Sympathy.* Our journey is not one of creating this ground, but of removing what obscures it. The little one, during the early days and weeks of life, may be directly oriented to this ground through his as yet unobstructed connection to Source. Lake noted that, in regression work, some of his clients accessed what he called *blastocyst bliss,* a direct experience of connection to the divine. Ideally, the womb of spirit supports the prenate's orientation to Source by mother's own spiritual presence and love.

The more a therapist feels supported by the creative forces of life, the more she/he can reflect this in the clinical holding environment. I believe that it is imperative for the therapist to have a spiritual context in which to hold the deep suffering that surfaces in clinical work. The particular spiritual orientation of the therapist, as long as it is not imposed on the client, is not as important as the intention to hold a spiritual level of truth. Lake did this through his Christian beliefs, I do it through my meditative practice, application of Buddhist principles, Taoist practices, and also the contemplative understanding found in the writings of Christian mystics like Meister Eckhart and Saint John of the Cross, and the anonymously written *Cloud of Unknowing.* However, a simple humility and awe in the presence of the creative forces at work in human-beingness is all that is really necessary.

Basic Needs of Being

Recognition, acknowledgment, and unconditional acceptance are the basic needs that support being. These qualities depend on the attunement and resonance of the holding field that mother and other primary caregivers provide. Mother, given the support, naturally enters a being-state that supports the little one's basic needs, allowing the infant to settle into his own innate being-state and know that "I-am" and "deserve-to-be." Fairbairn noted that the most basic need of the infant is for his love to be unconditionally received. Being needs are with us throughout life. We commonly seek the acceptance and acknowledgment of those around us to feel safe enough simply to be. In the pre- and perinatal period, and in early infancy, if acknowledgment and acceptance of being is denied, or rejection experienced, then a *wound at the level of being* may result, and defended self-forms will organize around that experience. Lake believed that some of the most defended and distorted self-systems organize due to this level of wounding. A wound at the level of being does not mean that being-itself is wounded, but that it has become deeply obscured to everyday consciousness. When being has gone into shadow, therapeutic work orients to its reclamation.

The term *discovery,* coined by Emerson, refers to the nature and quality of mother's discovery and recognition of the embryo within her. How the prenate is recognized and accepted by mother is ground for his developing sense of beingness and self-worth. Lake maintains that one of the deepest wounds the prenate or infant can experience is that of denial. For example, if a pregnant mother denies the existence of the prenate, is too busy to pay attention to the little one within, feels distraught or even disgusted by the pregnancy, or attempts abortion, the repercussions may be severe. The prenate may feel that its very being has not only denied, but, as Winnicott puts it, annihilated. A descent into non-being, meaninglessness, and true affliction is the consequence of this level of betrayal (Emerson Seminar, 1980; Lake, 1979).

If the need for recognition and unconditional acceptance is betrayed, then a distorted need for acknowledgment may later drive the person's self-system. Lacking support for a coherent experience of being, acknowledgment is sought at the level of self, in the conditioned things of life. Unfortunately, even when genuine acknowledgment is present, it may never reach the terrible wounding of being that was the consequence of the original breach of trust. Only the establishment of a new empathic holding field of unconditional acceptance, love, and acknowledgment can address this level of wounding and gradually help a person open to new potential, reorient to their being-nature, and reconnect to Source. Lake maintained that it is the Holy Spirit that does the healing at this level. From this perspective, the healing process is basically spiritual and shamanistic in nature. To my mind, whatever the cultural or spiritual context for understanding the vast forces that orchestrate life, healing the deepest wounding is fundamentally a psycho-spiritual journey.

Basic Needs of Wellbeing

Wellbeing relates to the little one's inner feeling response to his holding field. Whereas the satisfaction of being needs depends on the receptive nature of the holding field, the experience of wellbeing depends on how that field actively responds to the infant's presence. Wellbeing needs are met by the provision of spiritual, emotional, and physical sustenance and nurturance. Wellbeing arises as the little one senses in the actions and intentions of primary others, expressions of warmth, kindness, love, and attuned responsiveness, along with attentive holding, handling and object presenting. When the infant senses that mother and primary caregivers are attuned and appropriately responsive to his needs in a good enough fashion, he experiences positive feeling tones of wellbeing.

Wellbeing is also experienced via the response of primary others to the little one's own actions. In Fairbairn's terms, the infant experiences its taking from mother and others as an act of love, and he needs this to be seen and appropriately responded to. When its taking is truly received and responded to as an act of love, positive feelings of wellbeing are generated that support basic trust in the relational field and connection to innate being. The prenatal and early childhood experience of wellbeing supports self-esteem, openness to others, trust in one's relational environment, and the ability to negotiate personal needs.

The Good Enough Womb of Spirit

Obviously, mother's ability to attune to her child will depend on her inner state, her experiential world, and the support of her own holding field. Her attunements can only be somewhat partial and selective (Stern, 1985). Indeed, selective attunement is an aspect of the basic ambiguity all young beings meet in their relational field and a strong factor in shaping their developing self-system. Following Winnicott's lead,

Lake acknowledges this in his notion of *good enough womb of spirit*. In the good enough womb of spirit, the prenate or infant begins to trust primary caregivers, and learns also to trust that his needs will be met, even if the current circumstance is not ideal. Lake points out that less than ideal experiences, held within a loving and secure womb of spirit, will "vaccinate" the prenate against life's adversity (Lake, 1979). Meeting discomfort in a loving and trustworthy relational field allows the little one to meet the adverse conditions of life with resources and assurance. The internalization of safety and security, and the ability to cope with the adversities and disharmonies encountered in life, are hallmarks of basic needs being met within a largely attuned and responsive holding environment.

11

Umbilical Affect
and Primal Feelings

Lake's paradigm of self-formation is founded on the interplay between needs and feelings and the intensity of inner feeling-response to more and more challenging relational experience. He was a pioneer in putting forth the concept that self is generated in the milieu of feeling and affect experienced within the holding environment of primary caregivers, and in his understanding of the role of the autonomic nervous system in stress response and personality formation. The prenate and infant's experience of its holding environment, and of maternal attunement and responsiveness to its basic needs, generates particular feelings that Lake called *umbilical affect,* a term originally used by a another pioneer in pre- and perinatal psychology, Francis Mott (Mott, 1964). Affect has an underlying feeling tone, a most basic push-pull, at its root. As discussed earlier, this tonal quality is called vedanā in Buddhist psychology. The basic positive-negative valence given to an experience underlies more formed affects such as fear, frustration, anger, joy, warmth and satisfaction.

Lake's understanding of umbilical affect is that the feeling-inflow from the mother-prenate umbilical vein directly impacts or impinges upon the prenate's experience. The prenate senses umbilical inflow as a living experience, makes decisions about that experience, and takes shape accordingly. In a wider context, the prenate is surrounded by mother's psycho-emotional state as an energetic surround and is constantly permeated by the nature of that field. Here the infant experiences itself, its world, its needs, and its emotional life as non-separate from mother. This is obvious in the womb where there is direct connection via the umbilical cord, but is also, according to Lake, true for the first six to nine months after birth.

Lake found that the nature and quality of umbilical inflow and the umbilical affect it generates, lay the early foundations for a person's self-system and relational tendencies. The relational interchange between prenate and mother in the first trimester dramatically influences the child's later sense of the world and intimate others. In this period, mother's psycho-emotional life literally permeates the prenate and later manifests as the "background coloring of adult life" (Lake, 1979). The patterns of reaction and defense that the prenate engages in to protect himself from relational badness set up similar defensive patterns throughout life. Lake wrote:

> The prenate in the womb, especially in the first three months after conception, is invaded by the emotional states of the pregnant mother. The emotional chemistry circulating in her bloodstream … is transferred at the placenta into the umbilical and fetal circulation. If, for instance, she is fulfilled and joyful in responding to the care of husband and friends, or full of hatred and bitterness at the world's evil treatment of her, the baby also is transfused by these feelings. They are registered and remembered. They form the basis of a trustful personality, or of catastrophic persecution, melancholic affliction, and a sense of worthlessness. (Lake, 1979)

Due to the intimate nature of the emotional and energetic surround of the womb, the prenate cannot differentiate mother's states from his own. Boundaries between self and other are not clear, and confusion arises as to whose experience is whose. This is an early expression of primary identification, where the young child's emotional world is so continuous with the mother's that little differentiation is possible. Lake emphasized that this situation is the case from conception through the first six to nine months after birth. During this time, all affect is umbilical affect.

This does not, however, mean that the infant is lost in a merged state of primary narcissism. There is clear self-other experience from the beginning; but the feeling-world of the prenate and infant, and its experience of basic needs, is totally non-separate from that of mother and other primary caregivers.

For example, if mother feels unsupported in her pregnancy and in life in general, the prenate may also feel unsupported. This may generate a defensive self-system that has difficulty experiencing true support when it is on offer. Similarly, mother's mixed feelings about her own life may be experienced by the prenate as ambivalence towards his. Mother may feel let down by her husband, may even fear or loathe him, yet may feel good about having a baby, or vice versa. The prenate takes all of this in, but lacks the perspective, clear enough boundaries, and enough information to sort out what is being experienced. In this way, umbilical affects like fear, anger, anxiety, depression, etc., may arise and become linked to the experience of intimacy. From these and like observations Lake formulated his thesis and a significant contribution to the field: the little one experiences and responds to relational ambiguity from the very beginnings of life.

Categories of Affect

Lake categorized umbilical affect as positive, negative, or strongly negative. The fetal response to maternal umbilical inflow depends upon the intensity of the stress or distress experienced, its duration and repetitiveness, the perceived safety and holding in the womb-field, the input phase of the dynamic cycle it affects (discussed below), and the constitutional resources present. These all result in a personality system with particular ways of being and particular forms and tendencies of endopsychic structure.

Lake believed that strongly negative affect generates oppositional personality strategies, psycho-emotional splitting, defensive projection, and, in the extreme, the transmarginally stressed state of dissociation and disconnection. For example, if the umbilical inflow is sensed as negative or distressful, the prenate may push, or project this sense of badness back through the umbilical artery towards mother. Later in life, personality systems may develop that are based on projection and the perception of badness as out-there. Lake called this *projective displacement*. The internalized sense of insecurity is projected out and displaced, and intimate others may then be sensed as untrustworthy or dangerous. Indeed, in the extreme, intimacy itself may be perceived as painful, and the need for relationship may be denied. Lake discusses such strategies in terms of classic psychodynamic defensive processes, citing anxiety-depression, hysterical reaction, and schizoid splitting as having the earliest roots.

The three levels of umbilical affect outlined by Lake are these:

Positive Umbilical Affect

Ideally the prenate experiences an inflow of positive emotions, a consequence of the mother's joyful acceptance of pregnancy similar to the Rogerian concept of a field of unconditional positive regard, congruency, and non-judgment. Umbilical affect is largely positive, and arises in response to the presence of a loving, nurturing and safe holding field within which basic needs are largely met. The little one feels recognized, accepted, and welcomed. There is a strong sense of connection and communion with the other. The maternal field provides good enough sustenance and nurturing, and the prenate experiences joy and ease and a general sense of wellbeing. Within this responsive field, the prenate also learns to cope with periods when his needs are not fully met, for there is an expectation that eventually they will be. With the experience of positive affect, the womb of spirit is sensed to be trustworthy, and this can set the tone for a later sense of okay-ness and safety both in intimate relationships and in the world at large.

Negative Umbilical Affect

The basic needs of the prenate/infant cannot be continually met, even in the best circumstances, and some of the relational milieu will be experienced as unsatisfactory or relationally bad. This leads to the inevitable experience of negative affect. In negative umbilical affect, the prenate may sense some of mother's negative emotions, some absence of love, concern, or regard, or that his basic needs are not being met, and will then, in response, experience negative feeling tones. The perception of the loss of the empathic holding field, along with traumatic or shocking outer events, environmental toxicity, mother's illness or weakness, and any other kind of impingement that takes the little one out of the state of simply being, will generate negative umbilical affect and the experience of relational badness. This, in turn, sets the stage for the splitting and repression of the rejecting and needy self-constellations that organize around unmet needs, traumatic impingements, and unsatisfactory relational experiences. Hopefully the experience of positive affect balances out any ambivalence experienced, and a basic trust in a good enough holding environment is sustained.

Negative affect will strongly affect the forming self-system. For example, the prenate or infant may rightly or wrongly perceive that it is unseen and unnoticed, that its existence is disregarded or even denied by the mother or others. In later life, the child or adult may yearn for recognition, reassurance, and reflection from the other, yet due to the wounding, may not receive it when it is genuinely offered; or the prenate or infant may have a sense of being of no account and marginalized. He cannot emotionally thrive or sense love. He may be more aware of the mother's emotional needs than his own, and he may be distressed by them. As the prenate's wellbeing is dependent upon mother's wellbeing, he may feel compelled to help mother, to ease or prevent her pain in some way. Thus develops what Lake called the *fetal therapist*. After birth, the child's boundaries may be blurred, he may sense mom's distress or needs as more important than his own, and may continually attempt to make mother's state better, while ignoring his own needs. Thus is born the false self, the self that orients to the needs of others, while denying his own.

Alternately, the prenate or infant may internalize mother's distress or unmet need as guilt and self-blame. "I am the cause of mom's distress and must do something about it." Later in life he may dedicate himself to causes, may continually place himself in the role of helper; yet will disregard his own needs and may not be able to receive help from others.

Strongly Negative Umbilical Affect

In strongly negative umbilical affect, the prenate experiences an intense influx of negative maternal emotions and feelings, traumatic impingements, or forceful maternal rejection or denial. The negative feelings that mother is experiencing will permeate the prenate and generate strongly negative affect. Strongly negative affect, in turn, generates woundings in which the experience of simply being is denied or totally overwhelmed. This is the root of Lake's *Maternal-Fetal Distress Syndrome*. On one side is mother's suffering, her yearning, anxiety, fear, anger, disgust, bitterness, jealousy, and so on; on the other, is the prenate's perception of all this from within the womb of spirit. As Winnicott stressed, the prenate or infant cannot separate out his world from his mother's, as her emotional states permeate his experience. The infant prenate does not sense this as outside failure, but as internal self-failure. The prenate/infant is driven to respond or react to the distressed and distressing infusion of feeling by defending himself in some way, and so shifts from simply being. The sense of safety is lost, as is basic trust in the relational environment.

Lake writes, "Strongly negative 'umbilical affect' implies fetal distress at the influx of maternal distress" (Lake, 1979). The distress patterns of mother and prenate/infant become merged, and what Lake called *constricted confusion* results. The prenate must oppose the influx of badness in some way, yet is also dependent on the umbilical inflow for sustenance and survival. This intensifies the experience of relational badness and its repression, and increases the dynamic tension bound up in the resultant endopsychic structure.

Lake believed that strongly negative umbilical inflow was at the root of self-destructive and paradoxical feelings and behaviors. He writes:

> This "incompatible transfusion" of alien emotions leads to a variety of reactions in the fetus. It may cope with, or totally oppose it. The mode of the opposition varies with constitutional factors, intensities of stress and its duration, as well as with previous experiences severe enough to cause conditioned responses. If opposing the distress, in the name of life and growth, becomes too slight or far off, the fetus may flip into the paradox of transmarginal stress. Overwhelmed by dread and affliction, the organism longs for oblivion and death. (Lake, 1981)

Lake added that this life-denying behavior may take many forms, such as self-defeating interpersonal interactions, suicidal tendencies, or sado-masochism, or may be projected as antisocial behavior and violence (Lake, 1979, 1981).

In Lake's terms, the mixed bag of early relational and environmental experience generates a complexity of umbilical affect and a hierarchy of defended response in the prenate/ infant. He called this the *transmarginal stress hierarchy*, a model for understanding the formation of self-constellations and defended self-systems. This, coupled with Lake's developmental concept of the dynamic cycle, greatly facilitate understanding of how different personality systems are generated.

The Primal Spectrum of Emotion

Emerson describes the range of affects and emotions experienced via umbilical inflow as the *primal spectrum of emotion* (Emerson, 1988 seminar). This spectrum relates to the growing stress a prenate or infant is placed under as basic needs are overwhelmed or not met, negative umbilical affect is experienced, and the womb of spirit is sensed as increasingly untrustworthy or dangerous. This spectrum ranges from a deep and open love, in which an infant can totally relax, through states of anxiety, anger, and fear, to abject despondency and terror. The little one's emotional responses move through the range of the spectrum as the stress experienced by unmet needs intensifies.

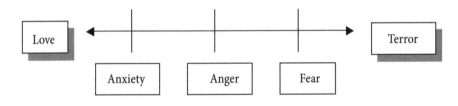

Fig. 11.1 The Primal Spectrum of Emotions

I have had the privilege of observing many babies and their families in my private practice, and it is obvious to me that an infant's natural orientation is to love, ease, and comfort. If his basic needs are not being met, the infant will first use its social nervous system to seek contact and help; that is, he will orient to mother or caregiver, make sounds and movements that indicate need, and wait for a response. If no response comes, or if the response is inappropriate or inconsistent, then the infant may become anxious and begin to shift towards a fear response. The parent may notice that the baby's cry changes as it expresses anxiety. Its movements may become less coordinated as a shift away from the social nervous system begins. If needs are still not met, the infant may then shift to a predominantly sympathetic nervous system response. The fight-or-flight mechanism will engage in forms ranging from anger, hitting, and pushing, to withdrawal and avoidance. In the fight response, his crying and motions may become sharper and more rapid as agitation and anger increase. The infant may even express rage and become oppositional in his response to mother. In the flight response, he may turn his head away, become withdrawn and avoid contact. If his basic needs are still not met, the infant may default to a parasympathetic state and collapse into protective reactions such as dissociation, freezing, and immobilization. These responses contribute to the formation of insecure attachment processes.

Some infants enter parasympathetic shock states unrecognized by either health practitioners or caregivers. In such a state the infant tends to sleep a lot, eat a lot, and generally stay very quiet. These behaviors can be confused with those of a 'good' baby, one who is content and in good contact with mother and caregivers. The difference between a shock state and contentment can be seen in the infant's responsiveness to mother, other caregivers, and the environment (Perry & Pollard, 1998).

As an adult, a person may have a tendency to default to the responses on the primal spectrum of emotion experienced in utero or early infancy. Under stress, some people become anxious, others respond with anger or opposition, some attack in a fight response, others run away in flight, and others dissociate and freeze. Knowing that these charged emotions have nothing to do with the current experience, being able to hold these emotions in awareness without becoming them is the first step in their resolution.

12

Lake's Developmental Paradigm

L ake called his developmental paradigm the *dynamic cycle*. He based his dynamic cycle on Fairbairn's three developmental stages outlining the movement from immature dependency to mature interdependency and the stages in the life of Christ.

The Dynamic Cycle and the Life of Christ

The dynamic cycle describes how the prenate and infant develop a sense of beingness, belonging, and wellbeing in the spiritual and emotional milieu of the womb of spirit. The dynamic cycle is an ontological view of human development. Its focus is the nature of being and the being-to-being relational field between mother and prenate and mother and infant. It is very different from the fixed developmental stages outlined by Freud, as it is conceived as a dynamic process that spirals throughout life as being and wellbeing are continually renewed.

The dynamic cycle is inspired by Lake's understanding of the life of Christ. Lake observed an alternating inflow and outflow in Christ's life as He shifts his attention from the world of men to "attend to his Father and to speak with God" (Lake, 1986b). This inflow, a shift away from the activities of the world to the Source of the world, reconnects Christ to the Source of his being. As Christ abides in God-as-Source, his being is acknowledged and his wellbeing sustained. An outflow, a movement back into the world of human beings, then follows the

God-ward movement. Supported at the deepest spiritual roots of being and wellbeing, Christ turns his attention back to the world and gives of himself in service and love. With his connection to Source secure, love and compassion naturally flow out into all relationships.

Lake saw this inflow and outflow mirrored in all human experience. Like a grand play of spirals within spirals, it cycles throughout life. The dynamic cycle represents, in essence, the archetype of life's constant movement. In the womb of spirit, mother represents the archetypal source-person who, via her being and spirituality, orients the little one to his own being and helps him maintain connection to Source. The self-status is then rooted in being and Source and can achieve its goals via compassionate relationship. This is the foundation of healthy human relationships and personality systems.

Developmental Cycles

The dynamic cycle describes the movement from a developmentally immature way of relating to a true sense of being and relational interconnection. It is an ontological model of health, rather than a model of pathology and disease. It describes the way innate being is acknowledged and sustained and comes to know both its own nature and the kind of world it finds itself in. It addresses basic needs that are with us our entire life, how these needs are hopefully met in a good enough empathic field, and the nature of the response to this field, especially in the first eighteen months of life.

The dynamic cycle has two basic phases: an input phase of *being* and *wellbeing,* and an output phase of *status* and *achievement.* These are connected by phases of what Lake calls *transition* and *return to source.* These phases relate to how being and wellbeing needs are met, to the umbilical affect experienced, and to the development of being and selfhood within the holding environment of mother and other primary caregivers.

Fairbairn's Developmental Stages

Lake was influenced by Fairbairn's ideas and his dynamic cycle mirrors Fairbairn's three developmental stages of immature dependency, transition, and mature interdependency (Fairbairn, 1994a, 1994c).

Immature Dependency: Being-in-Relationship

At Fairbairn's stage of immature dependency and Lake's being-in-relationship phase, the little one knows itself and its world solely in the reflection of mother's presence. In the early months after birth, he orients to mother via primary identification. During this time he is emotionally continuous and identified with mother as though the umbilical cord is still present, and cannot easily separate his feelings from hers as source-person. He is dependent upon mother to get his relational needs met, but cannot clearly differentiate his needs and emotional states from hers. It is as though the world of mother and the world of the prenate and infant are one and the same.

The un-traumatized infant naturally resides in a state of loving open-heartedness and connection, which is his inherent state of being. In this state, the infant senses a merging love with mother and connects this naturally loving state with his relationship to her. The infant cannot discern that its loving experience is not dependent upon mother's presence; he cannot yet differentiate his inner states from hers. For Fairbairn, the most basic need of the infant is for his love to be unconditionally received, and for his taking from others to be perceived as an expression of love. I am sure that you have seen a nursing infant glowing with love and contentment as it nurses from mother's breast. Its sucking, touching, looking, sensing, are all acts of the baby's love. The baby needs his taking from the other to be recognized as an act of love, and for this love to be unconditionally received. And he needs to know that he is loved purely for himself. Lake described these as being-needs of loving recognition, acknowledgment, and unconditional acceptance.

If the infant experiences that his love is denied or not fully received, he may feel his very being is also denied, as he experiences no differentiation between his own state of being and mother's. The badness sensed is experienced inwardly and the defensive processes such as introjection and splitting begin to arise. As we have seen, it is in this early phase that the prenate/infant encounters relational ambiguity and internalizes any badness sensed in order to keep the other all-good. In essence, the little one *becomes* the ambiguity and badness experienced in order to maintain an idealized sense of the needed other, This is an essential process that allows him to maintain integrity and connection to essential others.

As Lake stressed, if connection to mother as source-person is lost, the infant also loses connection to Source as, in the being-in-relationship stage, mother mediates that connection. The hope is that the relational field will be held in a good enough fashion that basic trust is maintained and the shift from being-in-relationship and immature dependency to being-in-itself and mature interdependency can be successfully negotiated.

Transition

In Fairbairn's concept, basic endopsychic structure is formed within the first two months or so after birth. However, even though the early experience of relational badness has been managed inwardly and the inner experience of badness repressed, the outer relational milieu is still relationally ambiguous. The defense of incorporation and splitting cannot change this reality. To deal with this, the infant engages in modes of relationship that Fairbairn calls *transitional techniques of relating*. With these techniques, the little one manages the ongoing experience of goodness and badness by introjective, projective, and dissociative processes. These transitional techniques allow the little one to stay in relationship to the source person in the midst of ongoing ambiguity.

Fairbairn believed that perceived indifference, neglect, or denial by the source-person at this stage would give rise to the most severe separation anxiety and primary trauma. The need to protect then would be intensified, and a wounded and defended self-system would be generated. In this state, the little one loses connection to innate being and identifies with the emerging closed and defended self. Then, as the Buddha maintained, the conditions and contingencies encountered obscure citta, the ground state of luminous sentience and wholeness.

Mature Interdependency: Being-in-Itself

Ideally, the child is held in a good enough empathic field so that a transition to mature interdependency occurs. In Winnicott's terms, the root of this transition is the experience of a cohesive and continuous state of being. In an attuned and safe relational field, the infant and child learns about his being-state and attains what Lake called being-in-itself, knowing one's own being without the need for the reflection of another. Innate being then becomes the foundation for the developing self-system, which does not have to organize around wounding or defenses. A cohesive sense of being is then present separate from the ups and downs of relational interchange. In Buddhist terms, the organization of the skandhas has knowing, a cohesive and stable state of sentience, at its core. The child can explore his world from this ground of knowing and begin to sense himself as separate from mother, relating to her as a unique being with her own needs. A basic sense of being-to-being interconnection with her is also sensed, and a more mature experience of mutual needs can be negotiated.

The maturely interdependent person does not need another in order to know his own being or to sense wellbeing. One's experience of wellbeing is an inner state that is not dependent on outer relationships, and the person can sense gratitude and love for another separate from whether or not personal needs are met. Here innate qualities of being, such as love, compassion, and joy, are experienced in relationship, but not dependent upon it. This is a monumental shift in relating from immature dependency, in which the little one depends on another person to fulfill his basic needs, while he does not recognize theirs; to mature interdependency, in which wellbeing is an inner experience not dependent upon another, and others' needs are directly perceived and honored. Relational life is then lived in a present-time, empathic, and negotiated way. In Lake's terms, as being knows its connection to Source, compassion becomes the prime motivation and movement in relationships, and basic needs are achieved in the ambiance of interconnection and interdependency.

Lake's Dynamic Cycle

Lake's dynamic cycle is an ontological paradigm of being and selfhood, a model of personality based upon health, rather than pathology. He posited an ontological cycle comprised of an *input phase, transition, output phase,* and *return to source.*

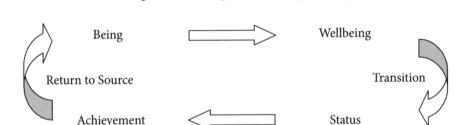

Input Phase
Being-in-relationship, immature dependency

Being   Wellbeing

Return to Source   Transition

Achievement   Status

Output Phase
Being-in-itself, mature interdependency

Fig. 12.1 The Dynamic Cycle
The qualitative experience of both input phases is based upon the prenate's perception of its relational field annd how its basic needs are met.

Input Phase

Lake's input phase relates to the basic needs of being and wellbeing, and how well these are met. Input is concerned with the interplay of the womb of spirit with the being-nature of the developing infant and the recognition and loving acceptance of the source person and the quality of nurturance and sustenance they provide. If basic needs are met in a good enough way in which basic trust is maintained, then the prenate/infant is largely protected from impingements, can rest in being, and not enter defended states too soon. This allows a more fluid self-system to coalesce around innate being and Source, and for secure attachment processes to ensue. In Winnicott's terms, at the heart of selfhood a cohesive and continuous sense of being is established. For Lake, this is the prerequisite for compassionate and appropriately responsive living.

Being

As in Fairbairn's paradigm, the input phase is one of immature dependency in which the prenate/infant's sense of being is dependent upon his relationship to mother. Lake calls this first stage *being-in-relationship,* as the little one only knows its being-nature through the presence and reflection of mother's being. Being is known via identifying with mother's being. The felt-experience of being is based directly upon the nature of this relational interchange and the felt-qualities of the relational field. Note again that this is not a narcissistically merged state, but one of intimate relationship where beingness and spiritual essence are experienced via the reflection of mother's own being, presence, spirituality, and loving acceptance.

The basic needs of being are supported within a receptive field of acknowledgment, recognition, and unconditional acceptance. As Lake wrote, "Acceptance makes 'being-itself' possible" (Lake, 1986). The developing self-system then organizes around a cohesive sense of being, and the possibility for felt-interconnection and mutuality of relatedness is potentiated. Lake writes,

> The baby has no capacity for separate personal existence. It can conceive of itself as 'in being,' or Alive, only by identity with the Mother's Being and Person ... Personal or spiritual being is the result of nine months (more or less) response of the baby to supplies of personal or spiritual being from the mother. (Lake, 1986)

If the maternal presence is experienced as largely attuned and empathic, and basic needs are met in a good enough fashion, then innate being is supported, coherency is maintained, and continuity of being is experienced. The little one then senses his own being-nature as personal or spiritual being, and this then becomes the foundation of the emerging personality system. A coherency of self oriented to fundamental being-nature emerges as being's way of being. As this occurs, innate being becomes personal being.

Wellbeing

The wellbeing phase is oriented to the sustenance and nurturance of being. Here mother and other primary caregivers actively provide spiritual, emotional, and physical support to the prenate/infant, and a growing sense of wellbeing emerges as he experiences an inflow of warmth and appropriate responsiveness from his relational field. It is the active sustenance of being that allows the generation of positive umbilical affect and the sense of wellbeing and relational goodness to be felt. Lake writes that wellbeing is dependent upon "the growth and enhancement of the personal being in communion with the mother's personal resources," and that "wellbeing is reached as the Baby abides in a Mother giving sustenance on all the levels of her being" (Lake, 1986). Thus being is maintained in a "giving-field" of sustenance. The basic needs of the child are actively met in a good enough way, and he discovers that he is worthy of this support. A sense of self-worth, self-esteem, and self-value begins to develop. The graciousness of mother's giving is experienced as "I-am-worthy-of-love." Being-worthy-of-love is sustained by mother's willing provision of a loving, resonant, and appropriately responsive empathic field, and wellbeing is sensed as a direct internal experience. In Fairbairn's terms, the little one knows that he is loved solely because he exists, and that his taking is received as an act of love.

Lake writes:

As non-being was met at "1" [input stage of being] by Being, so here, Emptiness is met by Fullness, with Satisfaction and Joy ... Being discovers its Meaningfulness, its value and worth to the Source. (Lake, 1986)

During the input phase, mother's presence represents Source-in-relationship and in this way reflects the Source itself. Self-worth is experienced and the coherency of the Source-being-self axis is sustained. Being now identifies with abundance, empowerment, and the grace of giving. This strengthens connection to the innate resources of Source with its energies of compassion and love. Source now can be actualized in life through compassionate action.

Hopefully, being is sustained in a good enough fashion and, in the balance of inner experience, a positive sense of trust in the relational environment is maintained and the little one can simply rest in being. As the infant explores its relational world within an empathic holding field, the felt sense of both being and wellbeing deepen and the little one is empowered to discover being-in-itself without anxiety intervening.

Transition

Lake writes about the importance of the transition between the input and output phases of the dynamic cycle, especially during the nine months just after birth. By the end of the transition period, the little one has hopefully directly experienced the nature of his own being. In the ambiance of a loving and reflective holding field, the transition from being-in-relationship to being-in-itself is encouraged. Lake calls being-in-itself a new relational phase where there the "mode of dependence is no longer by identification … but in a relationship of two persons; a duality" (Lake, 1986).

In the transition phase there is a shift from primary identification with the maternal holding environment as "I-am-if-you-are," to a separate "I-am-my-self." In this transition, the input of being and wellbeing is as it was before, but now there is a sense of being-in-itself and autonomy. The little one's sense of being is now no longer solely determined by its relationship to mother, and *being-in-relationship* becomes *being-in-itself.* The being and wellbeing experienced in mother's presence is internalized, and a continuity of being in the midst of changing conditions is also sensed.

Lake writes, "If all goes well, at the end of about nine months, the spirit, or Being, can gradually be born to an awareness of its now separable selfhood. An 'I-my-self' has been formed in the womb of spirit and has emerged into separate personal existence" (Lake, 1986). Ideally, in this process of individuation, the little one can maintain a coherent sense of his own being while also sensing his natural interconnection to mother and others. As in Fairbairn's mature interdependency, there is autonomy in interbeing.

Within the safe holding environment provided by mother and other primary caregivers, being as the I-am experience becomes the hub of self, the I-am-this experience. With the transition to being-in-itself, the little one has internalized its relationship to being; and the coherency between Source, being, and self is firmly rooted. Being's way of being is aligned with deeper truth, and from that a cohesive sense of selfhood emerges. Central-self develops schemas of being that are not driven by repressed energies. It can mediate being's natural connection to other beings via relation-seeking without the need to constantly protect or withdraw from contact. The infant and young child can then negotiate transitional processes in a good enough fashion and, over time, shift to mature interdependency, a mode of relating based upon the felt coherency of being and inherent interconnection.

I cannot stress too strongly that it is this alignment of central-self with the Source-being axis that transforms repressed energies. This is an essentially spiritual process, a natural process of maturation unfolding within a greater field of cohesion, presence, and interconnection. In this context, the person can rely on his or her own sense of being no matter what relational conditions are present. This movement away from dependency and wounding, to coherency of being and mature interdependency, is the backdrop to all depth psychotherapy and spiritual process.

Both Lake and Fairbairn note that the transition phase is one in which the little one may experience devastating separation anxiety. Lake stressed that if there is a breakdown in the empathic holding field before the transition period is complete, that is, before individuation has occurred, then anxiety may overwhelm the little one, as he is still dependent on mother's reflection to maintain connection to being, even as he is shifting to more independence and autonomy. Lake sees separation anxiety as potentially "more damaging and productive of personality distortion and neurosis" in this transition stage, when the little one still senses its being-nature via primary identification (Lake, 1986).

In the transition phase, the little one cannot conceive of itself as a being outside of mother's being. If strong separation anxiety is experienced as the infant seeks the presence and sustenance of unavailable, inconsistent, disconnected, or abusive others, panic and terror will arise, and he may be cast into the devastating experience of non-being. Lake writes:

Separation Anxiety is infinitely more damaging and productive of personality distortion and neurosis before the TRANSITION, while still in the identified period. The spirit (being) is specifically vulnerable during this symbiotic phase to periods of painful longing endured passively, leading to Panic, then worse, to Dread. (Lake, 1986)

If a wound at the level of being occurs, the developing self is infused by dread and the need to withdraw from open contact with other beings. The self that emerges as a way of being then organizes around the need to defend against relational contact and further wounding. Intimacy equals pain, as the presence of innate being and its natural interconnection to other beings is obscured. Selfhood then literally takes on a life of its own, unaware of its deepest roots. The perception of life shifts from the felt sense of I-am as an inner presence, to the experience of, and attachment to, I-am-this. As this occurs, connection to Source is also obscured, and life losses inherent meaning and joy. At best this will lead to oppositional and defended personality structures and insecure attachment; at worst, the little one is plunged into the abyss of non-being. Then an overwhelming sense of non-being and emptiness, as a primary wounding, drives the development of the self-system. Relationship is then denied and addictive and abusive behaviors emerge in order to fill the emptiness and desolation of non-being.

Output Phases

In the output phases, status and achievement refer to the condition and actualization of a secure self-system. These are expressions of 1) the nature of the experience of selfhood; 2) how self manifests within relationships; and 3) how self actualizes its basic needs.

Status

Status relates to the nature and organization of the developing personality system and "individual self-hood" (Lake, 1986). In a supportive, good enough womb of spirit, the self-system naturally develops into one that knows interconnection as a direct experience, yet is clearly individualized, self-confident, fluid, and balanced. The self-system is not organized around deprivation or wounding, but around coherency of being and an internal sense of wellbeing. This sets the stage for a "dynamic outflow of personal Being and Well-being towards the world of other people and things ..." (Lake, 1986).

When being and wellbeing are secured, the status of selfhood evolves from being and Source and not from wounding. Interbeing and a sense of connection to others is experienced. Source, being, and self are aligned, and the compassion that flows from Source is a lived experience. Meaning and motivation in life is derived from this unswerving alignment to Source and the coherency of personal being with its inherent being-to-being interconnection.

Achievement

Based upon status, achievement is the ability of self to actualize compassion and get basic needs met in meaningful relationships and meaningful ways. The compassion that flows from Source can now flow in all relationships. Lake conceptualizes this in terms of *service*. As Source manifests through being and self, the "actual use of this power of Being, in constructive activity, in play, in gaining skills, in work and in human relationships" can be actualized (Lake, 1986). No matter what one's activities, no matter what the nature of the relational field present, one can actualize compassion-in-relationship. The person has a direct experience of interbeing as the compassionate foundation for all actions.

Self can also respond appropriately to the variable nature of life in order to get basic needs met. Self approaches relationship from a position that is secure and not wounded, and there is clear discernment as to whether specific relationships meet basic needs. As the little one internalizes a sense of safety and boundary, it can more appropriately achieve his basic needs in the relational field. In Lake's words, as the infant and child explores its relational world, "... it learns to experience the input phases of the Dynamic Cycle in a new way, not 'by identification,' but in the clear duality of an interpersonal relationship between two separate beings. If the dynamic cycle has been adequately experienced, the child can proceed with development, without free-floating or fixed anxiety, without irrational fears, and with the power to accept isolated hurts. This all completed brings FULFILMENT" (Lake, 1986).

The little one has internalized the loving womb of spirit and can offer that to others in service. As the child was responded to in a loving field, it can now respond to others in a similar way. Life is full of meaning, which is actualized in service. This yields a sense of fulfillment.

Return to Source

The dynamic cycle is sustained by a continual return to Source that allows the ongoing sustenance of being and wellbeing. As Taoists maintain, the action of Tao is return: All things arise from Tao and return to Tao.

Being must be sustained in the world of action and meaning. This is a principle we see at work in all of our lives. We all seek relationships that are safe, non-judgmental, and supportive, which acknowledge us for who we are. At all stages of life, we seek the company of loved ones and the support and warmth of friends. We also seek space, holidays, rest and recuperation, all of which maintain our sense of being and wellbeing. Many of us seek spiritual and meditative forms that help maintain our connection to Source. We may take time out from daily activity to meditate or pray, go on retreat or to church, or seek a spiritual teacher or teachings, all to help maintain or renew our connection to Source. The renewing of this connection, like Christ's time in the desert, is the foundation for the dynamic cycle and our experience of life. The dynamic cycle depends on the actualization and continual renewal of the Source-being-self axis that enables compassion to flow.

Developmental Timing of Self-Formation

Lake's understanding finds its greatest impact in his claim that the roots of self-formation lie in the earliest prenatal period, and that the tonal quality of self is already set in the first three months in utero. Emerson echoes this claim when he states that a primitive ego, which he calls *body-ego*, forms before birth (Emerson, personal communications and seminars, 1979–2006). Thus the basic energies that later generate the territories of endopsychic structure are already present in fetal life. In Buddhist terms, sankhārās, or volitional tendencies, are forming from the moment of conception and become the underlying themes around which selfhood develops.

In Fairbairn's framework, basic endopsychic structure forms within the first two months or so after birth. During this time, the basic territories of central-, rejecting-, and needy-selves emerge. Stern has defined similar territories in the development of selfhood: In the first two months of life after birth, an *emerging self* arises, which is a coalescence of self-organization and self-other interchange. The emerging sense of self is based on relational information taken in through all of the senses, all at once. As moment-to-moment relational exchanges occur, the infant's sense of self and self-other emerges and manifests as internal representations of these exchanges. The development of the emerging self coincides with that of the basic endopsychic structure cited by Fairbairn.

At two to six months, a *core self* develops as an organized sense of self and other that includes self-agency, coherency of selfhood and self-other interchange, and a sense of continuity. This resonates with Winnicott's concept of the development of continuity of being. Similar to Fairbairn's concept of immature dependency, it describes the infant as able to perceive that it is separate from mother, but still unable to sense mother as an emotionally separate being. At the level of needs and feelings, again there is emotional, affective continuity between infant and caregiver. During this time, the infant's affective experience is modu-lated by the presence of self-regulating others. He learns to modulate his own internal state via the interactive mediation of mother, which includes the regulation of feeling-affects, attention, interest, curiosity, and cognition.

An *intersubjective self* then forms between seven and fifteen months, when the infant learns that he and others are mentally separate. Others' mental-emotional states may resonate with his own, or be very different. Experience then becomes subjective, and a more complex relationship with mother and outer others evolves. Both the development of the core self and intersubjective self occurs during Fairbairn's transitional phase, during which the infant learns to use projective, introjective, and dis-sociative modes in his relationship to others.

In Lake's terms, pre- and perinatal experiences underlie the various complex personality systems and reaction patterns that later manifest through central-self. By two months after birth, the basic self-territories generated in utero have coalesced into more discrete endopsychic structures. During the transition period, transitional modes of relating emerge, and more complex personality strategies are generated. These come fully into play by nine months after birth. Thus being's way of being, selfhood, and self-view, are formed by the end of Lake's womb of spirit period and become the foundation for attachment process.

Empathic Breaches and the Reflection of Wounding

Lake, Fairbairn, and Winnicott were convinced that an early breach or failure in the empathic relational field is the foundation for the deepest personal wounds. Such an empathic failure leads to what is called *basic or primal wounding,* which impels the infant to withdraw from relaxed and whole-hearted connection to those in its outer world and to shift to defensive and defended processes and positions. The greatest wound, in Fairbairn's terms, is one that disrupts ease of relation-seeking and intimacy and orients the developing self-system all too early to protective forms of relating. This also undercuts any resonance with mother or primary caregivers' own being, and the little one then loses the possibility of knowing innate being and interbeing in the reflection of primary other's being-nature. Selfhood then organizes around relational wounding and the need to protect, rather than a cohesive state of being.

Basic wounding emerges if the experience in the womb of spirit poses problems of safety and inconsistent needs fulfillment, or if the little one experiences deprivation or environmental or relational disturbance. The prenate or infant's developing sense of being and wellbeing are then disrupted by the breach in its holding field and by the strongly negative umbilical affect generated, which forces the infant either to oppose the perceived breach in some way, or to totally disconnect and dissociate from it.

In this relational ambiance, the nature of the self-systems of mother and other primary caregivers is of paramount importance. If the source-person is wounded at the level of being or wellbeing, there will be a lack of coherency in their Source-being-self axis, resulting in a self-system organized around basic wounding. As the source-person orients to the prenate or infant from a wounded self-system, true being-to-being empathy is impossible, and his or her ability to mirror the infant's own being is compromised. What is reflected to the infant is not being-in-itself, but the source-person's own wounding. Rather than a mirroring of being, only a lack of abundance and true openness, coupled with the caregiver's own defensive processes, are communicated. In this setting, the caregiver's wounds will, in some way, be passed on to the child. In the extreme, what the caregiver mirrors is non-being, an emptiness so deep that the little one is cast into the same barren transmarginal state.

As we have seen, Lake used the concept of the dynamic cycle to predict the outcome of relational wounds. He writes:

> We are assured that dependency, unconditional acceptance and sustenance are vital for the input phases (of being and wellbeing) which make for a normal healthy selfhood in infancy ... we can predict (from what we know independently of mental defense mechanisms) that interruptions, partial or total, of this dynamic cycle, particularly in babyhood and infancy (from conception through the first nine months of life) will lead to temporary, or (if they become fixed) permanent personality deprivation, conflicts and disorders. (Lake, 1986)

The womb of spirit includes mother's own Source-being-self alignment and her outer support system of husband or partner, family, loved ones, friends, and the society and culture in which she lives. There can be empathic failures in any or all of these factors that will impinge upon the little one and may be passed on in some way. These failures, and the basic wounding incurred through them, is the basis for the generation of adaptive psychodynamic processes and defensive characterological adaptations. The nature of these defenses depends on how the impingement arose in the input phases of the dynamic cycle and the level of its intensity as described in the transmarginal stress hierarchy. The most intense forms of basic wounding occur in the input phases of being and wellbeing. This gives rise to self-systems that are organized around the wounding, inherently protective and fragmented, and not open to life in the present moment. A sense of cohesive and continuous being is obscured, and the person then plays out his life as though the wounding is still happening.

Clinical Implications

An understanding of developmental process is a critical component of any psychotherapy form and is also extremely helpful in the general alleviation of suffering, in self-inquiry, and in spiritual practice. The usefulness of both Fairbairn and Lake's developmental paradigms lies in their inherent openness. They are both ontological models of development that support inquiry into the intrinsic wholeness of being. In radical ways for their times, they clarified the cyclical nature of the developmental process and stressed that self-formation is not fixed throughout time, but is continually being recycled, and is available for scrutiny and healing in this present moment. These paradigms orient us to the potential for healing the deepest wounds at any time in life.

From a Buddhist perspective, the developmental and cyclical nature of self is available to inquiry in the light of awareness. In an open and still state of mind, the potential exists simply to see process as process, as not-self. Seeing developmental process as a present-time activity holds huge potential for any healing form and all spiritual inquiry.

13

The Transmarginal Stress Hierarchy

The dynamic cycle reveals the ontology of being and selfhood. Similar to the Buddhist concept of dependent co-arising, it describes the cyclical stages that underpin psycho-emotional health and a fulfilled life experience. However, as we have seen, the relational field the little being finds itself in is inherently ambiguous and its good enough nature will become stressed and problematic at times. This next part of Lake's paradigm describes the prenate and infant's responses and reactions to increasingly stressful conditions experienced in the womb of spirit within the stages of the dynamic cycle. It fits in well with modern developmental models including the growing understanding of attachment and neural development (as outlined by Shore, 1995; Siegel, 1999 and others), with Porges' Triune Autonomic Nervous System concept (Porges, 2001) and with my personal clinical practice and understanding.

The term transmarginal comes from the work of Ivan Pavlov who formulated the original animal experiments on classical conditioning. He discovered that when dogs were placed under stress, their behavior dramatically changed. Pavlov deliberately placed these animals under conditions where their ability to cope with the conditions present were increasingly stressed and overwhelmed. They were pushed beyond the margins of opposition and endurance and entered what he called the transmarginal state. He noted various responses within this state. These included hypersensitivity to stimuli, inappropriate emotional states, an inability to experience pleasure, a lack of response to nurturing or the betterment of their conditions, paradoxical behaviors (what was formally pleasurable is now painful, what was formally painful now gives a perverse pleasure), an attraction to painful stimuli, and a collapse into apathy, immobilization, and frozen states. This sounds very much like the kinds of things therapists see in Post Traumatic Stress Syndrome, psychosis, and borderline states, with a clear correlation to a hierarchy of autonomic stress responses. Lake expanded upon this hierarchy, included the psychological, and filled the model out to describe what he found in clinical practice.

The transmarginal stress hierarchy evolves and is conditioned throughout the womb of spirit period and can be reinforced or engaged at any time in life. It manifests as four basic levels of response that are contingent upon the following conditions:

- the meeting of basic needs such as recognition, acceptance, safety, comfort, and sustenance within an attuned, resonant, and appropriately responsive relational field;

- the nature of umbilical affect experienced, whether positive, negative, or strongly negative; the more negative, the more intense the experience of distress and badness;

- the experience of increasing stress in physical and emotional conditions, or the perception of ongoing threat; at the extreme, the experience of denial, abandonment, or betrayal by a relational field that is perceived to be unresponsive, inattentive, or abusive.

As stress intensifies, the increasing need to defend generates protective and defensive strategies in response to physical, emotional, and environmental threat. These emerge as a hierarchy of responses that range from an ideal resting-in-being to the increasingly defensive reactions of coping, oppositional, and transmarginal.

The Ideal

The ideal level is one in which umbilical affect is totally positive and the basic needs of the prenate and infant are satisfied in every way. There is a wholly satisfying and pain-free interaction between infant and mother. The infant senses empathy, attunement, and positive regard from his mother, which is sustained throughout the womb experience. Being is reflected, and connection to Source is maintained. The birth process goes smoothly. It is not overwhelming or traumatic, and bonding between mother and baby is strong. The baby senses his being reflected back to himself in the loving eyes and attention of mother and other primary caregivers. When the baby expresses his needs, the caregiver responds in appropriate ways, and the infant has the felt experience of being seen and received and having his needs fully met. Lake writes:

> The epigenetic principle that the organism develops according to a ground-plan, as it interacts with its environment at the interface between them, is taking place so well as to meet the "ideal." The fetus in the womb is well-supplied in every way, the process of birth goes smoothly, maternal bonding is immediate and strong and all goes well thereafter. An ideal indeed! (Lake, 1979)

As we shall seen below, Lake did not consider the ideal to be the best situation for the prenate and infant all the time.

Coping Response

The womb of spirit is an inherently mixed experience, as the prenate and infant will inevitably meet conditions that are less than ideal. If negative umbilical affect is experienced within a good enough holding field, so that basic trust is maintained, then the next level of response, the coping level, arises. At this response level, maternal empathy and attunement are still experienced, and the prenate or infant's basic needs are well enough supported to permit continued growth and development. The conditions of interaction between the little one and his holding environment are not perfect, but are sensed to be safe and trustworthy enough to include bad or uncomfortable experience. At this response level, unmet needs are bearable. Trust in contact and intimacy is maintained and not breached. The infant knows that he is basically secure, and there is awareness that, although all needs are not being fully or immediately met, the unmet needs are not too great, and the situation is basically workable. Lake writes: "The conditions of interaction at the interface between the organism and its environment are not perfect, but 'good enough' for the basically-secure self to 'go along with it'" (Winnicott). There is an awareness that although all desires are not met in full, coping with the disparity is not too difficult" (Lake, 1979).

At the coping level, the little one is largely buffered from environmental and relational impingement, does not have to engage strongly defensive and self-protective processes, can carry on being, and learns to cope with moderate impingements in the good enough holding field. The support and safety present allow the difficult or negative aspects of the relational field, perceived as badness, to be included with increasing ease. A discrepancy between needs and their fulfillment is clearly present, but since basic needs are more or less being met, the badness experienced can be included without great distress. The infant can then orient to the ambiguity in his relational field trusting in its basic OK-ness. The good and bad aspects of relational experience all can be included; the pain present is bearable, and the prenate or infant copes without needing to react or oppose his experience. As endopsychic structure forms, central-self orients to the real goodness experienced, and the rejecting- and needy-selves are held in equilibrium. Central-self can then incorporate further good experiences, supporting self-esteem, and hold relational processes in a more and more discerning way. Developmentally, the little one is set up for the transition to being-in-itself, secure attachment processes, and mature interdependency.

Lake discusses three particular kinds of coping responses that relate to increasing stress experienced by the prenate and infant. The nature of the infant's response depends on the intensity of the negative umbilical affect experienced and how it can be accommodated in an ambiguous, yet still trustworthy, relational environment. The first response relates to a moderate level of stress experienced as manageable by the infant. In this process, the prenate and infant learns to tolerate delayed gratification and a certain level of discomfort by simply waiting in a trustworthy relational field. Thus the prenate or infant learns to develop suitable strategies and to respond appropriately to arising conditions and relationships. If the infant can meet discomfort within a secure and safe early environment, he will learn to cope, to get his needs met, and to appropriately regulate its emotional life. A successful response to discomfort, in which strong defensive processes do not have to engage and moderate stress is managed, is important in the formation of a fluid and healthy personality system and secure attachment processes. From this starting point, various other coping strategies may emerge which can positively affect later approaches to life.

Lake describes this coping response as a "vaccination" against future adversity. He believed that prenates and infants who have to cope with stress or discomfort in an empathic and attuned womb of spirit are better placed to meet stress in later stages than those who experience a purely ideal early environment. In the later phases of his career, Lake found this to be especially so in the first trimester of intrauterine life.

A second strategy at the coping level is called displacement, a defense via containment and physical projection. This strategy may be mobilized if negative umbilical affect intensifies and the balance of good and bad affect flow is periodically tipped toward badness. This pain is not so intense as to destroy the sense of trust in the womb of spirit, or to elicit oppositional response; but some kind of protective response is still needed. The badness is managed by displacing the felt discomfort and negative affect into the soma to make the negative inflow more manage-able. Affect may be projected into the musculoskeletal system as tension, or into the viscera as emotional tone, or some combination of the two. This is commonly coupled with some kind of meaning about the nature of relational life. For instance, feelings of badness may be displaced into the solar plexus area, associated with the experience of betrayal, tinged with affects like frustration and anger. This is the embodiment of Fairbairn's rejecting self-constellation. As this occurs, dependent on the nature of the response, the local tissues involved may contract and become hypertonic, or become flaccid and hypotonic. Lake believed that this kind of affect displacement could later give rise to psychosomatic ill-ness, hypochondriacal states, or ambivalent attachment processes. This strategy may find more intense expressions at the levels of oppositional and transmarginal; but at the coping level of response, unlike the later levels, there is still basic trust in the good enough relational field.

A third coping response may occur if the child is constitutionally strong, while his mother is perceived as under-resourced or in need of help. The wellness of mother is essential for the wellbeing of the prenate and infant, so the infant may act to protect mother as his source of life. He then takes on the burden of mother's pain, becoming, as suggested above, a *fetal therapist*. The infant does everything he can to alleviate or prevent mother's distress to the detriment of his own needs. This may become a lifelong mode of relating, so that, as an adult, the person takes on the role of perpetual caregiver and supporter, desperately attempt-ing to prevent or alleviate the pain of intimate others, while denying or rejecting his own needs. Likewise, he may get involved in various causes to alleviate the suffering of others, while remaining oblivious to his own needs.

While at the coping level, no matter what strategies arise, basic trust is maintained and the relational field is not severely damaged, if negative affect flow becomes too intense, the prenate may be pushed beyond his ability to cope and then have to shift to the next stage of the hierarchy, the oppositional state.

Oppositional Response

If the intensity or duration of negative affect and the stress experienced overwhelms the prenate's ability to cope, then a major shift in response occurs. Something truly traumatic has happened. An intolerable level of distress is experienced and he is brought to the margins of what is acceptable and manageable. The interface between self and other is sensed to be painful or even unbearable. Maternal empathy and attunement is either not present or not perceived, and the relational field is infused with danger and perceived as definitely *not* good enough. Unbearable impingement and strongly negative umbilical affect is experienced, basic trust is lost, and the little one is forced to shift out of the open and undefended state of simply being. The prenate or infant cannot cope with, incorporate, or include the badness, but *must* react against it. He seeks to oppose its inflow in order to end and repress the pain and distress in some way.

Thus the incoming badness is split off from direct experience and defensive strategies are marshaled to repress, displace, and contain the onslaught in some way. As this occurs, a wounding at the level of being or wellbeing is generated, innate being and its natural being-to-being interconnection is greatly obscured, and highly defended personality systems are generated. Characterological formation then revolves around the alleviation, avoidance, and repression of intense sensations, emotions, and feeling tones. A fragmented sense of both self and world then becomes the felt reality for that person. Lake writes:

> The first significant margin of pain has been reached. Pain of this order cannot remain connected up within the organism. It is split off. The catastrophic sensations are dissociated from the

accompanying emotions, and both gated off from the memory of the hurtful environment. Stable character is based on maintaining this, repressed. (Lake, 1979)

Fairbairn stressed that splitting and repression underlie all other defensive processes. Lake used this understanding as the starting point in his defensive hierarchy. Suffering of this order cannot be fully integrated into the infant's experience or sense of being. Strongly negative feeling tone and affect are experienced, and the ability to cope is totally overwhelmed. The intense or overwhelming sensations are split off from the accompanying emotions, and both are disconnected, or gated, from present experience. The dynamic tensions held within the developing endopsychic structure likewise intensify, and the affects of repressed badness may overwhelm any of the goodness constellating in central-self. This tension manifests as central-self, which continues to mediate the relational processes, manifests personality forms that protect against further pain. These distortions of relation-seeking needs may manifest in the idealization of the goodness of others; in withdrawing from or pushing others away; or in clinging to others in ways that are driven by distorted need and longing. These simple movements are at the root of all oppositional personality strategies.

Both Fairbairn and Lake discuss various personality modes that form in order to manage the inner experience of goodness and badness. In one common mode, the inner sense of badness is projected out. The badness is then out-there and can be opposed in some way. As the badness is split off and projected, a measure of control is felt; but this is based upon a projected false reality. As an adult, the person may play out her life experiencing a loss of basic trust in relationships and in the world in general. The more intimate the contact or relationship, the greater the need to defend against the onrush of bad feelings, and the more oppositional the person becomes. He or she may take an oppositional stance to life in general and to intimacy in particular, and close relationships of any kind may be difficult to maintain. Negative feelings are projected onto intimate others, the internalized badness is sensed to be in them, and they are pushed away or withdrawn from. Trust in relationship breaks down, and intimacy is sensed as painful and must be opposed in some way. In later life, the person yearns for connection; yet when intimacy is truly present, only danger, constriction, and discomfort are sensed.

At the extreme, the other is sensed to be the origin of all of one's pain, problems, and misfortune. Intimacy may intensify this oppositional stance until it manifests as a wish or will to do them harm or see them dead, symbolically or in reality. Or, as this rejecting-other is an inner experience, the anger felt may be turned inward, leading to depressive and suicidal states. Lake writes:

> The self cannot go along with this degree of pain. It cannot cope with it. The organism stops being its trusting self, open at the interface. In everything it reacts against the "badness." In too much pain, it may will the death of the now destructive "source person." Interaction for growth ceases. All is reaction against. (Lake, 1979)

All defended personality states and oppositional strategies have their roots in the need to oppose the inner sense of badness in some way. Rather than relating to others through interbeing and mature interdependency, relationships develop around a wound at the level of being, with the defensive engagement of oppositional personality strategies. These oppositional forms are described in many ways by different psychological traditions and range from active and aggressive characterological strategies, to passive, withdrawn, or frozen ones, running the gamut of autonomic and limbic responses. Displacement, containment, dissociation, and projection are common oppositional defenses. The prenate or infant may displace the feeling of badness onto some body part, attempt to contain it around the umbilicus, or symbolically displace it onto some image. Later, obsessional states, hypochondriacal states, phobias, or paranoid projections of badness onto others may ensue. Ambivalent or avoidant attachment processes result from this early experience.

Transmarginal Response

At the transmarginal response level, the intensity of pain or badness perceived overrides the prenate's or infant's ability either to cope or oppose. Overwhelming umbilical inflow is present, coupled with the intense experience of danger, denial, betrayal, and/or abandonment. There is a flooding of strongly negative affect; anxiety and fear intensify, and the little one is totally overwhelmed as his defensive and protective boundaries are breached. The little being goes into shock and implodes psychically, emotionally, and spiritually. This is a wounding at the most fundamental level of being. The connection both to Source and being is so obscured that the prenate or infant is cast into non-being. Life then is experienced as empty and meaningless and, at the extreme, is denied. In Fairbairn's terms, the little one is cast into the extremes of schizoid disconnection and emptiness as the splitting inherent in endopsychic structure is intensified. Lake writes, "The margin of tolerable pain has been reached. Beyond this threshold, Pavlovian transmarginal stress phenomena occur … The self turns in against itself, willing its own destruction and death … A longing for death supervenes as the affliction-threshold passes (is passed)" (Lake, 1986).

The only possible reaction to this intolerable situation is disconnection, dissociation, and withdrawal. The little one not only disconnects from his present relational field, but from his own being. The trauma is experienced as so overwhelming that disorganization and fragmentation of his core sense of being and selfhood results, and a depth of despair and dread permeates his existence. As endopsychic structure develops, central-self literally disconnects from the internalized badness, and the person lives a life dissociated from the body that holds the badness, and from all others who are sensed as dangerous and untrustworthy. In later life, the afflicted person cannot tolerate any pleasurable arousal, as a flooding of anxiety and anguish constantly overwhelms his experience. Their response to others is disconnection, freezing, or anger. It is a wound that affects every level of relationship. Relationship to family, friends, and intimate others is damaged by the need to protect against the underlying shock of overwhelming badness and the onslaught of despair and emptiness. The most basic sense of the inherent interconnection of self, being, other, and world is torn asunder.

As the body is permeated by badness, goodness may be relocated in the world of ideas and thoughts, or in the disembodied state of dissociation. Lake notes that at the extreme, the person may split his consciousness from the body and float unknowingly outside the body above the head. This dynamic is the foundation for the schizoid personality state (Lake, 1979).

In the transmarginally stressed state, it is impossible for the prenate or infant to feel safe or to connect with mother or primary caregivers, and the ability to regulate emotional affect appropriately is deeply compromised. This has significant repercussions for emotional development, bonding, and attachment processes. Disorganized attachment processes have their roots here. There is an ongoing need to defend against a core of inner badness and constant, overwhelming terror. In the most extreme forms, the overriding emptiness, disconnection, anger, and dread generate death wishes and self-destructive behaviors such as addiction, sadomasochism, and other forms of abuse. The great pain of transmarginal stress is that it deeply undermines the ability to be intimate, to nurture and be nurtured, to allow contact, and to feel any safety in relationship. Lake called this state true affliction (Lake, 1979).

14

Transitional Modes of Relating

The maternal holding environment is the first essential resource for the meeting of being and wellbeing needs and for successfully completing the dynamic cycle in compassionate relationship. As we have seen if this relational field is responsive in a good enough fashion, then the infant can rest in a state of simply being, and the self-system can then develop with a coherent sense of being at its core. If it is not supportive of being and wellbeing, then being's way of being becomes that of the strongly defended self. The more intensely ambiguous the field and the more the state of being is impinged upon, the more defended the developing self will become. In the following sections, we discuss the defended personality forms that may be generated in response to these interactions.

Fairbairn's Transitional Techniques of Relating

In the later stages of the being-in-relationship phase of Lake's dynamic cycle, the little one begins to sense mother and other primary caregivers as unique individuals with their own needs. Conflict may arise in this transition as the separateness of the other is sensed; yet primary identification is still active. Ideally, the infant shifts from primary identification, with its emotional continuity, to a process of emotional separation, as a growing sense of autonomy emerges. This is a shift from the stage of being-in-relationship, where being is only sensed in the reflection of the other, to the journey toward being-in-itself and mature interdependency.

The generation of internal endopsychic structures initially allows the little one to maintain an unambiguous relationship with mother and other primary caregivers. However, the reality of the ambiguous relational environment does not go away. Even though the infant has taken in the perceived badness in order to make the other all-good, the other is still experienced as ambiguous, sometimes relationally responsive, other times not; and so he begins to develop other transitional modes of relating. These are not pathological processes, but are natural adaptations that arise during this transitional phase. In Fairbairn's understanding, these entail the use of projective and introjective techniques (Fairbairn, 1994a). As he considered ego to be energy, this process is likewise energetic in nature. One can *feel* another's projections not just as mental or representational forms, but as energy having direction and impact.

The whole of endopsychic structure is involved in this process. For instance, in what Klein called *projective identification,* the badness is projected out onto the other and is then sensed to be *in* the other, not in the one projecting it. Projection is both energetic and infusive, and the person being projected upon may feel that the badness *is* his or her own. The therapist learns to negotiate projective processes so that he or she does not identify with them, but can draw on them for important clinical information.

Fairbairn outlined four basic introjective/projective interactions and named them after the more extreme personality positions that may arise if they become entrenched ways of being. I am simply calling them modes 1, 2, 3, and 4. Fairbairn discussed these as techniques of dealing with the intensity of affect generated by internalized goodness and badness and continuing relational ambiguity. While any transitional technique may become the predominant way of being, all may become engaged in relational processes and manifest in different schemas of being.

For instance, based upon early schemas of being with mother and father, one mode may be prominent in interactions with men, and another in interactions with woman; and different modes may be prominent in different attachment scenarios.

Mode 1

In Mode 1, the goodness and badness are kept within, and no projective processes are engaged. The self-constellations that were set up to manage relational goodness and badness all intensify, and the continuing outer ambiguity is sensed as an inner struggle between goodness and badness. The needy-self constellation, with its attachment to the internalized object and its longing for contact with the other, is countered by the rejecting-self constellation, with its rejection of the other. This dynamic tension commonly yields a depressive experience, but, at the extreme, can give rise to an obsessional personality in which the inner tensions are managed through active and repetitive processes. The inner badness is sensed to be infusive, and goodness is upheld through control and ritual.

Mode 2

In Mode 2, the conflict of holding both badness and goodness internally is overwhelming, and *both* are projected out onto primary others. Relationships then are experienced continually through the veil of projected goodness and badness. Outer others are sensed to be both dangerous *and* potentially fulfilling, and primary others are both longed for and loathed. As the child is still in a state of immature dependency and needs the other to be all-good, he cannot hold a mixed object, an outer other that is both good *and* bad. This results in continual shifts in relating, so that the other is first all-good and then all-bad, generating much anxiety and tension in primary relationships. And as *both* goodness and badness are projected out, so are all internalized objects. Even central-self is bereft of its idealized object, and a profound sense of emptiness and non-being results.

In extreme cases, phobic personalities may emerge as the badness is projected out onto things, people, or situations and experienced as terrifying. Rejecting-self then compulsively pushes the symbol of badness away. At the same time, needy-self compulsively clings to others that hold projected goodness and the possibility of salvation and safety. This situation of all-good, all-bad projections is inherently unstable. For example, an all-good projection can quickly flip as the promising other inevitably lets the infant or adult down, or until fear of identity loss via merging occurs. The person may then shift and project badness, experiencing the other as threatening, at which point rejecting-self then pushes them away. An intense manifestation of this transitional mode of relating is the borderline personality, discussed in greater detail below. In modes 3 and 4, the dynamic tension generated by the internalization of both goodness and badness is managed by holding onto one and projecting the other out. The inner conflict between accepting one or the other is then resolved.

Mode 3

In Mode 3, the inner conflict is managed by retaining the goodness, while projecting the badness out onto others. Self becomes strongly identified with the goodness of the internalized all-good object, while all of the badness, along with the bad object, is projected out and is constantly opposed by the rejecting-self. The person may develop life statements like, "I am innocent and good. They are bad, evil, out to get me, and the cause of all my problems, and I must oppose them." At the extreme, this mode of relating becomes a paranoid personality position, an all-good-inside, all-bad-outside perceptual experience. The person then continually finds himself in a hostile world where everyone is the cause of their pain and suffering, and no sense of personal responsibility or clear discernment of the intentions of the other is possible. The rejecting-self becomes the modus operandi, as outer others, now holding the projected bad-objects, are experienced as dangerous or bad, and must be opposed in some way.

Mode 4

In Mode 4, the reverse occurs. The dynamic tension generated by the interplay of internal object relations is resolved by retaining the inner experience of badness, while projecting out all sense of goodness. As the all-good idealized object is relocated out-there, the retained sense of badness intensifies and infuses the person's sense of selfhood. As this occurs, self becomes identified with inner badness, and an all-pervading sense of "I-am-bad" results. The rejecting-self turns inward and self-destructive behaviors manifest; while the needy-self is constantly seeking salvation out-there. An ongoing sense of badness, inadequacy, and worthlessness may result, while outer others are strongly idealized as better or all-good. The inner world is sensed as bad, even disgusting; no inner resource can be found; and all goodness is sought outwardly in others who are constantly perceived as potential saviors. At the extreme this can manifest as the hysteric personality adaptation, an all-bad-inside; all-good-outside, perceptual experience. The person lives with an overwhelming sense of inner badness and a modus operandi of longing and clinging, while his projections onto others of idealized goodness continually overwhelm any possibility of real relationship.

Table 14.1 Transitional Techniques of Relating

Diagram modified from Routledge and Scharff, 2000

Adaptation	Goodness	Badness	Entrenched Positions
Mode 1	Internal	Internal	Obsessional
Mode 2	External	External	Phobic
Mode 3	Internal	External	Paranoid
Mode 4	External	Internal	Hysteric

Lake's Concept of Embodied Adaptive Processes

Lake observed that prenates and infants employ embodied modes of primary defensive processes. As relational experience impacts the growing little being from conception onwards, negative umbilical affect may generate defensive body processes that Lake called displacement, containment, and dissociation. These processes help the little being maintain integrity in what may be an onslaught of difficult relational experiences, sensations, and feelings. This finding supplements Fairbairn's concepts of endopsychic structuring and transitional modes of relating to describe the embodied nature of introjection and projection.

Displacement

When overwhelming negative umbilical affect is experienced, the little one, especially while still connected to the umbilicus, may use displacement as an adaptive defense. As incoming relational badness is sensed via umbilical inflow, it may be projected or displaced into some part of his own body. This is common both in the prenatal period and during traumatic birth processes; however, embodied emotional displacement also can occur in adults as overwhelming intimate relational stress is encountered. Lake discusses displacement as the root of much physical pathology. For instance, the prenate or infant may displace an incoming inflow of badness, along with related anger or frustration, onto an organ such as the liver; or hold it as nervous system activation in the solar plexus. Later, digestive problems may arise along with an angry relational disposition. Any transitional mode of relating may be coupled with this process.

Containment

The prenate or infant may experience overwhelming umbilical inflow and attempt to contain it in some way. A common way of doing this is to tense against the inflow and to try to contain it in the umbilical area. I have noted that containment is a frequent response to difficult and overwhelming birth processes and is commonly coupled with the shock of sudden disconnection from mother, as when the umbilical cord is cut too soon. I have worked with many adults who have tense or overly sensitive umbilical areas, along with issues of low energy and low motivation. Emotional states such as frustration and anger frequently accompany these patterns and may be repressed, but will resurface under stress or relational challenge and in session work.

Dissociation

Dissociative disconnection is an adaptation to the shock of overwhelming experience and the modus operandi of transmarginal stress and the schizoid personality. The little one's needs were so violated that the only possible response was to split off completely from the overwhelming umbilical affects experienced. For Lake, dissociation is not just a mental process, but an energetic disconnection from embodiment itself by which a person literally displaces his self-sense outside the body and its feelings. The person then may live in his head, where goodness is found in the world of thought; or dissociate above himself, so to speak, living life disconnected from present-moment circumstances.

The Body Takes Shape

The works of Lake and Keleman contribute much to understanding how the body is impacted by, and takes shape according to, experience. The impingement of experiential forces begins from the moment of conception. Both Lake and Keleman describe how these impingements are embodied during embryonic development, through infancy and childhood, right until the moment of death. In a similar fashion to Lake, Keleman discusses defensive cellular processes that lead to over-bound (dense) or under-bound (flaccid) tissue structures and tissue fields. Lake discusses how the fetus or infant contains, pushes, or displaces bad feelings into various parts of his body, leading to physical tensions, tissue contractions, and protective densification or flaccidness of tissues that later can result in pathology. Keleman supports these concepts with extraordinary insights into cellular responses to stress, beginning with the single cell at conception and continuing throughout life, leading to the development of overall tension patterning of over-bound and under-bound tissue states (Lake, 1979; Keleman, 1985).

An example might be a young infant who experiences unattuned caregivers and empathic breaches in its holding environment, whose stress system is activated and autonomic and physical tensions are generated in order to contain the negative affect experienced. These may then manifest as tight or flaccid musculature, and inner tensions and tissue forms that are part and parcel of the person's personality defenses. Another example might be an anxious pregnant mother who is continually producing stress hormones that infuse the prenate's system. The prenate then may enlist its own protective autonomic and physiological processes in an attempt to protect itself from overwhelming impingement. Tensions and contractions may be generated in the developing tissue system, as may over-bound and under-bound states, all manifesting as an integral aspect of the developing self-system. I have worked with many clients whose tension patterns, such as tense neck, shoulders, or abdomens, were traced to their earliest experiences of relational life. These tensions were alleviated only when their relational issues were resolved.

15

Introduction to Personality Adaptations and Reaction Patterns

I n this next chapter, we will explore how endopsychic structure and transitional modes of relating become fixed personality forms, and how central-self manifests reaction patterns that help keep negative energies and painful affects repressed.

Reaction Patterns

As we have seen, central-self directly mediates being's natural connection to other beings via relation seeking and generates modes of relating that defend against repressed feelings and further wounding. Lake called these personality adaptations and defensive modes *reaction patterns*. They protect the individual from directly experiencing the repressed affects of terror and rage and of wounded need and longing. The reaction patterns explored below are all generated to maintain repression of intensely negative affects and bad object relations and allow for some kind of outer relationship, if in wounded forms.

Narcissism

The clinical concept of narcissism has its roots in Freudian theory and is a major theme both in analysis and psychotherapy in general. Freud postulated that infants have no sense of separation between self and other. He observed infants as merged in a state of *primary narcissism* with mother and the world in general, so that for them there is only a sense of everything-as-extensions-of-me. From this vantage point, the journey of personal growth becomes one of shifting from a merged state, to separation, and then to autonomy.

Research has shown, however, that infants do indeed relate to mother and others as separate; they have clear self-other relational awareness right from the beginning (Stern, 1984; Maret, 1997; Chamberlain, 1998; Schore, 2001a, 2001b). As we have seen, Fairbairn had a very different understanding from Freud's of infant-mother relations. He observed that infants can and do differentiate between self and other and relate to others accordingly. The infant experiences self-other exchanges via primary identification, so that, while clearly the other as separate, he cannot differentiate his own needs and emotional states from those of mother and other primary caregivers, resulting in a state of confusion, not of diffused merging with others.

Fairbairn saw that the natural developmental progression of narcissism is a movement from immature dependency to mature interdependency. This, again, is a dramatic departure from Freudian theory. As the schizoid position emerges, central-self initially mediates relation-seeking via primary identification and immature dependency. This is a basically self-centered narcissistic position in which the infant expects others will know his needs as their own and exist to meet those needs. There is no differentiation between personal needs and emotional states and those of others. If self-forms are fixed at this stage, then narcissistic distortions of relation-seeking will occur.

In this framework, the relational challenge is to shift from the immature narcissistic state to the narcissism of mature interdependency in which relational differentiation is possible, boundaries are perceived and respected, and others' needs are seen as equally valid to one's own. As the shift to mature interdependency is made, the I-it position, seeing others as objects to fulfill personal needs, shifts to the I-thou position, in which innate being becomes the hub of central-self and being-to-being relational awareness becomes possible (Buber, 1970).

As I have earlier proposed, sentience, a being-state, is present at the heart of the developing self right from the beginnings of life. This is the ground for self-referential experience. From this perspective, the prenate or infant is narcissistic in the best possible way. Narcissism can be viewed as a natural and healthy expression of the agency at the core of selfhood. It is from this core that relation-seeking emerges and around this core that selfhood forms. Kohut, following in the footsteps of Fairbairn, was one of the first modern theorists to challenge Freud's definition of narcissism as a purely pathological state (Kohut, 1966). He saw narcissism as having adaptive value. Similarly to Fairbairn, he understood personality development as the transformation of archaic narcissism, an immature state of self-other relatedness, to mature forms. In this process the growing child, adolescent, or adult shifts from immature relating, in which there is emotional projection and confusion of needs, to mature interdependency, in which selfhood manifests cohesively in creativity, empathy for others, and openness to the development of insight and wisdom. Kohut saw that a cohesive sense of selfhood is essential for maturational processes to unfold. Winnicott, too, saw a cohesive state of being as the crux of the matter. In our terms, a cohesive sense of selfhood, organized around innate being and its innate being-to-being interconnection, is the heart of a healthy or transformed narcissism capable of manifesting cohesive, interdependent self-other interchanges. As Lake maintained, being's greatest achievement is the manifestation of relationship based on the flow of love and compassion.

In its immature form, central-self's narcissistic position can intensify into a defensive personality adaptation called *narcissistic inflation*. As the internalized badness is repressed into the shadow world, its energies turn inward, generating guilt and low self-esteem, and the internal saboteur, enemy of true relation-seeking and trust in relational process.

In response, central-self may manifest a reaction pattern whereby the individual's narcissistic sense of selfhood, with an inflated sense of self-importance and lack of empathy for others, elevates her above others to counter her deeper sense of worthlessness and low self-esteem. A position of superiority is assumed to mask feelings of guilt and inferiority. It must be remembered that this is an adaptive state that helps keep painful feelings in check and has survival value. Lake writes:

> If the personality pattern is functioning well as an adequate defensive system, no part of the underlying anxieties emerges into consciousness. The panic and dread, emptiness and fear, rage and envy, are all dealt with within the repressive layer, and "appear" in consciousness only as their opposites, confidence and pride, capability and calm, compliance and generosity. The person is entirely unaware of the contents of his unconscious mind, and is aided and abetted by a variety of mental mechanisms in remaining so. (Lake, 1986)

Inflation protects against the inner sense of humiliation, guilt, and shame, and the associated lack of self-worth and self-respect. It helps maintain the repression of all self-directed negativity, along with its related feelings of terror, anger, frustration, and longing. Inflation maintains a reaction pattern oriented around, "I am too good for them. They are below me, and I am above all relational longing." The longing of needy-self is repressed, and the frustration and anger held in rejecting-self is transformed into condemnation, disapproval, and judgment of others.

Super-Ego Functions

Freud's concept of the superego has correspondences in both Fairbairn's and Lake's formulations. Fairbairn attributed super-ego roles to the repressed energies of bad object relations and directly influenced Lake in his discussions of anti-libidinal super-ego, libidinal super-ego, and reaction patterns (Lake, 1986). In his terms, both rejecting- and needy-selves, and the reaction patterns that constellate in relation to their energies, can manifest super-ego functions that protect against the overt expression of repressed anger and need.

It is not uncommon for a reaction pattern to manifest in a way that is diametrically opposite to the forces held in repression in order to protect against their expression in relationship. For instance, as the infant takes in relational badness and splitting occurs, the rejecting-self is infused by frustration and anger. But there is still an overarching need to maintain contact with and relationship to mother and outer others; so the frustration and anger are turned inward, generating feelings of inferiority, badness, and guilt. "It must be me. I must be bad for this to happen," etc. These secondary feelings act to restrain the surfacing and expression of the primary feelings of frustration and anger. Central-self may then generate various reaction patterns that further repress the painful experience of shame, guilt, and inferiority. As we shall see, there are many forms of reaction pattern that manifest this super-ego function of protecting the individual from the outright experience and expression of rage and longing. When repression fails, the negative energies may be so overwhelming that the person manifests dangerous or distorted behaviors, or is cast into the abyss of transmarginal terror.

16

Personality Forms Generated by Wounding at the Level of Being

The following descriptions are of strongly defended personality adaptations that arise within the oppositional and transmarginal territories of Lake's hierarchy. The first two adaptations are expressions of the intensification of basic endopsychic structure into schizoid or depressive personalities. The other adaptations discussed are intensifications of the various transitional modes of relating. They are based on whether the defense is by introjection, projection, or disconnection from the internal sense of goodness or badness. The different personality adaptations emerge dependent on which phase of the dynamic cycle is impinged upon and the intensity of the breach in relational safety and attunement. Different reaction patterns may be generated in response to different experiences and be layered into the personality system. For instance, a person may have an underlying anxiety depressive adaptation overlaid by a schizoid need to withdraw. Perhaps, during the being phase of the dynamic cycle, an initial breach in holding generated extreme anxiety coupled with oppositional processes. Later, a shocking experience may cast the little one into the transmarginal state, which overwhelmed his ability to either cope with or oppose relational exchanges. There is now terror at the root of the personality system. A dissociative response is generated that becomes the platform for a schizoid, disconnected way of being.

As the framework and terminology used below is largely analytical and has a pathological flavor, it is important to view the concepts presented with a non-pathological mindset. These personality adaptations result from deprivations or distortions in the satisfaction of the need for contact and relation seeking and must be understood in this context. All defensive patterns are adaptive in nature and help maintain contact with significant others and the world. For instance, a paranoid personality system is not an illness, but an expression of an early breach in the holding environment and unresolved relational wounding. It is an adaptation that helps the person maintain contact and relationship, even though it is energized by repressed pain and feelings. Even dissociation can be seen as an attempt to maintain integrity and some kind of relationship to internal and external objects. Thus the following characterological descriptions are adaptations for survival, attempts to maintain relationship even in the most desperate inner turmoil. It is also important to remember that all personality adaptations and self-other exchanges are energy in action, forms of energy exchange and energy process.

I offer below only an introductory overview of each adaptation and an outline of the healing processes for some of them. No matter what the defensive adaptation, the foundation of healing is the awareness of both practitioner and client, and the being-to-being relational field in which trust can grow. It is by maintaining a good enough, attuned, resonant, and appropriately responsive field that the therapist can best support the client's reclamation of relatedness and being.

Wounding at the Level of Being

Lake maintained that disturbances experienced in the being or wellbeing phases of the dynamic cycle had the greatest impact upon personality formation. Wounds incurred during the being phase were most pivotal. Both Lake and Fairbairn also noted that it is during the transitional phase, when the infant begins the process of emotional separation from mother, that the most extreme forms of separation anxiety may arise. During this period, the experience of the absence of mother, either physically or through her own defensive processes of emotional withdrawal or disconnection, is intolerable for the little one, with the potential to generate extremes of primary trauma. Lake stressed that severe separation anxiety has the potential to cast the little one into transmarginal stress, generating a wounding at the level of being with dreadful consequences.

It is important to stress that *wounding at the level of being* does not imply that being is actually wounded, but that its presence becomes deeply obscured to everyday awareness, as does the experience of inter-being and compassionate meaning derived from Source. This obscuration is accompanied by a change in orientation from Source and being to a wounded self-system. The deeper the wounding, the more the connection to Source is obscured, and the more fragmented and defended the personality system becomes. The experience of non-being, disconnection, and emptiness then permeates the individual's life. Lake believed that the *denial of being* generates the deepest and most painful wounds. These wounds occur when the maternal relational field does not acknowledge, or actively denies, the existence of the little one. Attempted abortion is an extreme form of this denial.

Wounding at the level of being also can arise when umbilical inflow and the holding environment of the womb of spirit are experienced as overwhelmingly inconsistent, bad, or dangerous. At this level of wounding, basic trust is lost, oppositional and transmarginal processes are generated, and the most defended personality systems arise. As far as I know, Lake was the first analyst to stress that ontological wounding is always coupled with physiological manifestations of the stress response. Thus autonomic activation, emotional cycling, states of anxiety and despair, dissociation, and freezing may manifest at any time in psychotherapy sessions. The clinician must be able to recognize these manifestations for what they are and help the client negotiate her processes without being overwhelmed again and cast anew into trauma.

Wounding at the level of being is a worldwide affliction. In the attempt to make meaning from the abyss of emptiness and non-being, addiction, fanaticism, abuse, and other dead ends are pursued. Whole cultures become caught up in this futility as wounds are passed on through generations. Vicious cycles are generated in which meaning is sought in the wrong places, wounding is projected onto convenient others, and more and more harm and pain are inflicted in misguided attempts to assuage the emptiness, terror, rage, disconnection, and alienation.

Wounding at the level of being severely compromises the infant's sense of wellbeing. Lake sites instances of negative umbilical inflow and perceived badness being displaced into the prenate's body parts and, when unresolved, resulting in degenerative diseases in these same areas.

Adaptations related to wounding at the level of being are the schizoid, anxiety depressive, hysteric, hystero-schizoid (borderline), obsessional, and phobic adaptations.

Adaptations Directly Based Upon Endopsychic Structure

The schizoid and depressive personality strategies manifest as intensifications of basic endopsychic structure. In the schizoid adaptation, the relational field was experienced as overwhelmingly bad, and the only relational possibility for survival was to disengage from both from the outer field and the internal bad object. This is a depth of wounding that throws the infant into the terror of transmarginal stress.

In the depressive adaptation, the love of the outer other is lost, but still longed for. The struggle between longing and rejecting intensifies and is fought within. One both loves and hates the object, generating an inner tension that manifests as an intense ambivalence to intimacy. This is a strongly oppositional adaptation set up to manage the extreme and paradoxical feelings of frustration, anger, and longing.

Schizoid Personality Adaptation

The schizoid personality is a defensive adaptation to extremely over-whelming experience and strongly negative umbilical affect. It arises from the depths of the transmarginally stressed state, and its defensive modes are withdrawal, dissociation, detachment, and introversion. Under the intensity of overwhelming experience, all the infant can do is literally to split off from the overwhelming infusion of badness. In the generation of the schizoid adaptation, an infusion of negative umbilical inflow permeates the prenate or infant's experience, and badness seems to pervade everything. If the breach in the holding field is so severe that the ability to cope with or oppose the experience is overwhelmed, then the infant is cast into panic and dread and descends into the transmarginally stressed state of primary shock, dissociation, and immobilization. All trust in the holding field is lost. Both the outer other and the internalized object are experienced as excruciatingly bad and withdrawn from, as the body is infused with painful or even terrible sensations. Any sense of goodness is displaced into the head with its world of fantasy, thought, and imagery, or out of the body altogether, as the dissociated psyche literally floats above the head, disconnected from all feeling and any chance of real contact or relationship. In Lake's terms, this initiates a shift in identity from knowing being by being-in-relationship, to non-being. Being-itself is lost, and any other sense of being is derived from thought and mentality (Lake, 1986).

In terms of basic endopsychic structure, the internal good object and all external good others are lost in terror, and an enormous emptiness is experienced. Needy-self's longing for the exciting or potentially fulfilling other is threatening, and all longing is repressed, as intimacy is experienced as dangerous. The individual withdraws from all objects to lead a disconnected, disembodied life, denying interbeing and withdrawing from relation seeking. Self-absorbed thinking predominates as the person retreats into an inner world where thinking is safer and more real than outer relationship. Fantasies may predominate waking life and become sexualized, but real relationship and consummation of sexual energies are avoided. The idealized object becomes the ideal thought.

Original motivation and meaning was found in relationship itself. Now meaning is lost, and love and intimacy are experienced as dangerous and even destructive. Emotions, sensations, feelings, and mental processes become disconnected from present experience, and lose cohesion, continuity of being is lost and a disconnection from Source is experienced. A great sense of disorientation occurs as the afflicted person lives a dissociated and disconnected existence terrified of the most basic need for contact. This state is the root of disorganized attachment processes, as the needed object is feared, terror underlies relational contact, and withdrawal and disconnection seem the only options. Thus the person in the schizoid state lives a disconnected life, afraid of relational others, never really entering into relationships or intimacy, avoiding any process that may activate the inner experience of badness and the emptiness of non-being (Lake, 1979, 1986). People living this state commonly report that they feel unreal, empty, and lost. It can seem as though they are living in a glass bowl cut off from both others and their own deepest feelings. They live as strangers in a strange land.

Schizoid Reaction Patterns

Central-self defends against repressed terror and dread by forming reaction patterns that remove the individual from the immediacy of his pain. Lake describes numerous reaction patterns that can overlay the schizoid state. One narcissistic reaction pattern is a defense via inflation that is mobilized when the moral defense intensifies into a loss of self-esteem with overarching feelings of inferiority and shame, and the underlying sense of inferiority is overlaid by feelings of superiority over and even contempt for others. The person lives a cerebral life, aloof from contact, totally unaware of the terror within. A basic life statement like,

"I don't need others" may develop as the person withdraws into a self-imposed self-sufficiency. This inflated pattern can and will extend into spiritual life. The person may be attracted to mysticism, feeling spiritually superior and assuming a holier-than-thou position relative to others. I have worked with many meditators who use their practices to feel blissful and superior, while only intensifying their dissociation. These people live in a kind of dual consciousness, one of spiritual inflation, and another deeper reality of impoverishment, alienation, and emptiness. True spirituality embraces life, directly senses interconnection from the level of being, knows the presence of Source as a moment-to-moment reality, and is a fully embodied and humble state of wonderment at the profound mystery of life.

Lake notes that, when the schizoid adaptation fails, or the person is drawn back into relational experience, an hysteric mode of relating may result. The inner world is sensed as overwhelmingly bad, and any sense of goodness is projected out, from a dissociated and disconnected vantage point, as ideas and ideals onto other people, causes, or things. The person may then engage in attention seeking, though appalled by actual intimacy.

Having lost any sense of internal goodness, central-self may also manifest as an overly compliant personality system, seemingly dependent on others, but in reality disconnected, disenfranchised, and terrified. Lake sees this reaction pattern as a last-resort protection from dread and despair. The person may likewise engage in other transitional modes, projecting all goodness and badness out as phobic states, or managing the internal split with obsessive behaviors. If the schizoid strategy and its various reaction patterns fail, that is, if the adaptations of repression and disconnection do not succeed at warding off the overwhelming emotion associated with the deep wounding, then the underlying panic, dread, and terror may once again infuse consciousness, along with an overpowering emptiness. The person may experience severe panic attacks and autonomic affects like cardio-respiratory symptoms, palpitations, tension, sweating, shaking, hyperventilation, etc. Even though the schizoid state is one of dissociation and withdrawal, the basic endopsychic structure usually remains intact. Fairbairn observes that if the basic schizoid position should fragment, psychosis and schizophrenia may arise. In these states the basic fabric of self has disintegrated and central self cannot mediate any form of relation-seeking or contact, or maintain any sense of inner coherency. These extreme states in which there is a fragmentation of internal self-constellations and dislocation from present reality are expressions of splitting at the extreme. They are intensely dissociated transmarginally stressed states.

Healing

The schizoid adaptation is an extreme response to devastating relational experience that entails a loss of being and selfhood at a root level. Healing of this adaptation depends on reclamation of being and interbeing. In a therapeutic relationship, the person using a schizoid adaptation has the opportunity to come out of isolation into real relationship. The first step is by necessity an inquiry into the dissociated and disconnected selfhood and a gradual reconnection to embodiment. The therapeutic holding field hopefully allows the client to settle into an inquiry supported by mindfulness practice and the direct reflection of a new empathic other. As the schizoid self re-embodies, the terror underlying the original rift must be negotiated in such a way that it becomes accessible to being-with, without becoming overwhelming or destructive. As terror is negotiated, a deep rage may surface—rage at being unseen, unloved, rejected, and/or overwhelmed. This, too, must be accessed and acknowledged in a safe and resourced field of relationship.

There is a period of testing out, clinging, and strong positive transference. As the client comes back into embodiment, the badness is directly experienced, and the push-pull of the rejecting- and needy-selves is clearly sensed. This leads to the experience of the depressive personality, in whom the struggle between longing for contact and needing to push it away come strongly into play.

As all of these dynamics are held in an empathic and reflective therapeutic field, a deeper settling may occur through which the client enters a being state in resonance with the therapist's own. As both settle into this present-time territory, the possibility of reclamation of being and Source awakens. Lake is clear, as am I, that healing a wound at the level of being is an essentially spiritual process. As healing occurs, there is a shift from the fixity of the closed self-system, to a more fluid and open relationship to life. This is more easily said than done and entails a journey into the unknown for therapist and client alike.

Depressive (Anxiety-Depressive) Personality Adaptation

As we have seen, in immature dependency, the infant needs its love to be unconditionally accepted, and its taking from the other to be received as an act of love. Throughout this early phase, the infant knows its own being only through its relationship to an attuned, loving, and reflective holding field. His most basic needs of being equate to being-loved and being-accepted in this field. If the infant experiences his love as rejected, or that the other is unloving and denying, then love itself is lost and may be experienced as dangerous and bad. When love is denied, being is also denied. A wound at the level of being results, and the depressive position of both longing for and rejecting the other intensifies. Basic trust is lost, and oppositional adaptations develop. The little one must oppose the badness in some way. Fight-or-flight energies are triggered, amplifying the dynamic tension already felt. The depressive position then becomes the depressive personality, an adaptive state that attempts to manage the intensity of longing and rage. Unlike the schizoid state, in which the object is overwhelmingly bad and pushed away, here the object is still needed, but its love—and love itself—is now sensed to be bad. Ambivalence to intimacy results: "I desperately need the other, but I am terrified and enraged by the loss of their love." The depressive personality is caught in this push-pull between the rejecting- and needy-selves, between loving and hating. These forces must be balanced in some way. The anxiety-depressive state evolves as a way of adapting to the intensity of this now torturous inner conflict. Lake describes this adaptation as a defense via ambivalence and repression of oppositional energies (Lake, 1979, 1986a).

In terms of basic endopsychic structure, the outer other is not to be trusted; but the idealized inner other is idolized. As the outer other and her love are lost, central-self organizes all self-other relationships around the now supreme internal ideal object. This inner object is held as unambiguously good, while the conflicting demands of the rejecting- and needy-selves are projected onto real others. The person's inner world of feelings and fantasy becomes more real than the outer one of people, places, and things. He cannot invest in real relationship, as a strongly ambivalent posture is taken towards all outer intimate others, who can never measure up to the internal ideal other. The past may be held as idealized fantasy. Nostalgia about past others, stripped of all guilt or fault, intrudes on present relationships, and these idealized past others are held as lost objects, making real, present-time relationship more difficult.

All experience is filtered through these veils, making it almost impossible to see intimate others for who they really are, or to receive the real relational goodness and love on offer. The more intimate a relationship becomes, the less the outer other can be trusted, the more the idealized object is clung to, and the more ambivalent the afflicted person becomes. The other is still needed, as is their love, but the fear of being unloved and the pain of the original wounding makes it impossible to love in return. Here the need for contact is present, only to be sabotaged by rejecting-self and the intensity of its rage. These are held in check as they may drive the needed other away. Rage is repressed as dangerous, yet may burst through at any time like a smoldering fire blown to life by the wind.

These dynamics are accompanied by an augmentation of the moral defense whereby the little one takes on the badness of the other. This intensifies into feelings of low self-esteem. The loss of the love of the other is then understood as, "It is my fault. I am guilty, unlovable, and unworthy." Because of these intense feelings of inferiority, the depressive may cling to an unfulfilling existing relationship, feeling incapable of finding another.

Lake sees the loss of love as equating with the loss of the other, resulting in a progressive loss of hope and a despair that, in turn, generate severe separation anxiety in the infant, especially in the transition phase of the dynamic cycle. As Fairbairn also describes, this intensifies the inner tension between longing and rejecting. These energies are repressed, but generate both autonomic activity and fantasy. The energies of the rejecting-self may manifest as aggressive fantasies, or as fantasies of power-over-others; while those of the needy-self may manifest as sexual fantasies, or as fantasies that idealize the potential for outer others to fulfill wounded needs. Dreams may be tumultuous and express the insecurity and low self-esteem felt by the depressive person. These energies, in the extremes of transmarginal stress, may take on masochistic, sadistic, or sadomasochistic form.

Depressive Reaction Patterns

Lake describes various depressive reactive patterns that become central-self's way of being. For example, needy-self may manifest its longing via the hysteric transitional mode of relating as attention seeking and clinging to others. Libidinal fantasies of lust, sexual conquest, and sexual nostalgia may permeate the person's waking life as well as his dream world, making real relationship even more difficult. The drive for sexual contact does not arise from the desire to give and receive love, but from the need to relieve the inner tensions generated by the depressive adaptation. There is no joy here, as the other is used as an object. Although this drive resonates with that described by Freud, it arises from a very different source: from the need to manage the intensity of inner badness, bad object relations, and strongly negative affects.

Lake describes four specific reaction patterns manifested by central-self to counter repressed feelings and the unmet needs that are their source:

The *compulsive compliant personality adaptation* may overlay the repressed rage of rejecting-self. In this organization of central-self, anger is rejected as too dangerous. Rage is managed through conformity, compliance, capitulation, and compulsive submission, and normal self-esteem is lost. The person will do anything to avoid confrontation and anger.

The *compulsive asexual personality adaptation* evolves to manage the excessive need and longing of needy-self. Individuals expressing this adaptation deny their sexuality and may isolate themselves and seem shy and retiring. They may be troubled by sexual fantasies, yet act prudishly and, due to their low self-esteem, be self-effacing. "I'm not important, intimacy with others is not important, and sexuality is disgusting."

In the *compulsive accepted personality adaptation,* central-self may organize an idealized self-sense in response to the anxiety and despair. Separation and aloneness are terrifying and, in essence, ruled out. The person cannot tolerate being alone, and his low self-esteem and longing result in an excessive clinging to the other, hidden by a superimposed attitude of calm, confidence, and secure belonging. But the separation anxiety and the terror of aloneness and loss of love lie just beneath the surface.

The *compulsive 'spirited' personality adaptation* manages the terror and despair at the loss of being and the descent into non-being. Here the person deeply represses his terror and despair by directing his energies out as activity and optimism. He cannot stop—to stop is to feel despair and hopelessness—but is in continual motion. He presents an energized persona with an indefatigable spirit, outwardly positive, inwardly fearful and despairing. He needs constant stimulation and activity to remain above the inner terror and despair. He may seek dangerous pursuits such as mountain climbing or skydiving to feel alive and exhilarated, showing a forced optimism and endurance. Inwardly the will to live is weak, while outwardly he shows a hectic appetite for life. He may take a moral high ground in relationship to others. Inwardly feeling worthless, he may outwardly adhere to a rigid morality, fiercely judging the actions of others. The moral defense and the sense of guilt it takes on are projected out, and others are seen to be the guilty or shameful ones.

At the extreme, the obsessional transitional mode of relating (Mode 1) may emerge to manage the energies of the inner badness, as may phobic projections (Mode 2). Lake notes that the intense energies of the depressive adaptation may be further defended against by conversion patterns, in which physical symptoms express the tensions of the inner conflict (Lake, 1986, charts Da, Db).

When a depressive client's anxiety-depressive adaptation emerges, great fear, rage, and/or longing, along with a near-suicidal self-deprecation, may accompany it, and these must be carefully negotiated in session work. The depressive adaptation is a highly activated state that may manifest sympathetic nervous system cycling, hypersensitivity, hyper-vigilant states, hyperactivity, insomnia, poor appetite, exhaustion, etc. Insecure attachment processes become the modus operandi of relationship, and anxiety depression may manifest in both child and adult.

Healing

The depressive adaptation cycles a huge amount of energy in the dynamic tension between rejection and longing. Healing processes begin with the acknowledgment of the loss of both the object and its love and a concurrent withdrawal of investment in central-self's idealized object. Letting the inner good-other go can be a monumental task for the client and demands persistent mindfulness of his inner states. He must be aware of both his inner world of fantasy and of the idealized others he clings to. A daily mindfulness practice in which he notes the push-pull between longing and rejecting, even while walking down the street, can be extremely useful, even fundamental, to healing. As he witnesses this projective process and truly senses its futility, an intense mourning process ensues in which the real loss is grieved, along with the unattainable idealized inner other. The terror and rage of both oppositional and transmarginally stressed states may emerge and must be held and discharged within the empathic holding of the therapist's presence. As these strong feelings are negotiated, the therapeutic environment offers the opportunity to grieve safely, to let go of past wounding, and to come into real relationship.

Over time, as wounding is processed, central-self may reorient to being and learn to absorb real goodness. When this occurs, central-self is freed from the over-idealization of the good object, and from the repressed dynamics of longing and rejecting, as well from their related guilt and shame. Again, over time, the empathic reflective environment held by the therapist, along with the therapist's ability to enter and hold her own being-state, allows the client to resonate with innate being. Mindfulness of inner states supports this process. As the client sees his arising thoughts and affects as process rather than as *me,* space is generated, and healing potential is activated. At this level therapy addresses the reclamation of being and a return to relatedness.

Adaptations Based Upon Transitional Modes of Relating

The next personality adaptations relate to transitional modes of relating as fixated forms of self-other interchange. These overlay the schizoid and depressive positions. When the infant finds, even after basic endopsychic structure is in place, that his relational milieu is still inherently ambiguous, he engages other modes of relating based on projection–introjection dynamics. When these become predominant, they can generate fixed modes of personality and self-view. These fixed modes include the hysteric, hystero-schizoid (borderline), obsessional, and phobic adaptations.

Hysteric Personality Adaptation

In Fairbairn's transitional technique of relating (Mode 4), badness is retained inwardly and goodness is projected out. If this mode becomes entrenched, the hysteric adaptation becomes being's way of being. Lake describes the hysteric adaptation as arising when mother is either physically or spiritually largely absent, as the infant passively waits for her return. She is inconsistent, aloof, and inappropriate in her responses. Even when present, she is a lost and unattainable object, and her unattainability is coupled with a narcissistic seductiveness that intensifies the energies of the infant's exciting or potentially fulfilling internal object. Fairbairn notes that the hysteric adaptation arises when the same single object, most typically mother, is both excessively exciting and rejecting (Fairbairn, 1994d). The little one longs for contact and love, senses this potential, yet is constantly disappointed by its absence. In Lake's understanding, critical to the development of the hysteric adaptation is the intense feeling generated in passively waiting for the longed for other, a mix of abandonment and titillation at the possibility of a fulfillment that is never realized.

Waiting for an inconsistent other who is absent in spirit even when present in form is devastating. The experience of abandonment generates severe separation anxiety, especially in the transition phase of Lake's dynamic cycle. The prenate or infant senses this relational milieu as an infusive badness, yet still desperately needs the other and longs for her attention. In the moral defense, as this pervasive badness permeates the experience of the infant, he takes on the guilt of the other and feels, "I am bad, and the badness is in me." Desperation and anxiety infuse relation seeking and contact with primary others. The need for the other to be all-good becomes, "I am all-bad-inside; she is all-good and will save me." This is wounding via abandonment and lack of attention, where mother's reflection of being via being-in-relationship is lost both symbolically and in reality, and being-itself is unattainable. The intensity of waiting for an absent yet seductive other generates a loss of the infant's most basic relationship, and a state of anxiety permeates his sense of being. This yields a wounding at the level of being. The prenate or infant remains unrecognized by mother, his existence is denied, and panic arises as he is cast into the emptiness of non-being, and a transmarginally stressed state infused with the shock of abandonment.

In terms of endopsychic structure, central-self's good object is lost in projection, all goodness is likewise projected out, and goodness is desperately sought out-there. As the other who is sought is both aloof and seductively present, needy-self's longing is amplified, and its potentially fulfilling object is projected onto others via intense clinging and demands for attention and contact. Rejecting-self's rage is turned inward, and the infusive badness intensifies, manifesting as low self-esteem, guilt, and self-deprecation. The infant's relational world organizes around the statement: "Never again dare I wait for attention, to do so would cast me into overwhelming panic, abandonment and loneliness" (Lake, 1986, chart Ha).

Thus the hysteric's inner world is sensed to be unworthy, and the afflicted person seeks goodness in outer objects or people. He desperately may cling to these, while never reconciling the inner badness. He may continually seek approval, reassurance, and acceptance from others, and become histrionic when acceptance is not experienced. In this bleak relational milieu, the other is still desperately longed for and clung to. Neither the being nor wellbeing stages of the dynamic cycle are supported, and an overarching impoverishment is experienced. Being and wellbeing must now be sought out-there, as all inner goodness is lost.

Hysteric Reaction Patterns

Lake discusses various kinds of reaction patterns that may overlay the hysteric adaptation. If central-self's hysteric adaptation is successful, the sense of inner badness is repressed, as are the underlying separation anxiety and panic. Although repressed, these energies still may compel compulsive attention seeking based on the underlying assumption that others are unwilling to pay attention. The longing of needy-self permeates central-self, which then manifests a reaction pattern of extroversion, compulsive attention seeking, attachment, and clinging to the projected idealized other. A person with an hysteric way of being may always try to bask in the seeming approval of others. In relationships and groups, they may continually attempt to be the center of attention, either with histrionics, endless questions, or exaggerated emotional responses. The inner sense, however, is of badness and emptiness; and no matter how much recognition, acceptance, and approval are received, they are never enough to shift this inner self-view. It is a very sad position to be in. When recognition is there, it is not sensed, and, in the extreme, the self may be felt to be so bad or evil that self-hatred arises accompanied by self-destructive behaviors.

If attention seeking is successful, the person manifesting an hysteric adaptation may also generate a compliant reaction pattern, compulsively adapting to others' needs and positions and agreeing with them no matter what is said, happening, or felt. They become overly dependent on the approval and presence of others. To be disapproved of, to lose the presence of the other, is to be cast once again into panic and emptiness. If attention is not gained by compliance and manipulation, the tyranny of the demand remains, and the person may become histrionic and exhibitionistic in their attention seeking, descend in giving way to cries, sobs, screams, threats, and extreme clinging—anything to regain attention.

Lake describes the hysteric adaptation as prone to lying, both to self and others, in order to maintain contact and approval. If attention seeking or approval are blocked, then the inner sense of badness and rejection may erupt, along with projected rage and blame. Lake notes that the hysteric personality is "a devil when thwarted" (Lake, 1986, chart Ha).

If attention seeking is rejected and unsuccessful, other reaction patterns may evolve. The conversion reaction, in which the pervasive badness and its related emotional pain are redirected into the physical and attention is sought via the symptoms that result, is one such pattern. The symptoms commonly are coupled with body tensions and restrictions, or with their opposites, tissue collapse and loss of resiliency. The conversion reaction is a defense against the overwhelming experience of absence and relational inconsistency via displacement and containment. Sometimes the badness as negative umbilical affect is contained via restriction in the navel area; sometimes it is displaced into limbs, organs, joints, etc., manifesting as tension, pathology, numbing, and body areas cut off from awareness. Alternately, the sense of goodness may be projected onto the body surface, and the person may keep up a very presentable and fashionable appearance, looking young and maintaining a fresh and smooth complexion even into late middle age. Outside, all looks good and presentable; inside, the person is seething and enraged. In this reaction pattern, the badness is repressed, and the afflicted person orients to an outer image of goodness, which also helps attract others into contact and relationship.

Lake cites the phobic reaction of anxiety hysteria as another mode of management of both the inner badness and projected goodness. Here everything is projected out, and the badness out-there is avoided via excessive attachment to an outer other, coupled with intense separation anxiety and phobic clinging. The bad is avoided by contact with the projected good object. Separation is devastating, as the badness is then all-encompassing.

If all reaction patterns and repression fail, which may occur with intense rejection, traumatic events, or other life-changing experiences, then the person may be plunged into the schizoid state and transmarginal stress. The only way to escape the intensity of infusive badness is to disconnect and dissociate, as overwhelming emptiness and a total loss of being are experienced.

Healing

In the hysteric adaptation, there is a rent in the cohesion of being and self, an all-permeating badness, and low self-esteem. Here it is essential to help the client build both witness consciousness and a sense of inner resources, of inner okay-ness to balance the overarching sense of inner badness present in hysteric adaptations. This will take time. Healing entails taking back what has been projected and, with the support of a stable therapeutic relationship, sensing goodness as an inner resource. As central-self incorporates this goodness, the infusive badness can be held in the light of awareness in a present-time, empathic, responsive, and non-collusive relational field. In a relational field that is constant in its intention to attune and witness, the client, in resonance, over time begins to sense her own ability to be present and witness. Insight into self-other interactions arises, and she learns to differentiate between real, present-time relationship and projection. This, again, entails a mindfulness practice, attention, and inquiry: "Where does my longing arise from?" "Where does my need to reject arise from?" "While feeling all of this badness, what tells me I'm okay?" "What is this for me?" etc.

As being and presence deepen, the underlying rage of the hysteric can emerge in the safety of the therapeutic environment. Grieving occurs, too, not only for the loss of the other and their love, but for the loss of being-itself. In Lake's context, the hysteric must learn patience, with both her own unfolding process and with the attention of the other. Ideally, a separation process begins, engendering a sense of agency and autonomy, along with cohesiveness of being and the experience of inter-connection. Here, too, the journey is one of reclamation of being and reconnection to Source and other beings. In Fairbairn's terms, it is a passage to mature interconnection, to being able to sense others' needs as separate and valid, while strengthening one's own agency and inner cohesion.

Hystero-Schizoid Personality Adaptation (Borderline Adaptation)

Both Fairbairn and Lake noted that sometimes a person with an hysteric adaptation may shift to the paranoid projective state, or descend into schizoid dissociation with a concurrent loss of selfhood. Associated with this behavior Lake observed an inherently unstable personality system that he called the hystero-schizoid personality (Lake, 1979). Now called the borderline personality, it refers to a transmarginally stressed state resulting from overwhelming primary trauma. If abandonment or betrayal, coupled with severe separation anxiety, are experienced early on in the transition from being-in-relationship to being-in-itself, they are sensed as a severe denial of being, casting the infant into transmarginal stress. Due to the early nature of the onslaught, an unstable self-system results, the hystero-schizoid adaptation, in which the dynamic tension held within endopsychic structure intensifies, and the relationships between central-, rejecting-, and needy-selves polarize even further.

In this milieu, central-self cannot fully repress the negative affects of frustration, rage, and longing, nor establish stable transitional modes of relating. Affect and response become unstable, and the individual may suddenly shift from one self-constellation to another, first expressing the longing of needy-self, then the anger and frustration of rejecting self, and then the idealization of central-self. The schizoid position of emptiness and disconnection is constantly present. The person may feel extreme anxiety-depressive tensions, as the experiences of goodness and badness are strongly polarized, and he may strongly project either or both out onto relational others. Thus any of Fairbairn's self-constellations and modes of relating may become active at anytime. From one moment to the next, the afflicted person may shift perceptions of himself or others from all-bad to all-good, and cling or reject accordingly. This is a black-or-white world, in which the afflicted person may shift from the hysteric projection to the paranoid, and then from the paranoid mode to a schizoid withdrawal from intimate others. Phobic and obsessional states may also manifest to manage the intensely polarized energies at work in the unstable self-system.

The hystero-schizoid personality bears a deep and abiding terror of further abandonment, colored by an inner perception of overwhelming badness. The latter is commonly projected onto intimate others as suspicion and faultfinding, and these people never know when or how the projections may strike. Taking the form of sudden anger, frustration, faultfinding or denigration, they may lack any obvious cause, and so can be very crazy-making to those on the receiving end. The targets for these projections are constantly walking on eggshells. Borderline processes and projections are energetically powerful. The afflicted person may shift back and forth from the rejecting-self to the needy-self, and feel anger, rage, and frustration; and then longing, terror, and fear; or he may disconnect from all affects and enter a deeply dissociated state of aloneness, aloofness, emptiness, and the despair of non-being. All of these states will be clearly sensed by relational others, and very painful dynamics of love, hate, and disconnection result. The projected emptiness, terror, or rage may infuse the other person, who may in turn feel persecuted by the borderline individual.

For instance, the afflicted person may manifest an hysteric adaptation as attention seeking and project all-goodness on the other person, to whom he shows strong attachment and clings when accepted. But when the other carrying the projection of all-goodness lets the borderline person down and fails to meet his needs or expectations, or when the borderline person senses danger or becomes suspicious, a quick flip in mode of relating may occur. Suddenly the goodness is retained inside and the badness is projected out onto the same person who was just all-good. Now they become the root of all evil: not angel, but Satan. Thus the borderline flips from the hysteric adaptation to the strongly paranoid. Lake saw the borderline state as originating in a denial of being so early, so devastating, so totally overwhelming, that it leaves no chance for stable relational modes to develop. To his understanding even the prenate in his first trimester in utero is vulnerable to this wounding. A breach in the relational field at this early stage, sensed as abandonment and/or betrayal, may generate a strong tendency to perceive all intimate relationship through the filters of suspicion and betrayal.

In Buddhist terms, an early sankhārā or volitional tendency is generated that infuses the later formation of endopsychic structure. While in the womb, during birth, or soon after, intensely negative umbilical affect overwhelms the little one, the relational field is experienced as extremely dangerous and denying, and a deep wound at the level of being occurs. Mother's presence is experienced as overwhelmingly bad, unavailable physically, emotionally and/or spiritually, oppressive, and/or unable to support being or wellbeing needs. In this early experience of denial, abandonment, and betrayal, both the object *and* its love are lost. The little one descends into the transmarginally stressed state and is thrown into an abyss of emptiness and non-being. With this abyss at its root, an unstable personality system develops, and being's way of being manifests equally unstable and dramatic shifts in modes of relating.

Thus in the borderline, self-sense and affect regulation are unstable. An all-pervading emptiness and unbearable sense of affliction are ever-present, and relationships are volatile, as the other is always sensed through the projection of what is intolerable. It is a loss of heart at the deepest level. Relationships of any kind may intensify the feelings of emptiness and loss, and intimacy is experienced as unbearable. And still there may be a simultaneous and desperate effort to cling to the other in order to avoid yet another experience of abandonment or betrayal.

The borderline adaptation is a wounding at the level of being in which the being-to-being connection, which is a heart connection, has been torn asunder. It is a state of misery. One's heart is broken. Schizoid emptiness permeates everything, and a great fear of abandonment and betrayal colors all close relationships.

Healing

We are confronted in the borderline personality with a loss of coherency and selfhood that permeates all relationship. Central-self and its modes of relating are unstable, and any and all modes of being and relating may emerge at any moment. The healing process for the borderline has been debated and written about by many people in many contexts. The key to the healing process is the consistent presence of a therapist who can rest in a being-state in the midst of great disturbance and projected energies. The stability of the therapist is critical. The maintenance of a being-to-being field between therapist and client will gradually potentiate the resonance of the client's own being, along with appropriate responses to the unfolding process. Help in the development of moment-to-moment mindfulness and awareness of inner states is essential, as is persistent orientation to present reality. There will be an intense testing-out period during which all of the borderline's modes of relating may be engaged. They must be challenged and clarified by the therapist, while she maintains a receptive and stable relational field and her own contact with present-time reality.

The development of a sense of inner resources and okay-ness is also essential. Hopefully, over time, the client will learn to witness his own arising process, related states of intense affect, and behaviors as separate from and independent of outer others, slowly reclaiming his projections and gaining the ability to come into real, present-time relationship.

Gradually more inner space is accessed, and a stability of central-self, with some sense of developing inner resources, may begin to emerge. This is a truly demanding process for the therapist, who may be challenged to maintain a cohesive being-state and connection to her own reality at every moment of the exchange.

Obsessional Personality Adaptation

The obsessional adaptation occurs when Fairbairn's transitional Mode 1 becomes a fixed way of being. Both the goodness and badness are retained and intensify within, and there is no projective process. The obsessive adaptation intensifies the polarity of the depressive position as transmarginal stress is experienced. This is a wounding at the level of being in which badness is sensed to be everywhere and fended off by separation ritual and repetitive behavior; while goodness is protected by ritual and sustained by repetitive behavior. The badness is infusive, overwhelming, sensed to be both inside and outside, permeating everything. The only defense against it is constant vigilance and containment through control, manifesting as obsessional, ritualized, and/or repetitive processes like maintaining order and cleansing. These serve to split off the badness as an internal other who must be defended against. Rituals must be repeated constantly, as badness is everywhere, and only temporary relief is possible. The obsessive is caught in a paradox whereby the sense of badness accompanies the goodness of support and nurturance; that which supports is also perceived as inescapably bad.

Phobic Personality Adaptation

The phobic adaptation evolves when Fairbairn's transitional Mode 2 is reified. As a response to wounding at the level of being, both goodness and badness are sensed as overwhelming and projected out. The badness is projected out onto objects as a terror out-there, and may imbue those objects with symbolic meaning. Irrational terrors of snakes, spiders, or other animals are examples of this dynamic. Another form this projection occurs when the early stage of the birth process is sensed as suffocating and crushing. In this case, the constrictive badness experienced may give rise to claustrophobia in later life. The badness is projected out, and tight spaces recapitulate the claustrophobia and perceived threat of annihilation.

Lake notes that early prenatal life, especially before implantation, may be experienced as 'great space.' If this space is infused with a sense of badness or toxicity, whether environmental or emotional, then space itself may be perceived as toxic or terrifying, as in agoraphobia (Lake, 1979). The experience may be amplified in the birth process if the baby is born into the great space of a hospital environment that is unwelcoming, devoid of contact, empty, or even menacing. In phobic projection, the whole world becomes a source of fear.

The good is also projected out, and refuge is taken in those objects that symbolically represent safety. To escape from the projected badness, the person may cling to others to protect him from the badness out-there, or gravitate towards religious fanaticism or cult behavior.

17

Wounding at the Level of Wellbeing, Status, and Achievement

Here we will explore wounds that occur at Lake's second input stage, that of wellbeing, and touch on the repercussions of wounding at the output stages of status and achievement.

Wounding at the Level of Wellbeing

In wounding at the level of wellbeing, the affected person's developing self-system orients to and organizes around the experience of deprivation. In the prenate or infant's experience, being may be supported in a good enough fashion, but deprivation of nurturance still takes place. The little one may encounter negative umbilical inflow or feel fear or distress, and engage in defensive adaptations to protect from these negative sensations. In Lake's paradigm the experience of deprivation gives rise to various coping and oppositional adaptations, making a lack of abundance a constant companion in all activity. Common life statements that relate to this lack of wellbeing are: "No matter how hard I try, I never get what I need"; "Life is a struggle"; "The world owes me a living"; "There is never enough"; "People are out to get me"; etc. Wounding at the level of wellbeing may give rise to feelings of jealousy, covetousness, and envy. The person may frequently experience humiliation and shame that contribute to a well of repressed rage and hatred projected onto an unsupportive world.

Central-self becomes organized around deprivation, and the rejecting or needy-selves may emerge very quickly. Needy-self may manifest in desperate longing for needs fulfillment and intimacy. The person may be overly needy and clinging when in intimate relationship; yet may feel that nothing can fulfill their needs. No matter how much is on offer, he experiences only neediness and lack. He may then shift to the rejecting self-constellation and push the needed person away. A vicious cycle of neediness and rejection is activated and patterns of insecure attachment develop, as the person alternates between clinging and pushing away, or avoids intimacy altogether. As a lack of abundance is constantly sensed, the afflicted person will not be able to actualize their needs in the achievement phase of the dynamic cycle. According to Lake's framework, the following adaptations occur when coherency of being is established, but not supported, sustained, or nourished: the paranoid, depressive, psychosomatic, and hypochondriacal adaptations. These adaptations are based upon transitional modes of relating underpinned by endopsychic structure.

Paranoid Personality Adaptation

In transitional Mode 3, goodness is retained, while badness is projected out. If this becomes an entrenched way of being, then the paranoid adaptation emerges. Lake defined the paranoid adaptation as a defense against badness via denial and projection. In the wounding associated with this adaptation, being has been supported, but wellbeing has been severely compromised by the experience of insufficiency and lack of nurturance. A strong paranoid reaction pattern results. Central-self maintains an all-good position and an idealized positive selfhood, while badness is denied and projected out. "It's not mine. I am good. The other is bad." This outlook defends its holder from underlying low self-esteem.

As the badness is projected out, the world, intimates, and others all may be sensed as antagonistic and betraying. The person feels himself in a hostile world, and no matter where he looks, badness is lurking.

Lake draws on the work of Klein in describing the paranoid strategy as a response to the good breast-bad breast dichotomy. In this adaptation, being-itself has been secured and there is a sense of continuity of being; but the physical, emotional, and/or spiritual support of being is insufficient or unjustly withheld. For the baby, feeding time becomes frustration time. The good breast is transformed into the withholding bad breast. The denial of the coveted breast gives rise to feelings of rejection. Closeness with mother then provokes painful longing and frustration, as it does not satisfy the craving for nurturance. This dynamic may manifest via umbilical inflow as well as the breast, and so can begin in utero as well as in infancy.

As this is still the early developmental stage of primary identification, the prenate or infant identifies with the lack of abundance experienced. Although being is secure, the badness experienced is sensed as a lack of wellbeing. The infant, or later the adult, humiliated that his rights have been denied, feels undervalued and betrayed. A sense of worthlessness, low self-esteem, and insufficiency, along with resentment and frustration, dominate relational experience. Being becomes "weak being" (Lake, 1986).

When intimacy is on offer to the paranoid personality, it cannot be trusted, and the intimate others may seem deceptive, betraying, or hostile, as he perceives projected badness rather than present reality. The angry, frustrated, rejecting-self is the modus operandi, and negative projections become the currency of relationship. A dichotomy arises between projected badness and the sense of goodness, as the badness is rejected, opposed, and projected, while the inner sense of goodness is split off and placed in opposition to "that which is bad." "I am good. They are betraying and menacing, and I must oppose them" is the paranoic's general outlook.

This is a very strong oppositional adaptation. In holding the all-good position, the afflicted person cannot admit mistakes or hear criticism; while rejecting-self projects a persecutory anger and frustration. The individual lives with a mightier-than-thou air, and is determined to assert his rights. In the process, he may detract from the achievements of others, suspect their motivations, and belittle them in order to maintain a superior position. Where needy-self longs, rejecting-self denies. The person with a paranoid adaptation may project strong envy and jealousy onto those who seem successful in getting their needs met, or who are in competition for the same good object. This is truly an adaptation of survival.

When under extreme stress, like the loss of a relationship or job, illness, etc., the paranoid's usual adaptive means may fail him, sending him into a depressive state in which he experiences an acute loss of wellbeing. A collapse into the transmarginal state, with concurrent feelings of low self-esteem, emptiness, and loss of meaning, is also possible. The negativity held within rejecting-self that was projected out to facilitate repression may come out of repression and turn inward. The lack of wellbeing, along with feelings of worthlessness, hatred, and abject despondency, overwhelm the present moment, and a dangerous state of suicidal depression may be experienced.

Healing

With the paranoid adaptation, the issue is not loss of being, but of wellbeing. The healing journey is one of reclaiming sustenance and the ability to be nurtured. It is critical to help the person build resources, test the relational field, sense true relational goodness, and develop mindfulness of inner states, feeling tones, and thoughts as they arise in clinical sessions. Over time, the client learns to trust the relational field with the therapist and develop his own presence and witness consciousness. The projection of badness is slowly retracted and, in the light of the client's awareness, gradually transformed. This is a process that commonly entails the surfacing of guilt and shame, along with a deep anger, all of which must be held within a the relationship of growing trust with the therapist. One client of mine compared her shift out of the paranoid adaptation to coming out from oppressive and murky gases and being able to breath fresh air again. The challenge is to learn to discern when nurturance is truly on offer and then to trust it. Central-self then has the opportunity to orient to a growing sense of wellbeing, as relational goodness is felt once again. Then doors open, but, as always, it is the client who must walk through them.

Depression (Depression without Anxiety)

Lake noted that depressive patterns can arise without any associated anxiety. This then is a true depressive state, sometimes classified as endogenous depression, manifesting as stasis, low energy or chronic fatigue, and low motivation. Here again, the sense of being has been supported, but has not been sustained or nurtured, and the wellbeing stage has been undercut. This lack of sustenance is experienced as shocking and as everywhere at once. The prenate or infant's body is infused with a sense of pervasive badness. Opposition is of no use, and the only escape is to contain the badness by contraction, numbing, and freezing. To survive is to close down. It is a passive mode of protection whose statement might be, "No matter how little I get, or how bad things are, I will not feel anything." The organism collapses into a state of parasympathetic immobilization with dissociative tendencies. Side-effects may include difficulties in learning and attention deficit states.

Depressive Reaction Patterns

Lake notes that a wellspring of repressed resentment, hatred, and envy underlies the depressive adaptation. The intensity of the badness experienced, and both the rejecting- and needy-selves and their related affects, are deeply repressed by numbing, but may, under extreme circumstances, break through in exhausting outbursts of hatred or jealousy. A paranoid reaction pattern may overlay the depressive pattern, as the badness is projected out onto others or current circumstances. "They are to blame for my state. My circumstances keep me down. I can't do anything about it," is a typical statement. More often, the person lacks the energy to blame anyone, including himself. This state of hypo-arousal is markedly different from the hyper-aroused state of the anxiety depressive.

Healing

In clinical practice, the first step toward healing for the depressive is the shift from a shocked and frozen condition to a more mobilized and energetic one. This can be a slow process of building inner resource as the therapist slowly helps the client to mobilize his autonomic nervous system. Acknowledgment and appropriate discharge of the underlying energies of disappointment, fear, and anger are critical as more energy becomes available. The challenge then is to shift perception from lack of abundance to a present-time appreciation of support and nurturance in both the therapeutic relationship and everyday life. A slow process of reclamation of energy and agency in a stable and appropriately responsive relational field then can unfold.

Psychosomatic Personality Adaptation

As Lake defined it, the psychosomatic adaptation is based on displacement of umbilical affect. In this process, a cohesive sense of being is present, yet relational sustenance is not maintained or is inconsistent. A lack of abundance is sensed and may be experienced as persecutory. The incoming sense of goodness (in terms of mother's presence) and badness (in terms of mother's denial of nurturance) become linked with a deep sense of insufficiency. The infusion of negative umbilical inflow evokes opposition, and both goodness and badness are displaced into particular areas of the body. An inner conflict between good and bad is played out in the body and its tissues, manifesting as pain and physical illness, hypertension, neurological disorders, and/or symptoms. Lake states that this adaptation may be a ground for anorexia nervosa, a rejection of both the badness and the sustenance of the goodness as the badness is starved. Reclaiming both the goodness and the badness reduces stress and opens the way for resolution of the conflict.

Hypochondriacal Personality Adaptation

The hypochondriacal adaptation is generated when the prenate or infant experiences very little nurturance or sustenance. Umbilical inflow is sensed by the little one to be meager and incapable of meeting his needs, or to be dangerous and, as in the psychosomatic adaptation described above, possibly persecutory. The scant nurturance may be due to toxicity, umbilical blockage of some sort, the mother's poor nutrition, or an unavailable or disconnected relational field, etc. The negative inflow is displaced into body parts, and the sense of being persecuted by the forces of badness is associated with illness, low sustenance, and pain. Any sense of goodness is limited, there is a prevailing fear of illness and loss, and the body is experienced as weak and vulnerable. Constant vigilance is maintained, as every sensation may be an expression of this badness and so need attention. Goodness is projected out, and needy-self constantly seeks helpers and those who are potentially fulfilling and nurturing. The expression of the badness and the dangerous states perceived to be within then become means to establish and maintain relationship with potentially-fulfilling others.

This is a very painful situation for all involved. When help is not on offer, the underlying resentment held in rejecting-self may manifest as anger and frustration, and a paranoid, holier-than-thou projection may surface. Here again, the building of inner resources is critical, along with the mobilization of the body energies. A safe holding environment in which health, rather than lack, is affirmed is the essential ground for the therapeutic process.

Wounding at the Level of Status and Achievement

According to Lake, wounding during the output phases occurs when the individual's status is challenged or denied, their motivations questioned, or their self-processes thwarted. Or in the achievement phase, they may find their attempts to actualize their intentions in the world are obstructed in some way. Lake sees these as stumbling blocks that potentially may affect the person and his or her sense of being and wellbeing. However, if a cohesive sense of being and wellbeing is already present, they can buffer the person against the negative effects of challenges or stressors arising in the output phases. But if basic wounding at the level of being or wellbeing underlies the person's personality system, then challenges or stressors in the output phases may reinforce this prior wounding.

The dynamic cycle functions throughout life. Being and wellbeing can be affected at any time by overwhelming circumstances. However, if the person has already established a ground of being and wellbeing and appropriate coping behaviors, then adversities can be met with the resources of the individual's self-system. When Source, being, and self are aligned, and the individual has a coherent sense of being and wellbeing, then she can access a natural resiliency and flexibility in response to the conditions in her world.

Summary

The seemingly complex forms of personality adaptation and interpersonal exchange have fairly straightforward roots. The healing journey, whether in the context of a psychotherapy or everyday life, leads us to increasing awareness of what has shaped us and our sense of selfhood, and to increasing freedom in the present moment of being. In the context of Core Process Psychotherapy, this journey is undertaken as a joint practice between therapist and client of holding arising process in the light of present awareness. In the end, there is nothing we can do to make ourselves freer. Freedom is inherent in each of us. What we can do is to learn to let go of what obscures our freedom and luminosity. That is a journey that will take us to the depths of our suffering and to the heights of joy of being.

18

Bonding and Attachment

The infant naturally seeks contact and relationship, not only to get his basic needs met, but also to know his own nature and that of the world he finds himself in. His early relationship with mother is thus primary, and the schemas-of-being that he evolves under impact of this and other primary relationships underlie all bonding and attachment processes (Stern, 1985, 1994). In the infant-mother dyad each participates in the reflection of being and Source and in meeting being and wellbeing needs. This mutual interchange leads to what is commonly called bonding and most clearly described in the work of John Bowlby.

Bowlby and the Origins of Attachment Concepts

Bowlby was a British psychoanalyst and the founder of attachment theory whose work evolved in reaction to what he saw as the over-theorizing of the analytical community, particularly Freud and Klein. Bowlby believed analysis should be based on what is directly observable. He did, however, draw on the work of other analysts of his time, especially Winnicott and Fairbairn. Fairbairn's observations on separation anxiety became a key aspect of Bowlby's attachment theory. It could be said that Bowlby, in his reaction to the analytical environment of his day, lost the essence of the inner world of the infant, the true foundation of all attachment schemas. His ideas did, however, open the door to research on the infant-primary caregiver relationship. The psychoanalytic community did not take them up, however; it was the psychologists who eventually explored Bowlby's theories further.

Attachment theory is a paradigm that attempts to describe the origins of relational ease and suffering. Attachment theory emerged from Bowlby's observations of maternal deprivation and loss and of the infant-mother dyad. It relates to the nature of the primary caregiver's attunement and response to the states and needs of the infant or child, and to the infant's or child's responses to his primary caregiver, to proximity and safety issues, and to the general nature of his relational environment. An attachment is an affectional bond that forms between the infant and his mother and other primary caregivers. Attachment connects mother and child in space and over time. It is a distinct motivational system that based on the human need for security and intimacy (Holmes, 1993).

Now a prominent paradigm among psychologists, analysts, and therapists, attachment concepts are sometimes misapplied to trace the origins of the human condition and of selfhood. Attachment is not the origin of selfhood, but is an important effect of relational interchanges and how prenates and infants inwardly process those interchanges. Attachment processes are outer expressions of the inner world of the infant and his developing self-system. In its various forms, it is a clearly observable outcome in all the adaptation strategies previously discussed. In the following exploration, we will attempt to relate Bowlby's attachment theory to those different adaptations and to the works of Fairbairn, Winnicott, and Lake.

A Spatial Theory

Attachment theory is both a relational and a spatial theory. It concerns the nature of the relational environment and the response that the infant or young child receives from his primary caregivers. The infant seeks proximity to, and security and nurturing from, his primary caregivers.

In Fairbairn's terms, this is the outer expression of the child's innate relation seeking needs. In Bowlby's terms, infants and children mediate their sense of wellbeing via proximity to their attachment figure. When a primary caregiver is too far away or too distant, anxiety arises and protest commonly results. Attachment behavior also applies in adult life. Holmes writes, "Attachment theory is in essence a *spatial* theory: when I am close to my loved one I feel good, when I am far away I am anxious, sad or lonely" (Holmes, 1993).

In attachment theory, primary caregivers ideally generate a *secure base,* or safe holding environment, for the infant, and the relational environment is hopefully perceived as safe and responsive to the little one's needs. A mutual attachment relationship forms between infant and caregiver. Attachment relationships are defined by the presence of the following three basic characteristics: (1) proximity seeking to the preferred person or people; 2) a secure base effect; and 3) separation protest.

For the infant and young child, proximity seeking is an expression of interbeing and relation-seeking needs. In Bowlby's theory, the infant or young child naturally will seek proximity to attachment figures in order to maintain a sense of security and safety. For Lake, proximity seeking is an expression of the deepest needs of being for recognition, acknowledgment, acceptance, and love. For Winnicott, it allows the little one to maintain contact with the safe holding field, a field of presence that protects him from impingements and allows him to rest in simple being and safely explore his world. In our terms, proximity seeking has very deep roots in the psyche of human beings and is an innate expression of mutuality and interbeing. When the attachment figure is too distant or remote, the infant or young child will respond by protesting in some way. This is called *separation protest.* Anxiety states, called *separation anxiety,* can arise if the proximity need is not met. Lake, Winnicott, Fairbairn, and other theorists as well all stressed the potential that separation anxiety has to generate insecurity and wounding.

In Fairbairn's terms, separation at the early stage of dependency when the little one is still in primary identification with his caregivers can generate strong separation anxiety. According to Winnicott, separation from the primary attachment figure, usually mother, is also separation from the holding environment and all possibility of safety and containment, from the buffering of impingements, from love being met, received and accepted, and from basic needs being fulfilled. Most importantly, the little one, as separation anxiety intensifies, is taken out of simply being into defensive and protective processes.

Lake associated extreme separation anxiety with a wounding at the level of being through which being's basic needs for contact, acknowledgment, and unconditional acceptance are overridden or denied. Lake maintained that the little one only knows its own being as being-in-relationship, and separation from the primary other is separation from my-very-being. This separation, he stated, causes the strongest separation anxiety, at its most extreme when it arises during the transition from being-in-relationship, when the infant is still emotionally identified with mother, and being-in-itself, when he attains an internal sense of continuity and cohesiveness of being.

Proximity seeking, separation protest, and separation anxiety are powerful processes and expressions of our most basic relation seeking needs. Even if an attachment figure is indifferent or abusive, the child or adult may continually seek his or her contact. In Fairbairn's terms, central-self maintains the relation seeking imperative in an idealized fashion, keeping the other as all-good.

Internal Working Model

Bowlby saw personality formation as based on an *internal working model* of the relational world that is generated by repeated patterns of interactive experience (Holmes, 1993). Attachment patterns are stored as working models of relationship and life. Similarly, Stern defined internal representations of relational experience as schemas-of-being-with and helped clarify Bowlby's concept of the internal working model by more clearly defining the infant's and child's inner developmental landscape.

In Bowlby's model, the child builds an internal model of his relational world based on the nature of his interactions with primary caregivers and the environment he finds himself in. Assumptions about the world and behavioral responses and norms all arise from this interplay. The working model contains his basic assumptions about life. It is an internalized representation of relationship and experience that includes his defensive processes, unresolved trauma, neurobiology, psycho-emotional processes, and behavioral tendencies. These, in turn, affect his self-constructs and coping behaviors. Value, self-sense, and self-worth all arise from this ground.

While *attachment* refers to the nature of one's attachments, *attachment behavior* refers to what one does to maintain proximity to one's attachment figure. In adult life, attachment behavior may include all of the personality and coping strategies that relate to the maintenance of an intimate relationship. An *attachment system* is the internal working model of intimacy that generates an individual's attachment patterns. It is an internalized relational blueprint or model of the world, very stable even in its disorganized forms, that is used to predict the outcomes of new relational interchanges. As Fairbairn pointed out, the self is a closed self-referring and self-perpetuating system prone to resisting change, and attachment processes are part of this wider system. It is an aspect of self's predictive and responsive functions where the internal working model of the world is used to predict the outcomes of new relational interchange and is very stable, even in its disorganized forms. It is this closed system of self and self-process that is observed and oriented to in therapeutic process.

The Strange Situation
and Attachment Categories

The Strange Situation is an experimental method developed by Ainsworth in the 1970s to study the ways young children cope with brief separations from their caregivers. In this study, a child was left alone while his mother or caregiver left the room. The child's response to the brief separation and reunion with mother was observed and classified. Four major patterns of attachment response and behavior were observed. These are *secure attachment* and *insecure attachment,* which in turn are divided into two or three discreet insecure categories. Ainsworth came up with two insecure attachment categories, ambivalent and avoidant; while Main later added a third, disorganized. These categories fit very well with Lake's transmarginal stress hierarchy, and we will use Lake's work, along with that of Fairbairn and Winnicott, to comment on these attachment categories (Ainsworth, 1978; Main, 1986, 1990).

Secure Attachment

Secure attachment is an expression of a developing self-system that has experienced a good enough holding field and developed adequate coping processes and a coherent sense of being at its hub. Mother and primary caregivers are experienced as secure bases from which to explore the world. Over time, this secure base is internalized as part of the developing internal working model of the world.

In the Strange Situation, children are usually distressed by the brief separation from their caregivers. They may protest and on reunion actively greet their caregiver, allowing themselves to be comforted before going back to their play or activity.

Secure attachment is formed during Lake's ideal and coping phases. The infant or child learns to cope with separation processes in a safe holding environment, while various coping strategies and personality tendencies develop that help mediate the relational experience. The child has experienced good enough caregiving and a sensitive and responsive relational field, senses a safe holding environment as a secure base, and knows that generally its needs will be met.

Winnicott describes the good enough holding environment as maintained within the ambiance of mother's reflective mirroring. The child is largely protected from relational impingements, basic trust is maintained, there is good enough attunement and sensitivity to the child's needs and inner states, the developing self-system does not have to generate defenses too early, and a secure attachment system results.

In Fairbairn's paradigm, secure attachment is based on a relational field that is not intensely ambiguous. Primary caregivers maintain an empathic environment, and a preponderance of goodness is sensed in relational exchanges. As dynamic endopsychic structure forms, central-self maintains relationship from this core of goodness, and the energies of rejecting- and needy-selves are less intense and do not interfere with relation seeking. An inner sense of security develops at the core of the individual's being, and a secure attachment system results.

Research has shown that in moment-to-moment relational exchange, both infant and the attuned mother are in feeling-resonance, a right brain function. In this field of attunement, the infant senses the feeling states of mother and other primary persons and internally processes this relational exchange as feeling tone and emotion. If mother is mirroring the infant's inner state from her own being-state and appropriately responding to the infant's needs and feelings, the infant learns to regulate his own feelings in relation to mother and others. As the brain develops in the milieu of feeling and affect regulation, attunement, resonance, and responsiveness, internal self-other schemas are generated that reflect the experience, and a secure attachment system results (Stern, 1985; Schore, 2001a, 2001b).

Insecure Attachment

In insecure attachment processes, the relational field is not maintained in a good enough fashion, the infant is not protected from relational impingements, and, as basic trust is lost, the self-system has to generate defensive forms too early. The energies of rejecting- and needy-selves infuse relation seeking. There are three categories of insecure attachment:

Insecure-Ambivalent

In the Strange Situation, the child is highly distressed by the separation and not easily comforted upon reunion. The child may seek contact, but will then resist by kicking, hitting, or turning away. He may continue to alternate between clinging and anger, and his play is inhibited.

In Fairbairn's terms, this is a response to a strongly ambiguous and ambivalent relational field and an intensification of the depressive position. Here the push-pull between rejecting- and needy-selves is predominant, and the child is caught between the need and longing for contact, and the need to push away and defend. Intimacy is experienced as both needed and dangerous, and the child is torn in the dynamic tension between loving and hating. In Lake's terms, this is a highly oppositional adaptation based on ambivalence and tied to the sympathetic fight-or-flight response.

Insecure-Avoidant

In the strange situation, the child shows few overt signs of distress when the caregiver leaves the room and ignores the caregiver on reunion. The child remains watchful or vigilant in relation to the caregiver and is inhibited in his activities.

In Fairbairn's terms, this pattern is an expression of rejecting-self's need to withdraw from contact and further wounding. It, too, is a highly activated state in which intimacy is experienced as suspect and danger-ous and avoided at all costs. In Lake's terms, it is an oppositional strategy tied to the flight response of the sympathetic nervous system in which withdrawal is the main mode of relating, while maintaining a state of active alert.

Insecure-Disorganized

In the Strange Situation, the child exhibits a range of behaviors that include rage, withdrawal, terror, freezing, immobilization, and dissocia-tion. This is a pattern of overwhelm in which the child abides in reac-tion, disorientation, and disconnection. There is no coherent pattern of relating or coping in the Strange Situation; and in intimate relationship, the child may quickly shift from rage, to clinging, to withdrawal, in a seemingly disorganized pattern. In Lake's terms, this is a transmargin-ally stressed and shocked state in which basic trust has been severely damaged and there is no sense of security, resulting in the child's experi-ence of emptiness, non-being, and disconnection at his core.

In Fairbairn's terms, central-self has internalized very little sense of goodness. The energies of endopsychic structure are intensified, and the child is pushed and pulled between schizoid disconnection and the neg-ative affects and wounded needs held in rejecting- and needy-selves.

Insecure attachment falls within the oppositional and transmarginal phases of Lake's hierarchy. In both the avoidant and ambivalent pat-terns, the contact and intimacy that are desired are also experienced as threatening. The stress response is attenuated, as the child is placed in a double bind. He does not experience a secure base or safe hold-ing environment and tends to perceive contact and intimacy through the oppositional phase of the hierarchy. In ambivalent behavior, the sympathetic fight response takes over, while in avoidant behavior, the flight response predominates. In disorganized insecure attach-ment, the child lives his life in an overwhelmed and shocked trans-marginal state. Intimacy is experienced as dangerous, shocking, and overwhelming. No coherent strategy of attachment or relationship can be engaged.

Any transitional mode of relating may be coupled with any attachment process and its related schema-of-being-with. For example, a Mode 3 paranoid technique of relating, in which an inner sense of goodness and self-righteousness is maintained while all internalized badness is projected out, may become a prominent mode of relating in ambivalent or avoidant attachment systems. As the person comes into intimate relationship, an inner sense of being in the right is experienced, while relational others are perceived as dangerous or continually in the wrong. Different attachment systems may develop in different kinds of relationships, as will different transitional modes of relating, one emerging with the schema-of-being-with mother, another with that of being-with father, another with grandparents, and another with other girls or boys, etc. These observed behaviors have important repercussions in the understanding of personality formation, behavior, and coping mechanisms.

Attunement and Attachment

Different patterns of attachment arise from different patterns of interaction, rather than from drives, temperaments, or instinct. Children may have different attachment patterns with each parent or caregiver. The quality of the interactions is more important than quantity. Stern states that the most important aspect is maternal attunement to the infant and his needs (Stern, 1984, 1998). The attuned mother moderates the infant's level of activity. If the infant is listless or bored, she will stimulate him; if he's overactive, she will quiet things down. She will also follow and reflect the infant's state via sound, movement, and play.

Brazelton and Cramer discuss four components of a secure mother-infant relationship that reflect Stern's concept of attunement. These are synchrony, symmetry, contingency, and entrainment:

Synchrony: Attunement to the timing of the infant's state and needs.

Symmetry: The mother mirrors and matches the actions of the infant.

Contingency: There is a mutual cueing between mother and child whereby each gives signs to the other as to states, needs, and current feelings. It is a conversation in which both are completely involved.

Entrainment: The mother's and child's respective states resonate with and reflect each other. It is as though each captures the state and responses of the other and reflects them back through his/her own state and responses.

The less attuned and synchronous the holding field, the more likely that insecure attachment processes will develop. Mothers of ambivalently attached children, although not rejecting, tend to ignore or override their baby's signals for attention and are generally inconsistent and unpredictable in their responses. Mothers of avoidant children tend to interact less, are rejecting, and seem to act in a merely functional way. They are not available for contact or connection, are unresponsive to basic needs, and may seem cold or uncaring. In disorganized attachment processes, mother or other primary caregivers are sensed to be dangerous, frightening, or frightened. There is no sense of security, and danger is sensed in every interaction—a truly tragic relational environment.

Some Clinical Considerations

In the framework of Core Process Psychotherapy, a secure base or safe holding environment is critical to allow for mutual exploration of a client's process. The establishment of a safe holding environment is in itself a therapeutic landmark, a necessary step in forming any therapeutic alliance. The holding of a nonjudgmental and empathic field of listening is key, as is the establishment of a clear, still, and receptive perceptual field. The therapist's goal is to attune to the process of the client, thus simulating the behavior of a primary caregiver who is attuned and responsive to the infant's needs. In this context, the client is free to tell her story and explore her process.

In this format, there is also the potential for the resolution of the organizing factors of self (sankhārās) and psycho-emotional processes; the exploration of internal working models, basic assumptions, and life statements; and the reevaluation of personality constructs. Defensive forms of selfhood and wounded attachment processes all will emerge in the therapy space.

Avoidant attachment clients may be remote and defensive. They may associate intimacy with pain and be constantly on the lookout for signs of the therapist's rejection or disapproval. They may test the relationship by avoiding anything, including the sharing of their inner states and history, that may draw them closer to the therapist as a relational other. A consistent relational environment that manifests real warmth and concern is essential to these clients, and the mobilization of frozen autonomic energies also can be of real benefit.

The ambivalent client may be resistant, prone to projection, and suspicious. He may not trust the therapeutic situation, manifesting a push-pull between accepting the secure base that therapy offers and being suspicious of the therapist. He will need absolute reliability, firm boundaries, and a gentle reorientation to the exploration of his own process. Again, the down-regulation and resolution of the fight-or-flight response is essential as part of the healing process.

The disorganized-dissociative attachment clients will be very fearful of intimacy and easily overwhelmed by arising processes. They will need slowly to build resources and trust. Building resources and self-skills is the important first step in processing their cycling autonomic energies and disorganized behavior.

The importance of the autonomic nervous system and its stress response in personality adaptations was emphasized by Lake and is clearly a factor in insecure attachments processes. An overview of this territory is undertaken in our next chapter.

19

The Autonomic Nervous System

L ake was one of the first theorists to stress the importance of the autonomic nervous system in personality formation and defensive processes. His transmarginal stress hierarchy is essentially a hierarchy of autonomic nervous system responses to stressful conditions. In the following sections, we will discuss the nature of the stress response and how it manifests in the transmarginal stress hierarchy. Knowledge of this territory is essential in any clinical setting, as expressions of trauma and shock in a client's system must be oriented to in particular ways to avoid a re-traumatizing experience. We will also discuss a paradigm of the autonomic nervous system developed by Steven Porges that resonates with and complements Lake's concepts.

Introduction

The sophisticated physiological processes that are employed in personal survival and species protection are rooted in ancient systems evolved over long periods of time. These have been so successful that we humans have come to dominate the planet and ironically now threaten our own survival through overpopulation, uncontrolled pollution, global warming, and weapons of mass destruction. It seems that humans as a species have had a hard time working cooperatively rather than competitively to meet survival needs. This may be partly due to the physiological mechanisms that mobilize us for action and survival. Flight-or-fight survival processes tend to be oppositional and confrontational in nature, and these processes are part and parcel of defensive personality systems and processes.

Stress

Stress is an integral part of our human experience. Indeed, we commonly live our lives at a pace that is stressful in itself. Almost any aspect of life can be experienced as stressful. Going to work on the underground or subway, walking down the street, driving a car, meeting new people, or forming new relationships all may be experienced as stressful. In this book I am particularly focusing on prenatal, perinatal, and early childhood stresses and their repercussions on personality formation. These may be compounded by later interpersonal encounters of almost any kind. Indeed, responses to any subsequent overwhelming experience, whether an accident, abuse, violence, crime, loss of a loved one, loss of work or home, or other shock, will be added to the fabric of selfhood. Prenates and infants are more easily overwhelmed by adverse experiences than older children or adults and will enter protective dissociative states more easily (Perry & Pollard, 1998). In Lake's terms, they are more liable to be overwhelmed by intense experience and enter transmarginally stressed states and dissociative responses.

The Stress Response

Our internal world must adapt in some way to the stressors encountered. This adaptation is called the *stress response*. The stress response is largely mediated by the neuro-endocrine-immune system, whose parts and functions are completely interdependent. This system runs constantly in the background of a life to insure its survival. It orients us to the external physical and interpersonal environment and monitors internal responses and processes. It helps the baby orient to mother and primary caregivers, vocalize and express his needs and get them met. It helps us discern and respond to danger, find food and mates, repair internal damage, and perform a host of other related functions. This system can be considered the command headquarters for all homeostatic and survival processes.

The stress response is mediated by certain nuclei (groups of neurons) in the central nervous system and related hormones and other neuro-active chemicals. There are many nuclei and brain areas involved in the stress response, all of which mobilize us to meet danger, stress, or challenge. This shifting into action is commonly called the *general adaptation response*. The system physiologically gears up to meet stress with instantaneous surges of neuro-active molecules that trigger responses throughout the body. Muscles, circulation, respiration, digestion, and other systems all respond in a symphony of complex interactions to protect and sustain life.

The initial response to stress involves two interrelated aspects: First is the activation of the sympathetic nervous system, the system that mediates arousal, vigilance, and action, along with increases in certain hormones, especially norepinephrine (noradrenaline) and epinephrine (adrenaline). Vegetative activities such as digestion are down-regulated, while the cardiovascular system, muscles, and limbs are geared for action. Secondly, a concurrent up-regulation of what is called the H-P-A axis (hypothalamus-pituitary-adrenal axis) occurs, yielding a surge of the hormone called cortisol. This mobilizes energies and helps maintain the adaptive response over time. Once the stressor is removed or successfully dealt with, the body physiology ideally then shifts back to a baseline state of homeostatic balance.

If the stress is repetitive, chronic, or prolonged, or if the traumatic incident overwhelms the system and cannot be processed at the time, then the body physiology may not be able to shift back to homeostatic balance. This can result in inappropriate expressions of the stress response, even though no new stressors are present. The ability of the system to maintain a fluid homeostatic balance is then compromised, and the system may become fixated in this state. The stress nuclei involved may then become hyper-sensitized to new input, and the ability to self-regulate in the normal way is lost.

As Lake pointed out, early stress and overwhelm have vast repercussions in personality formation. These responses become part of the developing personality system and its self-constellations and are the underlying energies of Lake's coping, oppositional, and transmarginal states. In later life, under stress, oppositional or transmarginal personality processes may more easily engage due to the nervous system's early sensitization to stressful relational input. Indeed, the person may live his life via these states. For instance, in the paranoid personality strategy there is a sensitization to relational input resulting from the loss of basic trust and wellbeing. Intimacy or interpersonal processes of any kind are almost automatically sensed to be dangerous and potentially bad, and the fight-or-flight response may more easily and inappropriately manifest in suspicion, anger, or withdrawal.

Inappropriate stress responses, including those arising from oppositional and transmarginal personality states, are commonly called *maladaptive responses*. These can be very disturbing, debilitating, and crazy-making to the person manifesting them, as well as to the people around him. Chronic maladaptive states can lead to both physiological and psychological dysfunctions, including immune deficiencies, auto-immune states, anxiety states, depression, dissociative states, sleeping and eating disorders, somatic dysfunctions of all descriptions, chronic pain syndromes, and psycho-emotional breakdown. They can have vast repercussions in the mind-body (Ogden, 2006). This is the territory of Lake's oppositional processes and personality strategies in which the system is highly sensitized to relational contact, and the fight-or-flight response is more easily engaged. The whole defensive personality adaptation may be driven by these energies, as the intention to protect inappropriately surges in relational interchange (Lake, 1986, chart Gd).

The Fight-or-Flight Response

The foundation of the stress response is the fight-or-flight response. This term was coined by Hans Selye in the 1930s to describe a most basic mammalian self-protective response to stress, danger, and other overwhelming situations. Fight-or-flight responses may even engage during prenatal and birth processes and can leave unresolved neurological cycling and stress-related processes in the infant's system that may manifest in oppositional and transmarginal personality adaptations.

The fight-or-flight response is mediated by the autonomic nervous system, which is comprised of two functions meant to balance each other. These are the sympathetic and parasympathetic systems. The sympathetic nervous system relates to arousal states, vigilance, the musculoskeletal system, and action; while the parasympathetic system relates to vegetative functions like digestion, elimination. rest, and repose, and orients us to meditative and contemplative states. These two systems function in homeostatic balance, unless maladaptive states are present due to unresolved trauma or other overwhelming experience.

There are four basic stages to the fight-or-flight response: the *ideal state, active alert, fight-or-flight,* and *overwhelm-shock.*

The ideal state is a fully resourced, relaxed, and present-time state. It is primarily a parasympathetic state in which the mind is quiet and the vegetative processes such as digestion and reproduction are at the forefront.

When novelty or danger is sensed, we very rapidly shift to an *active alert state,* sometimes called the *alarm state.* In this state we momentarily freeze to orient to the environment. This is a calm state mediated by a number of nuclei to produce heightened awareness and mental clarity.

If danger is present, we shift to the fight-or-flight response. This is a highly charged state in which the sympathetic nervous system surges.

Energies move to the periphery of the body, mobilizing it for action. The person fights or flees. Vegetative activities like digestion and reproduction are down-regulated, and the parasympathetic brake on the cardiovascular system is released as heart and respiratory rates surge. Ideally, when the danger passes, this state is naturally down-regulated, and the system returns to baseline homeostasis.

If the fight-or-flight process is thwarted, or if the intention to protect is totally overwhelmed, then we may enter another state, that of *overwhelm and shock*. If unresolved, this becomes the foundation for Lake's transmarginal stressed state. Here we may experience freezing, immobilization, and dissociation. The parasympathetic nervous system surges and overlays the sympathetic charge, although in this state of immobilization, there are still powerful sympathetic energies cycling. In the wild, animals are mostly able to process the cycling stress physiology and its associated energies and return to homeostatic balance; but in everyday human life, the resolution of stress response is commonly thwarted. Personal history, conditioning, or cognitive processes may get in the way, or past traumatization may hinder its resolution. The upshot is that some of those energies may be left still cycling. This can lead directly to chronic autonomic arousal, maladaptive states, anxiety and depressive states, immune disorders, and, over time, loss of the ability to respond fluidly to life.

Ideal

Resourced: needs met, safety experienced, can orient
to caregiver with appropriate emotional clues
(social nervous system)

Active Alert

Alertness when threat is perceived or sensed
Orienting response is engaged
(Parasympathetic nervous system, social nervous system, brain stem nuclei)

Fight or Flight

Mobilization states, protective intentions surge
(Sympathetic nervous system)

Overwhelm

Shock State
Dissociation/freezing states
(Parasympathetic nervous system, dopamine, endorphins)

Fig. 19.1 Stages of the Fight or Flight Response
(Only basic aspects of the fight or flight response are shown.)

Unresolved trauma cycling in our systems can led to inappropriate physiological and emotional response in times of stress or overwhelm. Perhaps with little real provocation a person gets angry and shouts or lashes out at their partner or colleague; or they are seized with terror when their boss flies off the handle; or they run away in fear from what seems a mild confrontation. These responses manifest in personality systems and may even be the driving forces behind many oppositional, dissociative, painful personal and defensive forms. In clinical work, these energies can be discharged and resolved in some way. Ideally, as clients manifest shock or oppositional states, they have the opportunity to resolve the underlying autonomic cycling. The ability to recognize these states is crucial in any form of therapy or counseling work.

Triune Autonomic Nervous System

Stephen Porges's pioneering work redefines the relationships and functions of the autonomic nervous system and sheds further light on both the stress response and Lake's transmarginal stress hierarchy. Porges developed some important clarifications related to the autonomic system, its mammalian defensive responses, and social orienting and communication activities that have to do both with how the nervous system has evolved and how its anatomy is organized (Porges, 1995).

Porges proposes a new model of a *triune autonomic nervous system* based on a refined understanding of the roles of different autonomic nuclei and on clarification of their phylogenic relationships. Phylogeny is the study of the evolution of life's forms and functions, from ancient simplicity to modern complexity. Porges's three-part autonomic system includes 1) the highest-level social nervous system; 2) the sympathetic nervous system; and 3) the parasympathetic nervous system. The social nervous system, along with the sympathetic and parasympathetic systems, is found in mammals. The sympathetic and parasympathetic systems are found in vertebrates; while invertebrate animals, like worms, depend uniquely on the parasympathetic system for their environmental responses.

In more detail and in order of evolutionary development, these nervous systems are as follows:

The most primitive *parasympathetic nervous system,* which sets a metabolic baseline for basic survival. Originating in the distant past when creatures were passive feeders in a liquid environment, the parasympathetic system has a small range of responses to novelty and stress in the form of adjustments in metabolic rate, including feigning death or freezing via down-regulation of the cardiovascular system. Examples of parasympathetic-only animals are worms and other invertebrates.

The parasympathetic system is in prominence in visceral, digestive states, in self-calming, meditative states, and in rest and repose. As we have seen, it is prominent in shocks states such as in transmarginal stress, and generates dissociative and freezing states that arise when a person is overwhelmed by traumatic experience. It also momentarily engages at the beginning of the active alert stage of the stress response to slow the animal down so that the orienting response can be initiated. If a person is left traumatized by past experience that sensitized the parasympathetic freezing response, then it may surge inappropriately during the active alert/orienting phase, preventing accurate orientation to the current situation and generating immobilized or dissociative states. Its unresolved cycling may leave a person in a constant state of vigilance dissociation, immobilization, and/or chronic fatigue.

The anatomy of the parasympathetic system consists of nuclei and nerves that coordinate the heart/lung cardiovascular, digestive, and reproductive systems, all via the vagus nerve and the cervical and sacral plexuses. Unmyelinated fibers control viscera and relate to calming, digestive, and eliminative functions. This system's major brain nuclei are the bilateral *dorsal motor nuclei* in the brainstem, which coordinate the major activities of the vagus nerve. Some also place the enteric nervous system (the gut brain) in the parasympathetic category.

The *sympathetic nervous system,* developed later, that generates increased physical mobility, better musculoskeletal coordination, and much quicker responsiveness to perceived danger. The sympathetic nervous system endows animals with more advanced musculoskeletal systems, including vertebrates all the way up the evolutionary ladder to mammals, with much wider survival options for finding food, finding mates, and escaping predators.

The sympathetic system is in prominence in active states, such as fast walking, running, sports, or physical work. As we have seen above, as part of the stress response, the sympathetic system mediates fight-or-flight processes, which are prominent at Lake's oppositional level of personality defense. If a traumatized person is left with unresolved sympathetic cycling, it may generate a constant state of fight-or-flight, hyper-vigilance, and hyperarousal, hallmarks of post-traumatic stress disorder.

The sympathetic system consists of nerves that modify the parasympathetic system and manage the striated muscles involved in mobilization activities and fight-or-flight. Particularly notable is the double chain of sympathetic ganglia running along either side of the spine and connecting with the spinal cord at the thoracic and upper lumbar levels.

The most recently developed system, the *social nervous system,* tremendously increases the chances of survival for mammals, particularly primates, by enabling sophisticated information processing and group behaviors. The social nervous system enables many important social behaviors, of which none are more important for survival than those of maternal bonding. As brain size increases, babies need enough time to mature and become independent. Securing this protected time is not a luxury, but essential. The solution is a complex set of structures, relationships, and functions that together create a neurophysiologic-biochemical phenomenon whereby the newborn baby can orient to and find mother, get her attention, communicate via facial expression and sounds, find her breast, nurse, coordinate sucking, breathing, and swallowing, and elicit profound care-giving motivations that endure for decades or even a whole lifetime. With this set of functions, ample time for sophisticated cortex development is secured, and the ultimate survival machine, the human being, is enabled.

As we have seen in previous chapters, the nature of being is to seek relationship with other beings, and the social nervous system directly mediates this most basic need. It allows the baby to seek and orient to primary caregivers, get its most basic needs met, and learn about the nature of the world it finds itself in. It also allows baby to orient to mother in such a fashion that her attention, attunement, and resonance are naturally elicited. The social nervous system is prominent at Lake's ideal and coping levels, and the modus operandi of self-systems that have a cohesive sense of being at their core. The social nervous system is the neural foundation of coping strategies not based on fight-or-flight or dissociative states. It participates in such activities as cooperative working, social gatherings, and friendships.

The social nervous system is commonly categorized as part of the parasympathetic system; but it is actually derived from an evolutionarily later set of nuclei. Its fibers are myelinated and run through the cranial nerves to neck and facial muscles, inner ear, and voice muscles. Its nuclei and nerves, particularly cranial nerves V, VII, IX, and part of X and XI, coordinate facial expression, voice, hearing, mouth, and head-turning, and regulate breathing and heart rate. Its major brainstem nuclei are the *bilateral nuclei ambiguous.*

The Triune System and the Transmarginal Stress Hierarchy

The three aspects of the triune autonomic nervous system are highly interactive and overlap substantially. Within this interdependent complexity, they generally operate in sequence. The newer systems operate by inhibiting and modifying the older; so the parasympathetic sets a baseline, the sympathetic acts on the parasympathetic, and the social acts on the sympathetic. In the presence of threat or novelty, this sequential scheme unfolds. We use our most sophisticated equipment first (social), then we try the older strategy (sympathetic), and if that fails we revert to the oldest (parasympathetic).

As we have seen, Lake's developmental model is based on needs and the affects experienced, as the basic needs of being and wellbeing are either met or not. As the prenate or infant becomes increasingly stressed when it experiences deprivation of basic needs, or is abused or overwhelmed, negative affects intensify and particular levels of the autonomic nervous system and transmarginal stress hierarchy are engaged. Porges's hierarchy of triune autonomic response integrates well with Lake's transmarginal stress paradigm. The social nervous system relates to the ideal and coping levels, the sympathetic to the oppositional level, and the parasympathetic to the overwhelm and shock of the transmarginal level. As trauma is experienced, if the prenate or infant is overwhelmed at any level, he or she can become fixated in its associated survival ploys. These energies then become linked to the developing personality system and will drive emergent personality defenses.

For babies, the social nervous system strategy is the most viable option, since they are too small and dependent to fight or flee. The infant's social nervous system is most powerfully overwhelmed by intense separation anxiety, whose deepest expressions are perceived denial, betrayal, or abandonment by a caregiver, whether actual or not. An infant initially will use the social nervous system as its first strategy to get its needs met. It will search for caregivers by orienting, and will express its needs via movement, facial expressions, and vocalization. If social tools are ineffective, if its needs are not met, if it has to wait too long for a response, if caregivers are unattuned or unresponsive, then it will shift to the sympathetic nervous system response, a fight-or-flight response of mobilization and activation. The infant's vocalizations and movements may become more demanding and forceful, and an emotional limbic nervous system response, such as anger or anxiety, may become activated.

If the sympathetic nervous system response is not successful, the system will then shift to the more primitive parasympathetic response of withdrawal, immobilization, and dissociation. Prenates and infants tend to default to this most primitive response much more easily than older children or adults. Indeed, the primal defensive strategy of a baby *is* dissociation and withdrawal. Fight-or-flight has little use to a little one who cannot move or protect himself; so the infant readily tends to move to his most primitive strategy. If prolonged, repetitive, or intense enough, this may lead to the terror of the transmarginal state, disorganized attachment processes, and schizoid personality adaptations. Recent research has shown that an infant may skip altogether the sympathetic response and devolve to the parasympathetic if quickly overwhelmed by his relational or environmental milieu (Perry & Pollard, 1998).

Summary of the Hierarchy of Responses

1. *Ideal and Coping Levels—Social Nervous System:* Social communication, orienting, self-calming, assertion of needs via facial expression, vocalization, and emotions. Orienting to caregiver and making needs known via sound, facial expression, and positive emotions. The social nervous system coordinates social contact and communication of needs and allows the infant to turn its head, to orient to mother's voice, image and face, to vocalize and express feelings, to smile and frown, and to suck, swallow and breath all at once. It largely mediates the ideal and coping levels of the transmarginal hierarchy and allows the infant to express its needs within an attuned environment. Central-self will use the social nervous system to express being's natural relation-seeking needs and intentions.

2. *Oppositional Strategies—Sympathetic Nervous System:* Mobilizing, anger, shouting, crying, and anxiety states. The sympathetic system mediates fight-or-flight responses supports Lake's oppositional level of the transmarginal stress hierarchy. When needs are not met through the social nervous system, the infant shifts to a sympathetic system response

to demand attention to get his needs met. The infant's demeanor will dramatically shift from social calling to crying, screaming, shouting, and anxiety states. These responses underlie the development of oppositional personality strategies and are their driving force when stress is encountered.

3. *Transmarginal Stress States—Parasympathetic Nervous System:* Immobilization, freezing, withdrawal, dissociation, feigning death. When needs are overwhelmed by separation, anxiety, perceived abandonment, betrayal, overwhelming emotions and experiences, etc., the parasympathetic system surges to protect the infant by initiating freezing and dissociative states. This system is in prominence in transmarginally stressed and dissociative states. It can engage very quickly, as infants are easily overwhelmed, and protects the infant by instigating withdrawal and disconnection from the pain and suffering encountered.

Clinical Repercussions

The clinical repercussions of this understanding are vast. When a client manifests various personality strategies as relational distortions and transitional modes of relating, these levels of response are always present. There are times in session work when these energies come directly to the surface. The therapist must then be able to relate to the arising of the transmarginal stress hierarchy and related autonomic states by empowering the client, as part of a growing awareness of their personal process and healing, to develop skills to moderate these states. If strong sympathetic fight-or-flight energies manifest, the client must be resourced enough to slow things down, bring awareness to the arising process, generate a non-dissociate witness, and complete the emerging sympathetic cycle by mobilizing and clearing his energies. Then he can then shift to an investigation of his oppositional and coping strategies without becoming overwhelmed by them.

If transmarginal stress emerges as shock and dissociative states, the therapist helps the client to develop inner resources, orient gradually and re-associate, and process the emerging parasympathetic state by discharging its energies and moving to a sympathetic, more mobilized process of clearing. This is basically a process of moving back up the autonomic hierarchy, from the parasympathetic state to the sympathetic, and then to the social nervous system.

Social nervous system responses will become conditioned at both opposition and coping levels of personality forms, and these can be witnessed and held with awareness as a basis for healing the deepest wounds, wounds at the level of being. Within the safe holding environment of the therapeutic alliance, clients gradually develop the abilities to witness and be with their personality process without becoming overwhelmed by it, to discharge autonomic cycling when appropriate, and, through the direct awareness of feelings, sensations, and mind-states, gain insight into the nature of that process. From this ground, the closed system of self that Fairbairn clearly described has the potential to open out and once again become a fluid expression of wholeness. The client then can develop a coherency and continuity of being at to support his or her life experience. This is a huge undertaking, yet is possible through the unfolding of the therapeutic process. It takes courage, time, and great patience.

20

Healing the Wounded Self

In the previous chapters we unfolded a paradigm of being and self that is ontologically oriented and intended to offer a useful working model that allows therapist and client to orient to the nature of selfhood within a developmental and relational context. The next important inquiry is, "what helps soften and open the intransigent nature of selfhood and heal its deepest wounds?" The corollary to this would be, how can a psychotherapist be trained to facilitate this process? Below, these questions are explored from the perspective of Core Process Psychotherapy.

The Healing Journey

Most people become engaged in a healing journey due to recognition of their own suffering. Commonly there is acknowledgment of the wounded self, that something is not completely satisfactory, and that help and guidance may be needed. However, a true healing journey addresses more than personal dissatisfaction. It facilitates a shift from identification with conditioned self, to a deeper resting in being and a more direct experience of interbeing. In Lake's terms, it is one of renewal and reconnection to Source as the dynamic cycle is completed in the generation of compassionate relationship; while in Fairbairn's, it entails a shift to mature interdependency, a state of interbeing in which there is clear differentiation of needs and feelings in real, present-time relationship.

This is not an easy journey to embark upon. Fairbairn noted the intransigent nature of self and the resistance to change inherent in its dynamic structure. Over two thousand years ago, the Buddha noted the cyclical nature of selfhood and the fundamental tendency to keep becoming what we have already become. Indeed, he initially hesitated to teach his insights, as he thought that most people were too set in their self-systems to understand his viewpoint, and that the deeper dynamics of selfhood would be too subtle for them to grasp. He is said to have been admonished by *devas* (angels) and gods to teach, as there were beings "with little dust in their eyes." He then, over many years, taught an approach to the alleviation of suffering that is particularly relevant in our modern context and has much to offer clinical practice.

My experience is that healing is both a multifaceted and many-layered process. There is a wide range of personal and interpersonal need, from those of strengthening the sense of selfhood, processing trauma and traumatized states, and creating more ease and coherency in everyday life, to completing the dynamic cycle, opening up entrenched ways of being, and returning to the very Source of life itself.

The following are some basic ideas that support this journey in the context of a therapeutic alliance of the most immediate and rewarding kind:

Presence

Our starting point in this inquiry must be that of presence and being. The therapist's primary intention is to establish his or her own orientation to being and Source, to enter a state of presence, and to orient to the client from this ground. Presence is not just an attribute of a particular person; it is a universal expression of interconnection and interbeing. As the therapist's presence resonates with the client, it is not so much about *his* presence or *her* presence, as it is about presence itself. The primary role of the therapists to be present and to maintain an aware, mindful space and a clear relational field in which the client's process can unfold. The establishment of presence in the clinical setting does not occur by the clinician's practicing or developing presence per se, but by her observing what obscures it. The therapist learns to rest in the truth of the present moment and orients to the client from this perspective. Bion's concept of O as the ultimate truth that informs the therapeutic space may be pointing to this presence (Bion, 1970).

An aspect of any depth psychotherapy, then, ideally is oriented to the reclamation of this inherent state of presence, or, in Pali, *sati*. Its Sanskrit root, *smrti,* has the connotation of remembering, recalling ultimate truth. The Buddha, in the Pali discourses, used the term sati, usually translated as mindfulness, in a number of ways. In the widest sense, sati is a state of inclusive presence, a spacious state of wakefulness that allows a person consciously to hold the whole of an arising process and all of its particulars in awareness.

As we have seen, in Buddhist understanding, each moment of consciousness, or viññana, is also a moment of *knowing.* Knowing is an expression of citta, an inherently radiant state of sentience and being, the heart of the core state. This state is commonly obscured to everyday awareness, masked by our self-process and the contingencies met in life. As sati or presence is developed, knowing, as a wider and deeper state of awareness and being, is also developed. In this state of knowing, when one orients to the arising of self-process via awareness of feeling tones, intentionality, ideas, thoughts, self-forms, tendencies, etc., then the arising of selfhood is *known* as contingent processes, rather than as *me.* As both therapist and client deepen their ability to be present, they discover that awareness is in and of itself transformative. When the light of awareness shines upon an arising process, be it internal or interpersonal, the potential for something else beyond suffering to emerge is galvanized. It is in this state that the potential for reclamation of coherency of being and reconnection to Source naturally can be realized. All of this unfolds within the ambiance of presence as the quality of the holding environment is established and sensed.

The Holding Environment

The nature of the early holding environment and the relational inter-changes that occur within it are crucial factors in personality development. Self is object-oriented. It is formed as being, manifesting its relation seeking intentions, meets its world of conditions. We are relational beings throughout life, and the nature of the relational field is critical, in the therapy setting as well as in utero and infancy. In order for basic trust to be established, the therapist must generate a holding environment that is experienced as both safe *and* non-collusive. This process is founded upon the therapist's ability to be present, to witness, and, when appropriate, to respond to the arising conditions and emergent life processes.

There are a number of relational axes that inform life and impact the therapy setting. These include the basic matrix of Source, being, and self, and the related axes which co-arise as expressions of our basic interconnection: the Source-being axis, the being-to-being axis, the being-to-self axis, and the self-to-self axis, all of which are mutually interdependent. It is within this milieu that relation-seeking, and relationship in general, takes place. It is also within this context that therapy work of any kind unfolds.

The safe holding environment has three essential aspects. The first relates to the Source-being axis. In the midst of her suffering, a client's connection to a deeper reality is obscured. It becomes the therapist's role to maintain openness to Source while orienting to the client and their arising process. In Core Process Psychotherapy, an orientation to what in Buddhist scripture are called the *Brahma Viharas* maintains this intention. In Buddhist awareness practice, when self-view is truly dropped, even momentarily, then the *Brahma Viharas,* the illimitable states of consciousness, naturally arise. These are inherent states of equanimity and presence, loving kindness, compassion, and joy. They are classically described as four interconnected states of *equanimity* (openness, spaciousness, stillness, and clarity); *compassion* (knowing the state of another through interconnection and being moved by interbeing to alleviate suffering; the direct sense that "your suffering is also mine"); *loving kindness* (an open-hearted state of interconnection); and sympathetic joy (joy-in-relatedness with others).

The *Brahma Viharas* are a unitary experience that has felt-tones of spaciousness, clarity, compassion, loving kindness to self and other, and a felt open-heartedness and joy in resonance with others. As we develop the ability to be spaciously present to immediate experience, compassion naturally arises as an innate response to suffering that might be described as awareness-in-action. When we reside in being and sense the inherent state of interbeing, then compassion comes to the forefront. In the clinical context, the therapist learns to hold a wide perceptual field, settle into a state of spaciousness, openness, and stillness, even when a client's process is very tight and fixated, and orient to the felt-movement of compassion, loving kindness, and sympathetic joy as these qualities emerge in the relational field. This takes clear intentionality and practice. How can one sense wholeness and sanity beneath disturbance and fragmentation? How can one be peaceful and resonant, and sense the natural movement of warmth, interconnection, and the energy of compassion, in the midst of transference, strong emotions, and fixed personality forms?

The second aspect of the holding environment relates to the being-to-being axis. Here again, the primary intention of the therapist is to orient to his or her own being-state and, through resonance, help the client settle into a state of *co-presence* until her own being-state naturally emerges (Laing, 1976). As the therapist settles into his state of presence, a resonance is established whereby the client begins to settle into her own being-state, develop the ability to be present, and bear witness to her own arising process. This is encouraged by both the therapist's own orientation to being and presence, and by the kinds of suggestions and interventions that he makes. It is this kind of field that provides the safe holding environment.

Orienting the client to an embodied exploration of her arising process helps generate *witness consciousness,* an expression of her most basic sentience and knowing. As this state deepens over time, both client and therapist engage in a mutual exploration of both universal and conditional forces and processes, opening the way for new ways of being.

The third aspect of the holding environment is, of course, the being-to-self axis. Here again, the role of the therapist is to maintain a state of presence oriented to the client's arising process. As the client's self-forms and self-processes surface, the therapist can hold these within the context of presence and being, and can respond appropriately, whether to transference, early wounding, primary trauma, particular modes of relating, the energies and projections of self-constellations and schemas-of-being, etc. Likewise, the therapist's own self-process may emerge in counter-transference and/or as inner states in self-to-self interactions. These kinds of relational processes will generate much useful clinical information and can help to orient the therapist to the felt sense of the client's relational processes.

All three axes of relating, Source-being, being-being, and being-self, orient the therapist-client dyad to supporting the basic needs of being and manifesting a new relational field of attunement, resonance, and appropriate responsiveness in a good enough way. It is in this kind of holding field that basic needs can be held and the roots of primary trauma explored. As the therapist generates a holding field, the client's needs of being and wellbeing will begin to resonate, defensive reaction patterns and their related affects will surface, projective processes will take relational form, and an informed inquiry into the nature of suffering can evolve. The therapist's role may then shift to one of more active inquiry. The relational process must be managed in ways that both acknowledge the suffering present and help the client open the cycling of their self-system to new potential. This must take place in a bounded and non-collusive field of inquiry that can help the client enter a state of being from which they can witness and make their own inquiry into inner states, self-forms, and behaviors.

Some intentions:

- The therapist holds an attuned, holistic, and receptive field of presence as a non-judgmental and non-interpretive field of listening.

- A unified field of co-presence is generated within which information is exchanged at subtle and energetic levels. The therapist becomes aware of non-verbal, tonal, and/or energetic forms of subliminal communication.

- The therapist's awareness and the client's process co-arise and are interconnected. The therapist receives the impact of the client's experience, is not separate from the nature of her suffering, yet does not take it on or identify with it.

- The therapist resonates with the client's process and appropriately responds to its arising conditions and dynamics in a good enough manner.

Transference and Countertransference

As the therapist-client relationship unfolds, patterns of selfhood emerge and are played out in the clinical holding space. Freud called the tendency for clients to project their inner world onto the therapist *transference*. This was initially thought to be an impediment to healing, but soon became its modus operandi.

Understandings and opinions about transference and countertransference, the inner response of the therapist to the client, vary widely. Freud thought *countertransference*, was a hindrance to the healing process and an indication that the therapist needed further therapy of his own. Klein described the basic interactions of transference in terms of *projective identification* and *introjective identification* (Klein, 1975). In projective identification, a person projects aspects of their inner world onto another and identifies those aspects as *out-there, in the other*. The other person, in turn, may experience *introjective identification,* by which the projected aspects are directly experienced as *inside-me,* and are partly taken over by them. Fairbairn's understanding of dynamic endopsychic structure and transitional modes of relating are an excellent framework for sensing and understanding the felt-nature of projective and introjective identification, both in the therapy space and in everyday life. They also provide, as previously presented, a clear sense of how these manifest in particular personality adaptations, and can help the therapist differentiate between her own process and that of the client's.

Fairbairn's idea that self is an energy form is directly applicable here. In my experience, projection and introjection are energetic processes based on real-time energy exchange. As self-self interchange resonates within, a person *feels* the projected energy of the other directly. This energy is no longer just in the other, but is now also *in-me*. This a cyclical process ensues in which one person projects on the other and the other projects back, both living in past-time, mutually playing out their inner worlds of selfhood. But in the light of the dynamics of field consciousness and the possibilities of direct mind-to-mind communication, the concept of transference moves beyond mental projection to mutual exchange at the level of interbeing.

Transference and countertransference are not rarified processes occurring only in the therapeutic space. We continually play out our internal object relations in our outer world of relationship. If we are unaware of this interplay, the entanglement of self-self interchange, with all its projections and introjections, becomes the stuff of everyday relational experience. For instance:

A man meets an attractive female. His central-self is infused with the longing of unfulfilled need and projects its ideal object onto her. She now *is* the ideal other. *Yes! She is the one who will make it all better for me, who will receive me like no other, who will really see my goodness, etc.* She, in turn, senses these projections inside herself, feels put upon, suffocated. *He is demanding and unresponsive. He doesn't see me, he's not there for me, etc.* She senses him as the dangerous one. Her rejecting self is activated and projects this danger back upon him as anger, or rejection. Now he is disappointed. She becomes his rejecting other, and he pushes her away. So the cycle of projection and introjection is interminably rerun.

Self is a very stable form, both conditioned and conditioning, with predictive and defensive functions. We see our relational world through the inner lenses of this self and the veils of the past defending against further pain in set ways. Self is a felt-experience, and every cycle of projection and introjection supports and reinforces the intransigent self-view. According to the Buddha, this cycling is a manifestation of dependent co-arising, and is an expression of ignorance, not seeing things as they truly are in present-time, and one of the root causes of suffering. In modern analysis, countertransference is understood as an aid to understanding and responding to the client: *As I feel the other, I know the other directly.* In this interplay, the therapist must clearly differentiate his or her countertransference from the client's defenses and projections. The key to this is the maintenance of witness consciousness, which can enable the therapist to discern clearly between self and other and respond wisely from his felt experience of the other. The intention of the therapist is to maintain the being-to-being and being-to-self axis, in which there is a sense of presence, connection, and interbeing, as the client's selfhood manifests in the therapeutic space. In Bion's terms, the therapist becomes the container for the client's projected process and self-forms. She contains and holds the client's inner world in her psyche and, as she does, a transmutation takes place in this holding environment so that the client can more easily metabolize the content of his inner world (Bion, 1967, 1970). In Core Process Psychotherapy, the interactive field of client and therapist is an expression of interbeing at a root level. The countertransference that arises in the therapist's mind-body does so as a direct felt-sense of the client's inner world, and this allows for appropriate response in the clinical process. The self-forms that manifest in the therapeutic field co-arise, and therapist and client partake in a mutual journey of self-inquiry.

Subliminal Mind

One further aspect of the relational field to consider is the nature of being-to-being communication. Once the therapist enters a state of presence, and the relational field settles and deepens, communication occurs on many levels. As described above, communication can even seem to occur subliminally, mind-to-mind. Maura Sills calls this state of resonance and direct empathetic knowing, *subliminal mind*. In an earlier chapter, I noted the possibility of mind-to-mind, feeling-to-feeling communication in early developmental processes, and discussed the direct emotional knowing that can take place between infant and mother. I believe that this state of direct knowing, mind-to-mind, heart-to-heart, can naturally arise in all forms of depth psychotherapy and is important to acknowledge. Quantum physics supports the view that the observer and the observed are not separate, and that each has a direct and non-linear relationship with each other, field-to-field. There have even been recent experiments that show that emotions directly impact DNA at a distance and that heart-based emotional information is communicated and received via field dynamics (McCraty, Atkinson, Tomasino, 2003).

In a clinical context, this means the direct knowing of another is possible, and the therapist's intuition and insight are not separate from the client's inner states and may be sensed via subliminal communication, mind to mind, field to field. It also means that the therapist's inner states and intentions are directly knowable by the client and will have impact on clinical process. The important differentiation here is that both therapist and client are directing their awareness and/or attention to the client's unfolding process. Part of the therapist's job then, is to be aware of both her own inner state *and* that of the client's. I believe that it is important to be open to the possibilities of subliminal mind and direct knowing in the therapeutic context and that, at the deepest level of our beings, we are not separate and not alone.

Mindfulness and the Cyclical Self

How can therapy break through the cyclical nature of self and loosen its fixity? As we've explored, the Buddhist concept of dependent co-arising describes the cyclical nature of conditionality that maintains a fixed sense of selfhood. The classic Buddhist approach to the opening of the cycle of dependent co-arising is to bring awareness as a state of presence, or sati, to one of its links. This entails a true opening-to-the-now.

In a major discourse, The Foundations of Mindfulness *(Satipatthāna Sutta)*, the Buddha gives clear instructions as to the nature of sati and of its prudent use in awareness practice. As we have seen, each and every moment of perception has awareness enfolded within it. As the inquirer settles into a state of presence and develops witness consciousness, awareness expands to hold the whole of the present moment. Attention is then given to the co-arising links in the chain of conditionality and the contingent nature of selfhood. A common staring point in this process of inquiry is awareness of the body, with an orientation to breath, feeling tone, and sensation. As awareness is brought to the arising of feeling tone and the changing nature of sensation, the closed nature of self and the cycling of dependent co-arising are held in a wider perceptual field. This is then expanded to include all that arises within the field of awareness—body states, feeling tones, emotions, sensations, cognitive processes, thoughts, qualities and states of mind, the tonal quality of mind-body as a feeling form, etc.

This kind of awareness can be actively encouraged as the therapist orients the client to his inner states, feelings, intentionality, and emergent process as an embodied experience. A simple suggestion by the therapist to the client, when appropriate, to notice what is emerging in present-time, to speak *from* his present-time embodied experience, rather than about it, initiates a witness consciousness that can hold self-process without totally identifying with it or becoming it. As this becomes more and more possible, the contingent nature of selfhood is held with greater and greater awareness. As self is experienced more and more as process, rather than as a fixed sense of *me,* the me-ness of self-structure softens. The client then can abide more and more in being and sense his inherent connection to other beings. In this state, compassion naturally flows and life becomes a lighter and more fluid experience.

The Buddha, in the Foundations of Mindfulness, encouraged the meditator to bring awareness to an arising process inwardly, outwardly, and as a whole. The meditator is advised not just to be mindful of an arising internal process, be it a sensation, feeling tone, thought, or state of consciousness; but also of its *relationship* to the external world and other beings and, more importantly, of the interrelated flux of experience as a whole. Thus one brings awareness to the inner world of the self and its internal object relations, to the relationship of that self to outer others, *and* to the interactive responses and states of self-other interchange as a unified arising process. Thus mindfulness practice is eminently relational in nature. This fact is sometimes overlooked in mindfulness training, but is the key to its usage and usefulness in psychotherapy practice.

The Buddha encouraged inquirers to be aware of their inner processes by being truly *in* the process. For instance, he encouraged the meditator to be aware of the "body *in* the body," "the feeling *in* the feeling," or "the mind-state *in* the mind-state"; in other words, to be aware of inner processes in a non-dissociative state (Nyānasatta, 1979). The Buddha stressed that this kind of holistic awareness can begin to open the intransigent cycling of the self-system or, as Fairbairn described, the closed system of dynamic endopsychic structure. These astounding insights into human nature and the possibility of true freedom were attained and put forth over 2,500 years ago!

The Foundations of Mindfulness include clear instructions as to which states and conditions lead to ease and the reduction of suffering, such as clear intention, energy, mindfulness, etc.; and which lead to further entanglement, such as sloth and torpor, confusion, automatic behavior, attachment to the self-system etc. Part of the meditative process is to be able to discern wisely between these states and conditions. As awareness is brought to an arising process, two important qualities emerge. These are called *sampajāna*, clear comprehension, and *yoniso manasikāra*, wise discernment. In the context of psychotherapy, these qualities are of supreme importance. As session work unfolds over time, both therapist and client learn to comprehend clearly and wisely discern the nature of the client's self-system and its dynamics. Over time, the therapist learns to comprehend clearly the nature of the client's process and relational tendencies and to discern wisely what is helpful and what leads to further entanglement. This is the ground for appropriate clinical responses to the client's needs and tendencies.

The Use of Mindfulness in Psychotherapy

Some current forms of cognitive therapy, such as mindfulness-based cognitive behavioral therapy, mindfulness-based stress reduction, and dialectical behavioral therapy, teach mindfulness practice directly, both in individual and small group settings, and demand that the client maintain a daily mindfulness practice. Cognitive therapies are not, however, oriented to the deeper organizing factors of self-form. They are geared more to affect and behavior modification. This certainly has its benefits; but in a wider reaching psychotherapy practice, in which a receptive field and long-term ongoing inquiry is the general mode, there are a number of things to consider in introducing mindfulness practice to an individual client.

The first principle is that therapy is client-led, based on the client's own emergent process. The therapist journeys into the client's world as fellow traveler, holder, clarifier, orienter, and reflective mirror. The therapist may help orient the client to his inner world, point the way in that direction, encourage present-time awareness, and provide the structure for further inquiry. As stated earlier, one essential aspect of the process is the generation of witness consciousness, which encourages the development of the client's ability to introspect and hold an arising process in awareness without identifying with it or becoming it. As the client mindfully observes the arising and passing of his self-process, something else comes to the forefront; a deeper sense of who he is, of spaciousness, presence, and interconnection. This is a most helpful resource both in the therapy setting and in everyday life.

As a client's process unfolds, so do his particular forms of endopsychic structure and transitional modes of relating. In Fairbairn's framework, every self-constellation is composed of a particular self-view and way-of-being, an internal object and an affect. As we have seen in the Buddhist view as well, self is object-oriented. As a client brings awareness to his inner world, its internal object relations and its relational interplay, he may sense the transitory nature of what was first experienced as continuous and solid. Then he can be encouraged to hold all of what is emergent in a wide and soft field of presence in which the volitional impulse, which is the key to any particular self-constellation, and its co-arising feeling tone and affect, may be held in awareness and sensed as process, rather than as *me*. In the light of this kind of wakefulness, a softening of identification to self and a realization of self-as-process can occur, as a deeper being-state begins to emerge.

I have noted a real shift in clients' work when they can hold aspects of themselves in inquiry, without becoming or acting out the emerging energies. With a growing ability to hold witness consciousness, volitional impulses subside and are not self-directed, and the real possibility of unraveling the chain of dependent co-arising emerges. Realignment to being and Source may then transpire, as identification to self-as-me is softened. As the state of presence, or sati, is maintained, a deeper state of coherency and being emerges, as does a greater sense of interconnection with other beings. Thus Core Process Psychotherapy is, in essence, a joint awareness practice. All of our suffering is relational in nature, a therapeutic relationship based on awareness and inquiry is a powerful healing tool.

On the other hand, a real balance has to be held in the psychotherapeutic setting between teaching processes such as mindfulness practice, and following the present-time flow of client process. When appropriate, I may orient a client to her inner state, ask her to speak from the embodied sense of an experience, help her become mindful of its arising nature, both inwardly and relationally, and to hold what emerges in present-time awareness. At another time, I may explain how this orientation to her felt sense of arising process, to her inner sense of her experience, to her feelings and sensations in present time, are helpful both in the therapy setting and in everyday life. Mostly the work of the therapist is that of following process, attuning to the client's inner state and emerging relational forms, orienting clients to a present-time embodied sense of their arising process, and being as appropriate as possible in clinical responses.

Embodied Inquiry

A further territory presents itself for exploration: How do you empower clients in their own inquiry without getting in the way of the natural unfolding of therapy work? What processes can orient her to innate being, while softening and opening her relationship to selfhood?

In addition to the establishment of presence, a safe holding environment, and the awakening of the inner witness outlined above, another very useful approach is Gendlin's focusing work. In his book, *Focusing-Oriented Psychotherapy* (Gendlin, 1996), he describes an approach by which the therapist helps orient the client to his or her inner world via awareness of immediate embodied experience, what Gendlin calls the felt sense. The felt sense is the embodied feeling tone that orients the client to the whole of an arising inner state. The realm of felt sense is found at the border between unconscious and conscious process. It is the emergent moment-to-moment bodily sense of the whole of something that is initially unclear and beneath the level of consciousness of a formed emotion, sensation, or image; yet includes all of these. Gendlin describes its holistic nature in this way: "Something makes me angry. The felt sense includes the anger, but also all the many facets that went into making me angry, all that has happened, what people did, what I am like, why I cannot easily change that, and all that goes with the incident—all as one uniquely sensed quality" (Gendlin, 1996).

An example of the felt sense realm might be experienced as one groggily wakes up from a dream in the morning. The dreamer at this stage has one foot in the dream realm and one in the waking realm; he or she is at the border of conscious and unconscious territories. The tonal quality of the dream is present, is felt as a bodily sense of something, but is initially unclear and ephemeral. In order to access the feeling sense of the dream, one has to stay with it at this level, sense it inwardly, ask it questions and wait for something to clarify. If one shifts too quickly to waking consciousness, the felt sense of the dream is lost and it subsides back into the unconscious. It is very much like this as one tries to enter the felt sense realm both in waking life and in the therapy situation.

In terms of Core Process, the felt sense orients the client to the whole of an arising self-form, conceived of either as the holistic emergence of a self-constellation and its object relations properties, including various affects and patterns; or, in the Buddhist framework, as the whole of an arising dynamic of the skandhas, the factors of self-process. The felt sense includes the whole matrix-like arising of consciousness colored by tendencies, past perceptions and conditions, and related feeling tones, all holistically sensed as an embodied, tonal and initially unclear form. As a process emerges, the client learns to settle into a bodily sense of it, hold the whole of what is arising in awareness, and gently inquiry into its nature. In Buddhist teachings, holistic awareness is a factor of sati, and it is this state of presence that can hold the whole of something in a soft and inclusive manner. This is one of the key qualities that the therapist needs to engender in work with a client. It is no accident that I was introduced to focusing by Gendlin in the context of a training in Tibetan yoga and meditation at the Nyingma Institute in 1980.

There are many factors that can encourage a present-time, embodied exploration of arising process. Obviously, the therapist must maintain a receptive, non-judgmental listening field. Within this orientation, the client's sharing must be heard; she must feel seen and received before anything deeper can occur. The therapist takes in the client's sharing and reflects it back in various ways to make sure what he is hearing is what the client really intends. The client may need to talk about her life and experiences, her analysis and judgments of her situation, etc. All of this must be received initially without interpretation or intervention. This is in keeping with the basic needs of being: recognition, acknowledgment, and unconditional acceptance. Until the client is assured she is being received, it is simply not safe enough to enter a deeper inquiry. Once the client feels received within an increasingly safe holding environment, then the shift can occur from talking *about* process, to talking *from* the immediacy of it. The intention is to support inquiry by orienting the client to the direct sensing of their process via an embodied awareness of its tonal nature. This brings them into the realm of feeling tone and affect, the glue of self-constellations. Rather than talk about their relational milieu, they shift to a direct inner experience of it, and can begin to talk from that. By asking the client to hold a wide awareness of the bodily sense of something The shift can take place from the history, situation, or condition arising, to the feeling sense of it in the body in the present moment. For instance, a client may feel aggrieved, angry, distraught. The therapist may orient the client to her inner body space from the neck down and suggest that she sense the whole of what is arising—in this case whatever it is that makes her feel aggrieved, or that is scary—in her whole body.

Initially the felt sense realm will be unclear and hard to grasp. Gendlin recommends a simple process to help clarify the felt sense and allow a more direct experience of it. The client is oriented to their present bodily experience and to a deeper something at its heart. Then she is asked about its qualities and perhaps encouraged to find a word or phrase that clarifies its nature. For instance, the client may feel frustrated in a particular relationship. Once her story has been heard, and some space arises in the interchange with the therapist, the therapist may orient the client to her bodily sense in the present moment. He may ask the client to find a word, phrase, or image that represents the nature of the relational problem with questions like, "What is the something that makes you frustrated right now?" or, "As you settle into an awareness of that in your body, what's the whole of this for you?" or, "As you sense that quality, is there a word or phrase that clarifies it for you?" This process is meant to clarify what Gendlin calls the *felt meaning* inherent in the arising process, Stern might call it the underlying narrative that drives the schema-of-being-with. In Buddhist terms, it brings the inquirer closer to the samskarā, or volitional impulse that underpins the particular self-view, or self-organization. Gendlin notes that when a handle is accessed, a *felt shift* occurs in the person's process that brings clarity and insight and allows a softening of the arising form. This, in turn, opens the client to new potential by opening the process of dependent co-arising, and helps the process advance to the next step. In essence, the client discovers that he is *not* the felt sense, but rather *has* a felt sense. This is equivalent to sensing that self is process and not me, and is a way to begin to inquire into the cyclical nature of selfhood. This is a very brief introduction to this area with my encouragement to read Gendlin's book, which defines the territory in much greater detail.

The Unfolding of the Healing Process

I have had conversations with many experienced therapists from different traditions. From these, a real commonality of experience was apparent that followed more or less along these lines: Once a safe relational environment is established, the healing process seems to arise in particular ways. Within the empathetic holding of the therapist, the client will communicate a substantial amount of information. This may come forth in waves in which many fragments of history, self-form, and relational dynamics will be communicated. Co-emergent shifts in emotions, images, and cognitive process may arise and infuse the therapy space at any time. The therapist holds and orients to all of this in a spacious field of presence, a state of simply being. Via resonance, a state of co-presence evolves. Information is shared subliminally, and all of the emergent factors of the client's schemas-of-being and relational dynamics settle into a kind of dynamic equilibrium. The therapeutic space is immersed in stillness, and a *particular* issue or relational process clarifies in the midst of these diverse conditions. This is really a monumental moment. The system is poised on the edge of a cliff. All is now in place for something to surface that transcends the conditions that have driven the self-system.

As this moment is held in awareness, an even deeper settling occurs. The client's psyche seems to enter a state of equilibrium. Conscious and unconscious processes come into balance. She enters a being-state and *knowing* arises. The conditions are known for what they are, and the client's mind-body system seems to process or let go of something. An emotion is gently expressed, insight occurs, and spaciousness and clarity infuse the clinical space. Wounding is resolved, and the client moves beyond the tendencies and conditions that have driven her self-system. Something new can now arise.

There is then a further period of acknowledgment, reorganization, integration, and completion. This can go on for a period of minutes, days, weeks, even months. This healing process is non-linear; it is more like being in the presence of spirals within spirals, fields within fields. The therapeutic imperative takes its own course in its own time, and the nature of its unfoldment cannot be guessed or analyzed. It is, by its own nature, a mysterious gateway to being-itself grounded in the reclamation of being and the reconnection to Source.

Final Thoughts on the Training of a Therapist

The therapist has his or her own journey. Its first step must be an inquiry into the nature of his or her own suffering. The next is the learning process involved in becoming able to hold the suffering of another. Both are enormous undertakings.

In the training of a therapist, a number of key skills must be developed. The first is the therapist's ability to enter a state of presence, a being-state that can hold both his own process and the client's with attunement and orientation. This is no small matter in itself. The next is the ability to generate an inclusive holding field that maintains, in a good enough fashion, attunement, resonance, and appropriate responsiveness to the client's arising process. Once those are in place, appropriate therapeutic skills must be learned and incorporated into one's way-of-being. Therapeutic skills are, in essence, life skills. These are not just about becoming and being a therapist, but about being a human being engaged in a journey of inquiry and healing. Training in counseling and psychotherapy ideally covers the whole gamut of theories and skills that orient to the following territories:

1. The development of presence;

2. The ability to generate and maintain a clear and holistic relational field and safe holding environment;

3. The ability to attune to the client's emergent process and self-system;

4. The ability to resonate with that process and to respond appropriately to its arising conditions, relational processes, and self-forms.

Formal training in presence and awareness practice is very helpful. It is not enough simply to ask a trainee to be present. Although presence is an innate expression of being, the ability to enter a being-state can be challenging, and the capacity to be present must be continuously refined. There is a vast number of contemplative practices that can support the cultivation of therapeutic presence and anchor the therapist in his or her being-state.

The first step in the practice of presence, however, is to simply become aware of oneself. This may seem obvious, but how many of us really take the time to become aware of our inner-most processes and their outer manifestations? This entails the development of a personal mindfulness practice; the ability to simply be with whatever is arising in terms of self-process, feeling tone, thoughts, tendencies etc. This is a process of awareness that includes self-other interchange, and whose development can have huge repercussions in everyday life. At its simplest, the development of presence is largely about learning what gets in the way of simply being, our innate ability to be still and know.

The challenge for the therapist is to settle under his or her preconceptions and self-forms, and enter a state of presence and receptivity oriented to the client's world and arising process. In this endeavor, it is essential for the therapist to put aside all theoretical concepts and ideas; to put aside any need to interpret or intervene, and to simply be open to each relational moment as it arises. It is the establishment of a field of presence that orients clients to innate being and enables them to hold the whole of an arising process in awareness. As the therapist settles into their being-state, and orients to the client's process, a being-to-being and being-to-self field is established. It is within this conscious field of presence that the therapy process unfolds and a safe holding field is established. The intention is to develop the ability to generate a safe and non-collusive holding field that can attune, resonate with, and appropriately respond to the client's emergent process. In this endeavor, students learn to appreciate the client's being and wellbeing needs, the nature of their primary trauma, relational wounding, emergent self-forms and related psychodynamics. Likewise, they develop the capacity to help clients develop their own state of presence and witness consciousness so that they can, in turn, develop their own capacity to hold the deepest relational wounds.

Therapy training is, in essence, a life training in which the student takes full responsibility for their own state and self-other processes and, at its deepest, it about reclamation of being and reconnection to Source. It is, however, a journey that is not unique to therapy. It is one that can be undertaken in many forms and circumstances, is essentially spiritual in nature, should be part of our training as parents, and could ideally be introduced to us in our earliest educational experiences. It is, at its roots, about the nature of our human condition and the possibility of real connection and interbeing.

Completions

I would like to conclude by acknowledging that the therapist's journey and process is not separate from the client's. Nor is their spiritual nature different. Even the nature of their personality shaping is not dissimilar. Their particular personality forms and defensive strategies may be different, but the process at its core is the same. Both are in this play of life together. Therapy is a mutual journey in which therapist and client

are fellow travelers in joint practice. It is within the joint nature of the
therapeutic endeavor that a cohesiveness of being may be reclaimed and
a mutual connection to Source directly experienced. I hope the journey
taken in this book has been useful, informative and thought provoking.
Its main focus has been to outline a paradigm of being and self that may
be useful in a clinical setting. On a personal level, this journey has been
of great use in the healing of my own relational woundings. I would like
to finish with a traditional Buddhist blessing:

> *May all beings be happy, may all beings be peaceful, may all*
> *beings be liberated from suffering.*
> *May we be happy, may we be peaceful, may we be liberated*
> *from suffering.*
> *May we all realize our inherent luminosity and freedom.*
> *Let it be, let it be, let it be.*

Bibliography

Addiss, S. and S. Lombardao, trans. 1993. *Tao Te Ching*. Indianapolis: Hackett Publishing Company.

Ainsworth, M., M. Blehar, E. Waters, S. and Wall. 1978. *Patterns of Attachment: Assessed in the Strange Situation and at Home*. Hillsdale, NJ: Erlbaum.

Analayo. 2003. *Satipatthana: The Direct Path to Realization*. Cambridge, U.K.: Windhorse Publications.

Anguttara Nikaya, I:10, Pali Canon, Pali Text Society.

Bion, W. 1965. *Transformations: Change from Learning to Growth*. New York: Basic Books.

Bion, W. 1967. *Second Thoughts*. London: Heinemann.

Bion, W. 1970. *Attention and Interpretation*. London: Tavistock.

Blechschmidt, E. and R. F. Gasser. 1978. *Biokinetics and Biodynamics of Human Differentiation*. Springfield, IL: Charles C. Thomas Pub.

Blechschmidt, E. 2004. *The Ontogenetic Basis of Human Anatomy*. Berkeley: North Atlantic Books.

Bohm, D. 1980. *Wholeness and the Implicate Order*. London: Routledge.

Bowlby, J. 1969. *Attachment*. Vol. I. of *Attachment and Loss*. London: Random House.

Braxelton, T. B. and M. W. Yogman, eds. 1970. Main and Solomon: Discovery of an Insecure-disorganized/disoriented attachment. In *Affective Development in Infancy*. Norwood, NJ: Ablex.

Buber, M. 1970. *I and Thou*. Translated by Walter Kaufmann. New York: Continuum International Publishing Group Ltd.; New Ed edition (21 Oct 2004)

Buswell, R. 1992. *Tracing Back the Radiance: Chinul's Korean Way of Zen.* Honolulu: University of Hawaii Press.

Calasso, R. 1996. *Ka.* New York: Vintage.

Chamberlain, D. 1998. *The Mind of Your Newborn Baby.* Berkeley: North Atlantic Books.

Cleary, T. 1997. *Kensho: The Heart of Zen.* Boston: Shambhala Press.

Corricall, J., and H. Wilkinson, eds. 2003. Schore: The Seventh Annual John Bowlby Lecture. In *Revolutionary Connections: Psychotherapy and Neuroscience.* London: Karnac Books.

Douglas-Klotz, N. 1999. *The Hidden Gospel: Decoding the Spiritual Message of the Aramaic Jesus.* Wheaton, IL: Quest Books.

Emerson, W. 1997. The Vulnerable Prenate. *Pre- and Perinatal Psychology Journal* 10(3), Spring 1997.

Emoto, M. 1999. *Messages from Water: The First Pictures of Frozen Water Crystals,* Volume 1. Tokyo: Hado Kyoikusha.

Fairbairn, R. 1994a in Birtles, E. and Sharff, D., eds. *Clinical and Theoretical Papers.* Vol. I of *From Instinct to Self: Selected Papers of W. R. D. Fairbairn.* London and Northvale, NJ: Jason Aronson.

Fairbairn, R. 1994b in Birtles, E. and Sharff, D., eds. *Applications and Early Contributions.* Vol. II of *From Instinct to Self: Selected Papers of W. R. D. Fairbairn.* London and Northvale, NJ: Jason Aronson.

Fairbairn, R. 1994c in Birtles, E. and Sharff, D. eds. The Screber Case and in Defense of Object Relations Theory, in *Clinical and Theoretical Papers.* Vol. I of *From Instinct to Self: Selected Papers of W. R. D. Fairbairn.* London and Northvale, NJ: Jason Aronson.

Fairbairn, R. 1994d in Birtles, E. and Sharff, D., eds. The Nature of Hysterical States, in *Clinical and Theoretical Papers.* Vol. I of *From Instinct to Self: Selected Papers of W. R. D. Fairbairn.* London and Northvale, NJ: Jason Aronson.

Fodor, N. 1949. *The Search for the Beloved: A Clinical Investigation of the Trauma of Birth and Pre-natal Conditioning.* New York: Hermitage Press.

Fox, M. 1983. *Meditations with Meister Eckhart.* Rochester, VT: Bear & Company.

Freud, S. 1914. Trans. Strachey, J. *Remembering, repeating and working-through further recommendations on the technique of psycho-analysis II,* Volume XII of *The Standard Edition of the Complete Psychological Works of Sigmund Freud.* The Hogarth Press (1975)

Freud, S. 1925. Trans. Strachey, J *The resistances to psycho-analysis.* Volume XIX of *The Standard Edition of the Complete Psychological Works of Sigmund Freud.* The Hogarth Press (1961)

Gendlin, E. 1978, 1981, 2003. *Focusing.* London: Rider.

Gendlin, E. 1996. *Focusing-oriented Psychotherapy: A Manual of the Experiential Method.* New York: The Guilford Press.

Greenberg, J. and S. A. Mitchell. 1983. *Object Relations in Psychoanalytic Theory.* Cambridge: Harvard University Press.

Greenberg, M. T., D. Cicchetti, and M. Cummings, eds. 1990. Procedures for identifying infants as disorganized/disoriented during the Ainsworth strange situation. In *Attachment in the Preschool Years: Theory, Research, and Intervention.* Chicago: University of Chicago Press.

Gomez, L. 1997. *An Introduction to Object Relations.* London: Free Association Books.

Grinberg-Zylberbaum, J. and J. Ramos. 1987. Patterns of interhemispheric correlation during human communication. *International Journal of Neuroscience,* 361–2: 41–54.

Grinberg-Zylberbaum, J. 1988. The syntergic theory. *Frontier Perspectives,* 41: 25–30.

Grinberg-Zylberbaum, et al. 1992. Human commmunication and the electrical activity of the brain. *Subtle Energies,* 33: 25–41.

Grof, S. 1979. *Realms of the Human Unconscious: Observations from LSD Research.* London: Souvenir Press.

Grof, S., 1993. *The Holotropic Mind.* San Francisco: Harper San Francisco.

Grotstein, J. S. 2000. *Who Is the Dreamer Who Dreams the Dreams?* London: The Analytic Press.

Guntrip, H. 1961. *Personality Structure and Human Interaction: The Developing Synthesis of Psycho-dynamic Theory.* London: The Hogarth Press.

Hanh, T. N. 1975, 1976. *The Miracle of Mindfulness.* Boston: Beacon Press.

Hartman, D., and D. Zimberoff. 2003. Deintegrate, disintegrate, unintegrate: A Buddhist perspective in heart-centered therapies. *Journal of Heart-centered Therapies,* 6:27–87.

Heidegger, M. 1962. *Being and Time.* Translated by J. Macquarrie and E. Robinson. Hoboken, NJ: Blackwell.

Ho, M. W. 1998. *The Rainbow and the Worm: The Physics of Organisms.* Singapore: World Scientific.

Holmes, J, 1993. *John Bowlby and Attachment Theory.* Brunner-Routledge.

Holmes, J. 2001. *The Search for the Secure Base: Attachment Theory and Psychotherapy.* Hove, U.K.: Brunner-Routledge.

Johansson, Rune E. A., 1979, 1985. *The Dynamic Psychology of Early Buddhism.* London and Malmo: Curzon Press.

Jung, C. G. 1970. *The Structure and Dynamics of the Psyche.* Vol. 8 of *The Collected Works of C. G. Jung.* Princeton: Princeton University Press.

Jung, C. G. 1976. *The Development of Personality.* Vol. 17 of *The Collected Works of C. G. Jung.* Princeton: Princeton University Press.

Karpman, S. 1968. Fairy tales and script drama analysis. *Transactional Analysis Bulletin,* 726:39–43.

Keating, T. 1986. *Open Mind, Open Heart.* New York: Amity House.

Keleman, S. 1985. *Emotional Anatomy.* Berkeley: Center Press.

Kohut, H. 1978. *The Search for the Self: Collected Writings of Heinz Kohut, 1950–1978.* Vol. I. International Universities Press.

Klein, M. 1975. *Envy and Gratitude and Other Works, 1946–1963.* New York: Delacorte Press.

Kohut, H. 1984. *How Does Analysis Cure?* Edited by A. Goldberg. Chicago: The University of Chicago Press.

Laing, R. D. 1976. *The Facts of Life.* New York: Pantheon Books.

Lake, F. 1979. *Studies in Constricted Confusion: Exploration of a Pre- and Perinatal Paradigm.* The Clinical Theology Association.

Lake, F. 1981. *Tight Corners in Pastoral Counseling.* London: Darton, Longman and Todd.

Lake, F. 1986a. *Charts.* Oxford: Clinical Theology Association.

Lake, F. 1986b. *The Dynamic Cycle.* Oxford: Clinical Theology Association.*

Larimore, T. and G. Farrant. *Universal Body Movements in Cellular Consciousness and What They Mean,* Primal Renaissance, Vol. I, No. I.

Laszlo, E. 1996. *The Whispering Pond: A Personal Guide to the Emerging Vision of Science.* London and New York: Element Books.

Laszlo, E. 2003. *The Connectivity Hypothesis: Foundations of an Integral Science of Quantum, Cosmos, Life, and Consciousness.* Albany, NY: State University of New York Press.

Laszlo, E. 2004. *Science and the Akashic Field: An Integral Theory of Everything.* Rochester, NY: Inner Traditions.

Leighton, D. and Yi Wu. 2000. *Cultivating the Empty Field: The Silent Illumination of Zen Master Hongzhi.* Tokyo and Rutland, VT: Tuttle.

Llinás, Rodolfo R. 2001. *I of the Vortex: From Neurons to Self.* Cambridge: MIT Press.

Lui, H. C. 1974. *Tao Te Ching.* Class notes of Franklyn Sills.

Maret, S. 1997. *The Prenatal Person.* Lanham, MD: University Press of America.

---

* Lake's writings are available via Bridge Pastoral Foundation, www. bridgepastoral.org.uk.

McCraty, R., M. Mike Atkinson, D. Tomasino. 2003. *Modulation of DNA Conformation by Heart-focused Intention.* Boulder Creek, CA: Heart-Math Research Center.

Mott, F. 1964. *The Universal Design of Creation.* Edenbridge, U.K.: Mark Beech Publishers.

Nyānasatta 1993 *The Foundations of Mindfulness,* Buddhist Publication Society: Wheel Publication No. 19.

Nyānasatta 1979 *The Foundation of Mindfulness,* Satipatthāna Sutta, in Hanh, T. N. *The Miracle of Mindfulness,* p. 111–128, Boston: Beacon Press.

Ogden, P. 2006. *Trauma and the Body: A Sensorimotor Approach to Psychotherapy.* New York: W. W. Norton & Company.

O'Keane V. and Scott J. 2005. Obstetric complications to a maternal-foetal origin hypothesis of mood disorder. In *British Journal of Psychiatry,* 186: 367–368.

Parkes, C. M., and J. Stevenson-Hinde, eds. 1982. Ainsworth: Attachment: Retrospect and prospect. In *The Place of Attachment in Human Behaviour.* London: Tavistock.

Payutto, P. A. 1994. *Dependent Origination: The Buddhist Law of Conditionality.* Bangkok: Sahadhammika Co.

Pereira, F. and D. Scharff. 2002. *Fairbairn and Relational Theory.* London: Karnac Books.

Pereira, F. and D. Scharff, eds. 2002. Matos: The Problem of Melancholia in the Work of Fairbairn. In *Fairbairn and Relational Theory.* London: Karnac Books.

Perry and Pollard. 1998. Homeostasis, Stress, Trauma, and Adaptation: A neuro-developmental view of childhood trauma. In *Child and Adolescent Psychiatric Clinics of North America,* 7:31–51.

Ployé, P. 2006. *The Prenatal Theme in Psychotherapy.* London: Karnac Books.

Polt, R. 1999. *Heidegger: An Introduction.* London: Routledge.

Porges, S. W. 2001. The Polyvagal Theory: Phylogenetic substrates of a social nervous system. *International Journal of Psychophysiology,* 42:123–166.

Pribham, K. 1970. *Biology of Memory.* New York: Academic Press.

Pribram, K. 1971. *Languages of the Brain: Experimental Paradoxes and Principles in Neuropsychology.* Upper Saddle River, NJ: Prentice Hall.

Radin, D. 1997. *The Conscious Universe: The Scientific Truth of Psychic Phenomena.* San Francisco: Harper Edge.

Radin D. 2004. Experimental investigation of event-related EEG correlations between isolated human subjects. In *Journal of Complementary and Alternative Medicine,* 10:103–112.

Scharff, D. and J. Scharff. 2000. *Object Relations Individual Therapy.* London and Northvale, NJ: Jason Aronson.

Schore, A. 2001a. Effects of a secure attachment relationship on right brain development and infant mental health. In *Infant Mental Health Journal,* 22:1–2, 7–66.

Schore, A. 2001b. The effects of early relational trauma on right brain development: Affect regulation and infant mental health. In *Infant Mental Health Journal,* 22:1–2, 201–269.

Sheldrake, R. and David Bohm. Morphogenetic fields and the implicate order. In *Revision,* 5: 1982.

Sheldrake, R. 2003. *The Sense of Being Stared At: And Other Aspects of the Extended Mind.* London: Hutchinson.

Siegel, D. 1999. *The Developing Mind: Toward a Neurobiology of Interpersonal Experience.* New York: Guilford Press.

Stern, D. 1985. *The Interpersonal World of the Infant: A View from Psychoanalysis and Developmental Psychology.* London: Karnac Books.

Stern, D. 1998. *The Motherhood Constellation: A Unified View of Parent-Infant Psychotherapy.* London: Karnac Books.

Stone, R. B. 1989. *The Secret Life of Your Cells.* Atglen, PA: Whitford Press.

van der Wal, J. 1998. *The Speech of the Embryo: A Phenomenology of Embryonic Existence,* English text based on De spraak van het embryo, Een fenomenologie van het embryonale bestaan, from Leiber amicorum Steven de Batselier, Betty Reiners, editor, English edition May 2002.

Varela, F. 1991. *The Embodied Mind.* Cambridge: MIT Press.

Verny, T. 1981. *The Secret Life of the Unborn Child.* Summit Books.

Wilson, S., ed. 2003. Radin: Thinking outside the box: EEG correlations between isolated subjects, in *Proceedings of the 46th Annual Convention of the Parapsychological Association.* Vancouver: Parasychological Foundation.

Winnicott, D. W. 1987. *Babies and Their Mothers.* London: Free Association Press.

Winnicott, D. W. 1965b. *The Family and Individual Development.* London: Tavistock.

Winnicott, D.W. 1965a. *The Maturational Environment and the Facilitating Environment.* London: The Hogarth Press.

Index

About the Author

FRANKLYN SILLS is the co-director of the Karuna Institute, and has pioneered trainings in Craniosacral Biodynamics and Core Process Psychotherapy. His work is dedicated to integrating Buddhist self-psychology with Western object relations and developmental theories. He lives in Devon, England.